Learning Change

Learning Change

One School District
Meets Language
Across the Curriculum

Nancy B. Lester *and* Cynthia S. Onore

BOYNTON/COOK PUBLISHERS
HEINEMANN
PORTSMOUTH, NH

Boynton/Cook Publishers
A Division of
Heinemann Educational Books, Inc.
70 Court Street   Portsmouth, NH 03801
Offices and agents throughout the world

The authors would like to thank the following for granting permission to
reprint material in this book:

Pages 7–8: From *The Medusa and the Snail* by Lewis Thomas.
Copyright © 1977 by Lewis Thomas. All rights reserved. Reprinted by
permission of Viking Penguin, a division of Penguin Books USA, Inc.

Pages 25–26: From "Negotiating the Curriculum: Programming for
Learning" in *Negotiating the Curriculum: A Student-Teacher Partnership*,
edited by Garth Boomer. Copyright 1982 by Ashton Scholastic.
Reprinted by permission of the publisher.

Library of Congress Cataloging-in-Publication Data

Lester, Nancy, 1946–
    Learning change : one school district meets language across the
curriculum / Nancy B. Lester and Cynthia S. Onore.
        p.   cm.
    Includes bibliographical references.
    ISBN 0-86709-254-8
    1. Language arts—Correlation with content subjects—New York
(State)—Case studies.   2. Language arts teachers—In-service
training—New York (State)—Case studies.   3. Teachers—In-service
training—New York (State)—Case studies.   I. Onore, Cynthia S.
II. Title.
LB1576.L49   1990
428'.007—dc20   89-36956
                                                              CIP

Cover design by Jenny Greenleaf.
Text design by Vic Schwarz.
Printed in the United States of America.
90 91 92 93 94   10 9 8 7 6 5 4 3 2 1

Contents

Acknowledgments

Somebody should have studied us as we researched and wrote this book. Not only did we plan and analyze and question together, but we even found ourselves writing as one person, finishing each other's sentences as we composed. Some people may describe our relationship as dependent. Other people have trouble telling us apart. In fact, a guy stopped alongside us at a traffic light as we were driving home from Charmont and asked us if we were twins! We have discovered along the way that we are truly collaborative people.

But our collaborative nature extends well beyond our relationship to one another. And so we are grateful to all of our collaborators in this project. When we say, as authors often do, that without the help of so-and-so this book would not be possible, we really mean it. First and foremost, we want to thank all of the teachers, administrators, and school board members whom we worked with in Charmont and who continue to strive to make change possible. They are Tara Arturi, Fred Blais, Kathy Buckhout, Joan Courtney, Viola Davis, Ralph Defino, Debbie Donovan, Lynn Doughty, Joan Egan, Janet Farnham, Helen Fogel-Egan, Jeannette Gabriellargues, Shirley Gillis, Mildred Gilman, Barbara Gochman, Barbara Hirschman, Loretta Hirschmugl, Adele Josiger, Judy Kamlet, Charles Keir, Jean Kennedy, Karen Leitner, Priscilla Liebowitz, Robert Lish, Barbara Lofthouse, Christine Louth, Robert Manthey, Jane Martin, Kathe McBride, Maggie North, Lynn Pedraza, Samuel Plummer, Linda Reich, Lorraine Rossi, Howard Rubin, Barbara Schlieper, Laura Seitz, David Siegel, Carol Stark, Ann Ten Eyck, Fran Varady, Cindy Wilkins, Art Wulfhop, Doug Young, William Zablinis, and Joe Zajac.

While we did choose to use pseudonyms throughout the book, that in no way diminishes our respect and admiration for all of our collaborators in Charmont. In order to acknowledge the debt we owe these people, the names we did select are names of our most respected and best loved teachers from kindergarten through high school. We hope thereby to be simultaneously honoring both groups of influential people in our lives.

Because we see ourselves as collaborators, we wish to acknowledge a particular group of our professional colleagues. During the past four years, we have shared our work in progress at the L. Ramon Veal Seminar at the NCTE Spring Conferences. Those who attended, too many to name here, were supportive throughout and helped us to see the possibilities and limitations of our questions and the answers we were formulating.

Sarah Benesch worked with us during the second year of the language and learning in-service program in Charmont. Her help with workshops and classroom visitations, as well as her insights about what was going on, provided an additional perspective from which to view the process in action.

When it came time to actually let others read the book, we chose four people whose work we respect. The perceptive and penetrating responses we received from Rita Brause, Fordham University; Toby Fulwiler, University of Vermont; Carol Lefelt, Highland Park High School; and Gordon Pradl, New York University, were invaluable. Their responses were incredibly thorough, especially given the timetable we gave them. We thank them for being prompt, generous, and enthusiastic.

Bob Boynton and Peter Stillman have treated us with trust from the start. They helped us know that we were on to something interesting before we fully believed it ourselves. Thanks also to Dawne Boyer for her help during the production of the book.

Cindy's colleagues at City College, particularly Norman Shapiro and Laurie Engle, gave us the extra time we needed by deftly juggling schedules, deadlines, and demands.

We got support from Stash Karczewski in his role as photographer, as well as in his role as Cindy's husband. Even during those times when it appeared that Cindy was more wedded to Nancy than she was to Stash, he helped us in every way he could by listening, questioning, cooking, and bartending.

If it were not for John Mayher, we may never have begun our collaborative relationship. John was Cindy's dissertation chair and introduced her to Nancy. He says he was never sorry about that. John's roles in this book are probably too many and too deep to define very clearly. We know that he read the text as it was emerging and the manuscript in every stage. Our trust in him is immeasurable. We talked with him about the project almost incessantly for four years. The way that his ideas about teaching and learning have influenced our own is inexpressible.

Picture Nancy, Cindy, Stash, and John at The Noho Star restaurant in New York City every Friday night for a year and a half talking about how work on the book was going. You can see and hear John and Stash over the cacophony, commiserating in our depression and delighting in our accomplishments. Without those dinners at the Noho Star this book would not be possible. Cheers!

NANCY B. LESTER   CYNTHIA ONORE
The Write Company   City College of New York
New York, New York   New York, New York

Prologue

Change as Possibility

The year was 1985. The time 7:00 A.M. on a September morning. We were driving to Charmont, a small, suburban community about one hour from New York City. This could have been just another trip to just another school district to work with just another group of teachers. But it wasn't. This book is an attempt to describe why things were different right from the start. But we have to backtrack a bit in order to set the stage for the work we did with the Charmont School District from 1985 through 1988. We think that it's important for us to say a little bit about who we were and how we thought about in-service education prior to this time. We want to recreate our histories as in-service educators from 1982, when we first began to work with each other.

Although we had been working exclusively with English and language arts teachers before 1982, by the time we joined together, we had already broadened our focus to include teachers across disciplines. We had learned by 1982 that developing students' writing abilities was the province of all teachers, not just English teachers. Our goals had been to help teachers in all subject areas use writing as a way of supporting students' grasp of subject matter and, at the same time, increasing the amount and variety of writing students would do during the school year. In terms of these goals, we were successful, as evidenced by a writing sample survey we conducted in one school district we worked in from 1982–1985. We documented an increase in both the amount

1

and variety of writing that students engaged in across the curriculum (Onore, 1984).

What we did in workshops from 1982 to 1985 was similar to what we planned for Charmont. We would use learning logs, writing, sharing, and revising, professional readings, small group work, and the like. We had a set of successful strategies ready at hand. Because we were still learning and still developing our professional know-how, we didn't always understand the implications of what we were doing. We constructed purposeful writing tasks, but we didn't see the relationship between such hands-on experiences and the complete learning that can come with distancing and reflection. We didn't encourage explorations of personal learning histories, because we hadn't yet fully realized how important it is to understand learning in order to change teaching. We and the teachers talked a great deal in these workshops, but we didn't talk about why we were talking. We didn't understand when and how to share responsibility and decision making. We used small groups and decentered our workshops, but we still believed that motivation and ownership could come as a result of our engaging writing tasks and our engaging personalities. We didn't see engagement or motivation as generated from the inside out. In fact, we worried sometimes that the teachers' desire to try out new strategies derived more from personal loyalty to us and a desire to please than from a commitment to the new ideas and strategies themselves. And so we were anxious about how much the teachers would be able to carry on without us. As beginning professionals in in-service education, then, we lacked the experience to analyze and interpret our own teaching in such a way as to bring to light the implications of our actions.

We didn't have enough experience to reflect thoroughly on our in-service work, but we did have a growing sense of dissatisfaction that teachers' efforts at incorporating writing into their classrooms were neither developing students' writing abilities in ways we thought could be possible, nor supporting students' learning to the extent we hoped writing could. Once we became dissatisfied by what we had been doing, we had to discover what was missing from our work. We asked ourselves what we were doing, or not doing, that was contributing to the results we were seeing in teachers' classrooms. In trying to pinpoint where we got the insights to question our practice, we keep recalling the many visits we made to classrooms as part of our in-service programs. The ostensive purpose of these visits was to help teachers integrate and apply writing activities to their subject area and grade level. We couldn't help teachers in this process without bumping up against a whole range of things teachers were doing that seemed to undermine the writing activities.

A visit to a special education class of five students in 1983 was pivotal for us. During the writing activity that we observed, the students were allowed to choose their own topics and encouraged to share their writing with one another. The classroom was purposefully noisy and excited as students read to and commented encouragingly on one another's work. As this writing time slipped into time for science, there was a not-so-subtle change in the class-room environment. Students returned to their assigned places and all talking ceased except for the teacher's lecture.

In trying to help this teacher in the post-visit conference, we began to explore along with her some of the reasons why the two events we observed seemed to contrast so starkly. Together we discovered that perhaps the students were receiving mixed messages: while they seemed to have a right to their own language and ideas when producing their own written texts as well as being free to share and talk and explore collaboratively, that right didn't belong to them when learning science. There, student talk was not an appropriate vehicle for learning, nor were sharing and collaboration.

Incidents like this had a cumulative effect on us. Before long, we knew we had to broaden our focus to include all language modes, not just writing. And further, we began to sense more acutely the role students' language, oral or written, plays in their learning. Writing, then, became only the tip of the iceberg, while the parts that were submerged became more threatening, but clearly unavoidable: in order to do writing purposefully and intentionally, students also needed to collaborate through talking about their ideas; in order for writing to be a successful way of learning subject material, it must be the kind of writing that is exploratory, tentative, and risky, like talk among peers.

The effect on us of making these connections was to consider changing our in-service focus from writing across the curriculum to language and learning across the curriculum. Not only did we need to spend time exploring the connections between language and learning, but we also needed to examine the role of talk in the classroom. We also needed to broaden the professional readings from a focus on writing to one on how reading, writing, talking, and listening contribute to learning.

At about the same time that we began to consider changing the focus of our in-service programs, we also began to consider changes in our processes of instruction. Our conferences with many teachers following our visits to their classrooms were "talking back" (Schön, 1983) to us. What they said was that explicit, conscious reflection on what we and the teachers were doing was imperative to round out the learning cycle. The "talk" during these conferences was, indeed, helping us learn more about what we were doing and thinking. What we began to recognize as essential in our workshops was that this process of distancing, or reflection, had to be linked to whatever immersion or hands-on activities we engaged in. We began to ask the question "*What* and *how* did you learn?" of ourselves and the teachers.

But there's more. Once you ask, "*What* and *how* did you learn," you begin to explore the implications of all the teaching strategies and all the theories of language and learning for classroom structure. With this question in mind, let's return to the special education class we just looked at. *What* the students were learning was that learning writing wasn't like learning other subjects. Perhaps the students were learning that writing was more fun than science or even that writing was less important academically than science. It was certainly more fun at least because they could talk to one another, get up from their assigned seats, and be themselves. It might have seemed less important for the same reasons.

Many educators tell us that "real" learning in school must be serious. If students seem to be enjoying themselves when they learn, then can they really be learning? The students in this special education class certainly seemed to us to be enjoying their collaboration, their freedom to make their own decisions, and the informality that allowed them to move about the classroom as they worked. When the class shifted to a focus on science, however, all of these attributes connected with writing time disappeared. The underlying message this shift must have sent to the students was that science is a rigorous, academic subject that demands a serious classroom climate, whereas learning how to write is just plain fun. By implication, then, learning to write must not be as important as learning science.

Of course, the enjoyable part of learning to write in this classroom has serious implications when it comes to thinking about the *whats* and *hows* of learning. We can speculate that what might have been fun about this learning time was that students were making independent decisions about writing. The teacher's decisions about what they were to write about and how they were to help each other were kept to a minimum, and then only to facilitate students' decisions, not to impose her will on them. Rather than having one expert in the classroom, all the students considered each other as experts and sought out help from one another as a result. And, because students were writing on a variety of topics, most of which reflected their personal knowledge, there was not, in contrast to the science segment, a body of knowledge they were either unfamiliar with or expected to sit quietly and take in. They were all producing knowledge themselves. Because the teacher was doing all the science teaching herself, she was learning little about what her students could do in science or knew in science. In contrast, the teacher was learning quite a lot about her students' strengths and weaknesses as writers and as collaborators in the processes of writing.

They were all learning that they had different roles to play when they studied different disciplines. Receiving the material from an expert comprised the *hows* of the students' learning of science. In writing, the process was to share, through talk, their different meanings and expressions. To the extent that their teacher shared her role of expert with them, she became a facilitator and collaborator. When she didn't, the *hows* of her teaching involved controlling the content as well as the processes of learning.

We see two different views of learning here that reveal contrasting underlying assumptions or beliefs about how knowledge is constructed. We were finally discovering that changing any one aspect of a classroom, in particular, how language is used, isn't possible without simultaneously changing who has power and control over knowledge. Anything other than a thoroughgoing reconceptualization of learning would result in what Peter Elbow (1986) has called "the pedagogy of the bamboozled." If we change the gimmicks we use to teach, but don't change what we think teaching is, then students are drawn into a trap in which they believe that they are empowered over their own learning when their learning is controlled solely by the teacher. Our insights about knowledge construction had far-reaching implications.

These implications took on life in applications in our workshops in Charmont. But like all new insights, "knowing that" and "knowing how" turned out to be very different things. It took us the full three years in Charmont both to understand and to act on our understandings. We were continually trying out new structures and mechanisms. The trying out taught us about the subtleties, which, in turn, helped us refine the strategies. Our trial-and-error process taught us more and more about the complexities underlying shared power.

Story as Research

We've spent time sketching our collaborative professional autobiography because we believe that our research can be best understood and appreciated if our readers know something about how and what we think. We've chosen to tell stories in order to reveal our point of view. We have situated ourselves in the stories that are to follow because we are the narrators and two of the characters in the stories. For Clifford Geertz (1988), this sort of research depends upon a particular view of the question of "authorial presence":

> The establishment of an authorial presence within a text has haunted ethnography from very early on, though for the most part it has done so in a disguised form. Disguised, because it has been generally cast not as a narratological issue, a matter of how best to get an honest story honestly told, but as an epistemological one, a matter of how to prevent subjective views from coloring objective facts. The clash between the expository conventions of author-saturated texts and those of author-evacuated ones that grows out of the particular nature of the ethnographic enterprise is imagined to be a clash between seeing things as one would have them and seeing them as they really are. (p. 9)

Like Geertz, we believe that there is no difference between "seeing things as one would have them" and "seeing things as they really are." In the stories we're about to tell, we could not have chosen the "luxury" of cool distance on the characters and events. For us, there cannot be a construal—a story—without a construer. This is after all, *our* story.

We have been studying ourselves, the participants, and the schools in Charmont as institutions since the inception of the three-year program. We can't quite pinpoint the exact moment when we said, "Hey, this would be an interesting book to write." What we do seem to be able to track is the evolutionary nature of the study of the central question of this book: "What are the factors, both individual and institutional, that promote and enhance or inhibit and stifle change?"

This book begins, then, with Part I, "Learning and Teaching," which includes Chapter 1, "Toward a Philosophy of Democratic Schooling," a description and an explanation of the theoretical lenses through which we currently view teaching and learning, and Chapter 2, "Philosophy and Structure of the In-Service Program," which introduces the Charmont School District and presents the design of the in-service program. Part II, "The Teachers," contains the next four chapters. "The Nature of Knowledge: Two Views," Chapter 3, creates portraits of two teachers who illustrate the central hypothesis of this study. The next three chapters, "The Teacher as Reflective Practitioner," "The Teacher as Learner: 'Contradictions of Control,' " and "The Teacher as Leader," each focus on one teacher who exemplifies a distinct process of change. Chapter 7, "Teachers Face the Institution," which comprises and titles Part III, broadens the discussion of change to include school, district, and community constraints on the change process. In the *Epilogue,* we look at what we have learned and what we believe the future holds for Charmont.

The function of our inquiry was to generate hypotheses that could account for what we saw and what we learned. With the question, "What are the factors, both individual and institutional, that promote and enhance or inhibit and stifle change?" guiding our seeing, we systematically collected and analyzed a variety of data we hoped would give us insight. Having entered into this collection and analysis process with a Kellyan framework (Kelly, 1955), we were looking to identify teachers' personal constructs as they related to the teaching and learning process. (An explanation of Kelly's theory of personal constructs is contained in the methodological introduction to Part II.) We identified seven categories of constructs that seemed to infuse the participants' work and growth in the workshops as well as their practices in their own classrooms.

As we plotted the course of these constructs for teachers during the period of their involvement in the in-service program, one of these constructs began to emerge as having overarching power. This one, the core construct, is the one by which an individual defines the nature of knowledge, and by that we mean what knowledge is, how people acquire it, and how we decide whether knowledge has been acquired or not. (See Douglas Barnes, *From*

Communication to Curriculum, particularly chapter 5, for a similar view of the connection between a teacher's concept of knowledge and teaching practices.) This superordinate construct, as Kelly has defined it, has predictive value. The central hypothesis we generated, then, is that teachers' definitions of the nature of knowledge account for the degree and kind of change they will experience. We also found changes of varying degree and kind in the six remaining satellite constructs. We agree with Kelly that a person's core construct does not change, although the subordinate constructs that derive from it may change. Thus, we are suggesting that there is a significant correlation between the core construct and who changes in what ways and how.

The Individual as Social Being

This hypothesis and the framework guiding it clearly point to the individual as the central player in the drama of reform. Though we recognize that the world shapes the individual, what we are attempting to emphasize by our hypothesis is the contribution individuals make in shaping both their worlds and the larger social world of which they are a part. In this project, we worked with individuals who happened to be teachers, but we also tried to get to know the context in which we all worked. In addition, we acted as advocates for them in helping to change the social context of their schools. But what the teachers did and how they grew had profound effects on their students, the worlds of their classrooms, the structure and organization of their schools, and, not so incidentally, on us.

This is not, of course, to deny the role that the institution of school plays in shaping individual teachers' views of teaching and learning. The radical literature that we have become familiar with and used extensively in this book makes a substantial case both for how schools influence and shape those who teach and learn in them and how schools must change philosophically and politically, as well as structurally, if teaching and learning are to change. Although we do, in fact, devote a chapter to exploring how teachers deal with institutional constraints (Chapter 7), our analysis rests on a transactional or dialectical view. That is, we are not convinced that school structure alone accounts for how teaching and learning proceed in school. After all, structures are, in this case, not concrete objects, but people. Each, then, the institution and the teachers, can form the center of an analysis, because what each brings to the relationship will ultimately affect the nature of that relationship as well as the entities that comprise it.

Lewis Thomas (1979) comes closest to describing what we see as the relationship between the individual and the social context in his definition of a truly transactional relationship between the Medusa and Nudibranch:

> When first observed, the nudibranch, a common sea slug, was found to have a tiny vestigial parasite, in the form of a jellyfish, permanently

affixed to the ventral surface near the mouth. In curiosity to learn how
the medusa got there, some marine biologists began searching the local
waters for earlier developmental forms, and discovered something
amazing. The attached parasite, although apparently so specialized as to
give up living for itself, can still produce offspring, for they are found
in abundance at certain seasons of the year. They drift through the upper
waters, grow up nicely and astonishingly, and finally become full-
grown, handsome, normal jellyfish. Meanwhile, the snail produces snail
larvae, and these too begin to grow normally, but not for long. While
still extremely small, they become entrapped in the tentacles of the
medusa and then engulfed within the umbrella-shaped body. At first
glance, you'd believe the medusae are now the predators, paying back
for earlier humiliations, and the snails the prey. But no. Soon the snails,
undigested and insatiable, begin to eat, browsing away first at the radial
canals, then the borders of the rim, finally the tentacles, until the jellyfish becomes reduced in substance by being eaten while the snail grows
correspondingly in size. At the end, the arrangement is back to the first
scene, with the full-grown nudibranch basking, and nothing left of the
jellyfish except the round, successfully edited parasite, safely affixed to
the skin near the mouth.

It is a confusing tale to sort out, and even more confusing to think
about. Both creatures are designed for this encounter, marked as selves
so that they can find each other in the waters of the Bay of Naples. The
collaboration, if you want to call it that, is entirely specific; it is only this
species of medusa and only this kind of nudibranch that can come
together and live this way. And, more surprising, they cannot live in any
other way; they depend for their survival on each other. **They are not
really selves, they are specific** *others*. (pp. 4–5)

It is clear from Thomas's description that each of these creatures is
knowable as an independent entity. Knowing them as entities, however,
requires knowing about features and characteristics of the other. That, we
think, expresses metaphorically the relationship between the individual teachers with whom we worked and the context in which they worked. Moving
from the metaphorical to the literal, then, this book is mainly about people and
the chapters that follow are case studies of them.

Our Work in Relation to Research on School Reform

In thinking about what school knowledge is and in coming to understand
how individual teachers' views of knowledge affect their classroom practices,
we've been influenced by the work of Michael Apple (particularly, *Education*

and Power, 1982) and Linda McNeil (1986). In attempting to analyze the role of school in society, and particularly the means by which schools transmit the dominant culture, McNeil (and others) suggests three different conceptualizations of how this has been achieved: reproducing culture, producing culture, and transforming culture.

Cultural reproduction suggests that the role of the school is to preserve the inequalities that already exist in the larger society. Apple asserts that schools don't just reproduce the culture, but they produce their own kind of culture, one in which the goal is to develop the particular kinds of knowledge required for a labor force that will contribute to and support, rather than be critical of or impede, the production of capital. In building on Apple's analysis, McNeil develops the idea that the educational process itself is designed to support the culture that schools make:

> After being processed through worksheets, list-filled lectures and short answer tests, the cultural content, regardless of whose interests it may have served before, comes to serve only the interests of institutional efficiencies. . . . Its meaning is whatever meaning the assignments have in helping students meet the institutional requirements of their credentialing. (1986, p. 13)

Schools, then, support cultural and economic reproduction as well as they do because schools themselves embody the kinds of mechanisms that make bureaucratic control both possible and sustainable. The kind of knowledge that is valued in such places is knowledge that controls students and teachers, not knowledge that either students or teachers make for themselves. Schools are structured and knowledge is delivered to disempower rather than to empower all the players.

In attempting to contribute to this analysis and enrich it, we found ourselves continually raising two sets of questions: The first, how does a teacher's individual belief or construct system contribute to creating and supporting this system? And how does the system contribute to the teacher's individual belief or construct system? Most teachers have been willing participants in the system in the sense that their views of knowledge are compatible with the aims and roles of schooling. And to return to the metaphor of the medusa and the snail, the individual and the larger social context have as some of their features categorical features of the other.

The second set of questions raised by McNeil's research include: What happens when a teacher's view of knowledge is incompatible with the school's? How does a teacher deal with the "contradictions of control"? And lastly, in the context of an in-service project that supports an opposing view of knowledge from the school's, how are a teacher's classroom practices affected by and how might a teacher come to effect change in the larger school context?

This book is an attempt to explore the answers to these questions as well as to contribute to the larger, professional conversations about school reform.

Why Language Is an Agent for Change

As will be evident as this story unfolds, *subject*: language and learning was at the same time *process*: language and learning. This implies that we attempted to make our teaching practices as congruent with and reflective of the philosophy and practices we were engendering as we could. In addition, because we ourselves had learned the value of talk in terms of contributing, modifying, and creating knowledge, we gave talk a central place in the workshops as an instrument for learning. In other words, language was both the object of study as well as the means for study. Taking a more comprehensive and, perhaps, richer view helps us understand why language is an agent for change. We think it's no accident that the language across the curriculum movement, in general, has had such a profound impact on the classrooms and schools where it has served as the philosophy of instruction and a disaster in those that took on the name, but not the substance. As Garth Boomer writes in *Metaphors and Meanings* (Green, 1988):

> The language and learning movement . . . was however trying to get across policies of a different and arguably far more fundamental kind. The focus was not: let's improve literacy and language performance. It was: let's improve learning by looking at how language affects and shapes learning. This involves school and faculty policies focused on matters of thinking and meaning and learning. (p. 152)

From Boomer's perspective, it has been the express intention of language across the curriculum to have an impact on a wide range of school issues and not just on how much language or what kinds of assessments and pedagogical strategies are used. We believe that the reason for this lies in the fundamental nature of language, its connection to knowledge construction and to learning and its power to shape people and the world. Like the individual and the social context, language and learning are medusa and snail. Once allowed its full capacity to support and extend learning, language becomes a tool for empowerment. Through language, learners become more engaged in learning, they expose their ideas, beliefs, feelings, speculations, and contemplate them. They collaborate through language with one another to build meanings and webs of support and encouragement, and they reflect on their own growth and change. As a result, learners take action, redefine their own knowledge and their relationship to knowledge and to "those who know." All of these contribute to the fundamental changes, the visible reorganizations of people and institutions that characterize reform. We wanted to know what would promote or inhibit change. In the process of investigating those issues, we found that we had the very instrument to promote change at our disposal—language.

Beyond Language Across the Curriculum

The original request that the Charmont School District made to us was to help teachers develop a comprehensive, district-wide writing curriculum. Like other school districts, Charmont was operating within a commonsense view of the world of schooling (see Mayher, 1990, for an in-depth discussion of commonsense vs. uncommonsense schooling). They had a problem that they wanted to solve—students weren't writing well enough to get high test scores and there was no fixed curriculum to help them improve. Having no other source of ideas for how they might go about improving writing instruction, Charmont called upon knowledge they already did have. Science and social studies, for example, had a set curriculum, so it seemed natural to propose that a writing curriculum would best serve the teaching and learning of writing. Further, if students weren't doing well on tests of writing, then teaching them how to pass such tests would certainly improve results.

Charmont employed us at a time when we had shifted from a focus on writing to one on language in learning and, finally, to one on learning in the context of schooling. As a result, we convinced them that both focusing on writing alone and producing a K–12 writing curriculum would not, in fact, meet their expressed objective for improving students' writing abilities. Their positive response to this allowed us to explore with the Charmont teachers the relationships between language in all its forms and learning. From the beginning, then, and with an increasing depth of understanding on our part about the central place that exploring learning has, not only on changing how language is used or writing is taught and learned, but on changing the fabric of schooling, we and the teachers we worked with began, and we continue with this book, to challenge the system of schooling.

Part I

Learning and Teaching

Chapter One

Toward a Philosophy of Democratic Schooling

Putting Learning First in Teaching

September, 1985, the beginning of the program in Charmont, represents a significant moment in our development as in-service professionals. We were struggling at that point to know ourselves better. We were trying to examine our own beliefs and assumptions about teaching and learning and trying to make the work that we did with teachers in Charmont help them to examine their beliefs. We were sometimes getting in our own way because we didn't understand as fully as we needed to what our actions and choices as in-service leaders implied, the extent to which we might be inhibiting rather than supporting teachers' efforts to examine critically their own work. Once teachers' questions or actions posed contradictions or dissonances for us, we could begin to reflect on the beliefs that underlay what we were doing and begin to reconstruct our actions so that teachers could be free to learn about and for themselves.

In our search to discover the causes for the dissonance and dissatisfactions that we began to recognize in our practices, we ally ourselves with James Britton (1969/1986) and Judith Lindfors (1984) in their attempts to understand why learning happens when it does and what role teaching plays in the process of learning. We began to notice when we asked our students to tell us *what* and *how* they were learning that what we were teaching didn't necessarily look at all like what our students were learning. Britton cautioned us not to equate teaching with learning years ago when he wrote:

> We teach and teach and they learn and learn: if they didn't, we wouldn't. But of course the relation between their learning and our teaching isn't by any means a constant one. From any given bit of teaching some learn more than others; we teach some lessons when everybody seems to learn something, and other lessons when nobody seems to learn anything—at all events, not anything of what we are "teaching." (1969/1986, p. 91)

Since our initial reading of Britton's formulation of the problem, we've learned more about the potential differences between teaching and learning from Lindfors, whose descriptions of "teachers' instructional activities" and "learners' sense-making activities" have clarified instances in which teaching and learning don't match. Lindfors argues, even more strongly than Britton, that teachers need to focus their attention on what learners are doing and derive their teaching from learning. Once we began to listen more carefully to what teachers were telling us about our teaching, we understood the "profound confusion" between teaching and learning that was driving our own practices.

From our present-day perspective, it's now easy to see that we wouldn't have even recognized the confusion between teaching and learning if we didn't hold a constructivist belief about knowledge, that knowledge is the active creation of meaning by each learner. From this perspective, the sense-making activities of learners have primary importance in the teaching/learning act. If, on the other hand, we had held an objectivist belief about knowledge, that knowledge is an entity capable of being transmitted from one who knows to one who doesn't know, then teaching acts have primary importance in the teaching/learning act. Thus, we are suggesting that being able to recognize the potential differences between teaching and learning rests on a fundamental belief about knowledge.

We reasoned that because beliefs about knowledge are fundamental, then such beliefs would imply other beliefs about teaching and learning as well. We thought a view of knowledge might relate to the roles teachers and students assume in the classroom. Beliefs about knowledge might also explain how they use language, how they assess learning, and how they develop the curriculum. We began to envision two different classrooms: the autocratic classroom, one built on an objectivist view, and the democratic classroom, one built on a constructivist view of knowledge.

Envisioning these two classrooms involved us in a process that we can now see as one of developing our own philosophy of instruction. Our purpose in presenting portraits of these two kinds of classrooms is to create an understanding of the philosophy we were trying to enact in the in-service project because we were beginning to define one of our major goals as helping teachers develop their own philosophies of instruction. We were trying to establish a democratic setting for the in-service workshops and hoping to work with teachers to examine the implications of democratic schooling for their own classrooms. We want to construct a picture of these democratic principles in action so that you can see how the teachers, whose stories we will tell later in this book, understood these principles. We will also see how they enacted their understandings and how they confronted the problems and conflicts that arose when they examined their own beliefs and brought those beliefs to life.

We will contrast the beliefs and resulting actions of the democratic classroom with those of the autocratic classroom. All of the current research on American classrooms (see, especially, *National Commission on Excellence in Education,* 1983; Apple & Weis, 1983; Aronowitz & Giroux, 1985; Boyer, 1983; Cuban, 1984; Goodlad, 1984; Sizer, 1984) suggests that what we are calling the autocratic classroom is the dominant and most acceptable form of education. Because it is so pervasive and so commonsensical, it isn't easy to critique, nor is it easy to envision alternatives. By attempting to uncover the beliefs that are implied by the "time-honored" practices (Cuban, 1984) of teachers in autocratic classrooms and by juxtaposing these beliefs with the alternatives to them implied by the principles of the democratic classroom, we hope to understand both better. We need to understand, as fully as possible, what *is*, to listen to what these classrooms we are calling autocratic are telling us, in order to envision what *might be*. When we know what beliefs underlie autocratic classrooms, when we know why we see the practices we see, we may then be able to envision what is possible.

Autocratic Classrooms

Our portrait of the autocratic classroom draws on the research and reform reports cited above. We've synthesized these studies with our experiences in such classrooms and, as a result, have created a stereotype, which, like all stereotypes, has no exact equivalent in the world.

Beliefs Underlying Autocratic Classrooms

Autocratic classrooms are places where teachers and their knowledge are at the center of learning. Teachers are the only experts because what they know determines what students must know. All knowledge, that which teachers have and that which is contained in textbooks and curricula, is a fixed entity or a commodity, bounded by teachers' interpretations and understandings, texts, tests, and time. Knowledge doesn't seem to have been produced by any one. What matters is that students consume whatever knowledge teachers and textbooks have, not that students come to know how to make knowledge for themselves. Knowledge is transmitted from those who know to those who don't. The mind might be described as a kind of duplicating machine that makes exact copies.

Some have described the relationship between teachers and students as that of producer and consumer (Bowles & Gintis, 1976). Freire (1970) has called this relationship "the banking concept" of education. No matter what metaphor you use to describe these relationships between teachers and learners, the concept is the same: those who have knowledge have power. Their power is derived from the fact that they choose when knowledge will be transmitted, how knowledge will be transmitted, what knowledge will be transmitted, and, finally, how it will be determined whether or not successful transmission has occurred. Students are always dependent upon someone else for knowledge; thus, they are placed in consistently subordinate positions as consumers.

Based on this conception of knowledge and the role the teacher plays in transmitting it, learning is a passive process of reception. The better students are at swallowing and regurgitating teacher and textbook knowledge, the smarter they are considered. They don't have to work at making meanings or interpreting the meanings made by others. All they have to do is receive and reproduce what is transmitted. Because learners' intentions and knowledge don't figure at all in this model, it really doesn't matter if there are conflicts, gaps, or misunderstandings. There's no reason to ameliorate differences in the kinds of knowledge each participant brings to the situation or to generate mutually supporting intentions. Any conflicts, gaps, or misunderstandings that arise are interpreted as resistance, stupidity, and/or disinterest. If students don't learn—get the knowledge—it's because they're dumb, or haven't listened hard enough, done their homework, taken notes, or memorized the textbook.

In the autocratic classroom, then, teachers decide who may speak and when; whose questions get raised and answered; what is relevant and not; what counts as knowledge; who has learned and who has not. The point should be clear: teachers, acting as experts in all these areas, control all decisions, all actions, all choices. Another expression of the power teachers wield in this setting is that they help shape students' assumptions about what schooling is. If students view school as competitive, alienating, disenfranchising, and irrelevant, then, we think, the objectivist view of knowledge is largely responsible.

Language is the primary vehicle through which power is expressed. Transmission, the way knowledge is given and received in autocratic classrooms, rests on a "code theory" of language. Code theory (Sperber & Wilson, 1986) describes one point of view about how language and thought are related. By analogy, we also think it describes the hypothesis teachers have about how they communicate knowledge to their students and how students come "to know." Code theory suggests that speakers—teachers—possess a system that encodes language from their minds into a message that is carried through the air (or telephone, or typewriter, or computer, or the chalkboard) and is, pretty much verbatim, decoded through a matching system that listeners possess. The kernel notion here is that there is a one-to-one correspondence between what the teacher says (encodes) and what the learner receives (decodes). Knowledge encoded by the teacher will be "learned" as the student decodes the message. This is the only way students can learn.

Teacher talk dominates classroom interaction for 75% of a student's day, according to Goodlad (1984). Moreover, teachers tend to be the ones who ask questions and the questioner controls the conversation. Even when teachers are attempting to reduce this kind of control and ask a question like, "What is your interpretation of the relationship between Romeo and Juliet?" a question that appears to encourage students to make their own meanings, teachers are still setting the agenda for the exploration that is to follow. The type of talk that generally goes on in classrooms—the oral workbook—is of a variety found in no other context (Brause & Mayher, 1983). In addition to the short-answer, fill-in-the-blank characteristics of a workbook, there is another important element to classroom talk: teachers automatically evaluate, either through their oral responses or their body language, each answer a student supplies, indicating whether it is right, wrong, relevant, or irrelevant.

This learning model rests on a very strange communication situation: the teacher tells students things that they don't necessarily want to hear, and the students, at exam or evaluation time, tell the teacher what the teacher has already told them. Since one of the basic pragmatic principles of communication posits that you don't tell people things that they already know or things they don't care about or are intending to care about (Grice, 1975; Searle, 1969; Sperber & Wilson, 1986), then this communication context is bankrupt. Real questions, questions that engender genuine exchanges of ideas, are rarely posed or answered. Classroom questions are primarily examination questions because teachers ask questions for which they already have the answers. The teacher's goal is to find out if anyone else has the answers, another violation of normal communication situations. Successful students are those who recognize the rules of this particular game, those who are able to set aside what they already know about communication out of school and substitute, from years of experience in school, this somewhat bizarre set of rules. Learners who succeed in autocratic classrooms do so primarily because they understand the rules and play by them.

Practices Typical of Autocratic Classrooms

Let's look at a few of the ways the autocratic classroom operates. If knowledge is viewed as a commodity, then the most efficient means of transmitting it from teacher to student is to deliver it to the whole class all at once. The criteria for evaluation are speed and efficiency of reproduction. Covering the curriculum is the most important goal and, since whole-class teaching is the most efficient mode, then questions of how individual students learn or what they're learning can't figure into the teacher's planning. Teachers do the lion's share of the talking because they have the knowledge that counts, the knowledge that has to be consumed.

Periodically, teachers need to find out whether or not the students have learned what's been transmitted. Informal testing goes on all the time when teachers use the oral workbook technique as well as when they ask questions for which they already have the answers. Formal tests are a regular feature of autocratic classrooms. The most efficient assessment is the short-answer or multiple-choice test because there are right and wrong answers. Even essay questions, however, can be made mechanical (Langer & Applebee, 1987). A short essay about the causes of the Civil War, a discussion worthy of book-length exploration, is really designed to reveal whether the student remembers and can reproduce the causes that have been detailed in the classroom.

Tests are central to teaching because they provide the rationale for learning. They reflect only the teacher's knowledge and intentions, so students, in order to be successful, must recognize that their job is to reproduce the contours of the teacher's thinking. Testing, when used in the autocratic classroom, nullifies students' intentions because tests set the goals and requirements for learning.

Testing sets the pace of learning. The test signals the end of a learning episode. What or whether learning has occurred is not as important as moving on. The test lets all know that they can forget what has been tested and that it is now time to accumulate another commodity. Subject matter knowledge is not developmental, but discrete, because each new topic can be introduced, covered, and tested without reference to anything that has come before or anything that may come after. Although teachers often complain that students don't remember anything that has been previously "covered" in the curriculum, they may not recognize that the pattern of teaching and testing might be responsible for what is perceived as students' amnesia.

Control has a variety of faces of which testing is but one. The most easily recognized form of control is discipline. Classrooms that are quiet, clean, smooth, and orderly represent the best environments for teaching and learning. As long as students sit in their rows, face the board, and copy quietly into their notebooks, their classroom is effective.

Another form of control is control of the content of what is to be learned. Textbooks and teachers' lectures are designed to set the parameters for what's appropriate to learn. Textbooks define the scope and sequence of learning. From the history textbook that fails to mention the contribution of African Americans and other minority soldiers during World Wars I and II, to the science text that excludes any reference to theories of evolution, to the literature anthology that, like a version of *Reader's Digest Condensed Books*, presents selections from Shakespeare's plays as if such piecemeal excerpts could convey the essence of the longer versions, to the basal reader whose vocabulary and sentence structure is controlled by readability formulas that make these texts harder to read than real literature might be, textbooks consistently limit the field of knowledge by limiting the access to knowledge and limiting potentially diverse interpretations to single, partial, and partisan points of view.

Teachers' control over knowledge is, in many ways, similar to that wielded by textbooks. Another dimension, however, is that teachers are living human beings in the classroom, so the knowledge they are attempting to transmit is in more danger of direct challenge than the disembodied textbook. After all, teachers are present and can be exposed to students' challenges, scrutiny, contradiction, and disbelief. What strategies do teachers use to stave off these attempts at reducing their control? Linda McNeil (1986) discovered four— fragmentation, mystification, omission, and defensive simplification— in her ethnographic study of four Wisconsin high school social studies classes. These strategies shape how content is delivered and aim to protect the teacher's control of knowledge in autocratic classrooms.

Fragmentation involves "the reduction of any topic to fragments, or disjointed pieces of information—lists" (p. 123). This ensures, or at least promotes, the impression that all information is factual and agreed upon by the experts in the field. Not only does fragmentation eliminate interpretation and incompleteness, but it makes

> efficient use of time, avoid[s] arousing discussion, and present[s] information in a manner that facilitates quantifiable testing. When filled with lists, the course content appears to be rigorous and factual. It makes the teacher appear knowledgeable and gives students a sense of fairness in the grading: they know they have to memorize the lists. Lists and unelaborated terms reduce the uncertainty for both students and teachers. For this reason it is clearly the dominant mode of conveying information. (p. 124)

Any complex or controversial topic can be made accessible through the strategy of *mystification*. An idea is presented as "very important, but unknowable" because it is too difficult to learn in the amount of time allotted. By rendering the topic mysterious, by transmitting only the label, the teacher can retain control of it. Naming a topic counts as covering and learning the topic. To probe and explore this kind of topic would demystify it and allow students to share in control of it because it would open it up to multiple interpretations.

The teacher may anticipate controversy and choose the strategy of *omission*. McNeil discovered that a subject like the Vietnam War might receive no attention whatsoever in a twentieth century American history class. Rather than deal with a topic upon which students may have divergent opinions, or even attempt to mystify or fragment it, the teacher can choose to exclude it altogether. Orderliness and safety are not only features of classrooms where student behavior is controlled, but also features of classrooms where, under strategies like mystification, fragmentation, and omission, students' intellectual lives are controlled.

Topics that cannot be omitted, mystified, or fragmented are treated to a strategy of *defensive simplification*. Out of fear or in expectation that students will not be able to grasp the information without working to build a rich context in which such information could fit, "the teacher will win the student's compliance in a lesson by promising that it will not be difficult and will not go into any depth" (pp. 128–129). These topics are made knowable via a process similar to the application of readability formulas to literature. Teachers, convinced that students cannot handle the study of richer contexts, decontextualize these topics and thus, ironically, make them more difficult to grasp. Yet teachers feel confident that they have covered the curriculum in a way that matches their students' abilities and tests easily.

Fragmentation, mystification, omission, and defensive simplification seem to have students' best interests at heart, if we assume that students find school boring and irrelevant. The teacher who uses these strategies doesn't want to increase alienation. In fact, teachers hope that these strategies will make school a little more palatable. But McNeil found that "ironically, [the teacher's] very attempt to minimize student cynicism by simplifying content and avoiding class discussion only heightened students' disbelief of school knowledge and foster[ed] in students greater disengagement from the learning process" (pp. 116–117).

McNeil discovered further that, while a teacher might achieve an orderly and controlled classroom through the use of these strategies, one of the contradictions of this control was that students tended to resist in more subtle ways by refusing to believe in school knowledge. Eliminating discussion and controversy undermines the students' already rich knowledge base acquired outside of school and prevents them from activating their intentions. Students will naturally compare what they already know to what's being presented in school. Where these versions of reality clash, students tend to silently dismiss the school version in favor of their own personal knowledge.

By barring the students' personal knowledge and intentions from the classroom, the teacher is sending a subtle, but strong, message that their knowledge and intentions have little value. Rather than building new knowledge by beginning with what students already know or helping them question their assumptions, these strategies suppress any but the most rudimentary or superficial learning. The result then is control gained, knowledge lost.

These strategies have consequences for teachers as well as learners. Teaching is controlled and defined by the same strategies. How much pleasure and excitement can teachers derive from teaching when they believe they have to pare down, gloss over, and cover up complex ideas in their fields? Their emotions, their feelings, their points of view have as little place in the classroom as those of their students. As Goodlad (1984) has shown us, the sterility of the environment is all encompassing.

Democratic Classrooms

The democratic classroom we present here is our idealized world of teaching and learning. The teachers we worked with in Charmont taught us what a democratic classroom might look like in practice. We have also learned about democratic schooling from reading, among others, Dewey (1933), Freire (1970), and Giroux (1988).

Beliefs Underlying Democratic Classrooms

Another set of beliefs and practices leads to a very different picture of teaching and learning. These we've termed constructivist. From this perspective, knowledge does not exist independent of a knower, but, instead, is brought into being through a transaction between the learner and the environment. Learning is not reacting passively, but building constructively, actively, and passionately "a theory of the world in the head" (Smith, 1975). Transactions are not one-directional. A classroom built from a constructivist perspective would be a place where learning is initiated by both teachers and students, and students, teachers, and their knowledge are all "simultaneously conditioned by and conditioning the other[s]" (Bentley & Dewey, 1949).

In the autocratic classroom as we've described it, learners' intentions and purposes are not a necessary part of teaching or learning; in the democratic classroom, it's essential for learners' intentions and purposes to be voiced. In such a setting, open-mindedness, authenticity, wholeheartedness (Dewey, 1933), attitudes, and dispositions that are central to learning, are generated and supported. The democratic classroom acknowledges that each human being brings a whole range of experiences, feelings, beliefs, knowledge, and assumptions to bear in every learning situation that influences what, how, and why they learn. Intention, commitment, and ownership are outcomes of giving expression to learners' experiences, feelings, and beliefs.

In this model, teaching and learning work with, rather than against, each other. Teaching is a response to learners and to the learning situation, rather than a separate act, which at the best of times might match how learning proceeds, and at the worst of times might obstruct learning. In the democratic classroom, the intentions of all participants are brought to light and negotiated, creating what Freire (1970) calls "cointentional education." This blurs the distinction between teaching and learning.

A shift from an autocratic to a democratic classroom demands a shift in how language is viewed. One belief underlying how language functions in the democratic classroom is that it is transactional. It is an integral part of the meaning-making process. It is not simply the dress for thoughts and ideas and, as such, is neither transparent nor unimportant. Language is the vehicle through which we build up and work through our understandings. Texts, for example, are not just the words on the page. If they were, then we would all respond to the same text in the same way. But reading a text involves using our own language to understand and make meanings of the text's language. The relationship between thought and language and language and learning is, therefore, dialectical. (See Vygotsky's *Thought and Language*, 1962, for a thorough discussion of these relationships.) Language is a powerful tool for restructuring knowledge and building relationships.

Douglas Barnes (1969/1986) has described what happens when language use is altered in a nontraditional classroom setting:

> It is when the pupil is required to use language to grapple with new experience or to order old experience in a new way that he is most likely to find it necessary to use language differently. And this will be very different from taking over someone else's language in external imitation of its forms: on the contrary, it is the first step towards new patterns of thinking and feeling, new ways of representing reality to himself. It is not enough for pupils to imitate the forms of teachers' language as if they were models to be copied; it is only when they "try it out" in reciprocal exchanges so that they modify the way they use language to organize reality that they are able to find new functions for language in thinking and feeling. (p. 38)

From Barnes' description, we can see that more than language is at stake here. Language is being used in new and creative ways, and, as a result, the relationship between teachers and learners is also changing. In the autocratic model, teachers' power was derived, in part, from their control of the language of learning, where it was demanded that students reproduce the teacher's language in order to succeed in learning. By contrast, when learners try out new ideas, they often use language differently from the way teachers do. This trying out presupposes an inclination on both the teacher's and learner's part toward risk taking, incompleteness, and approximation. Such experimentation can only take place in an environment of mutual trust and respect, where errors are signs of progress, rather than occasions for punishment. Further, as Barnes says, these trial-and-error stabs at meaning making are conducted in "reciprocal exchanges," which to our minds happens only in collaborative learning environments, where the teacher's traditional role is revised. No longer analyzer of deficiency or sole possessor of knowledge, the teacher becomes co-learner, facilitator, and advisor.

As we saw in Linda McNeil's work, when power over the content and processes of learning is consolidated in the teacher, students often resist, or drop out, or disbelieve. When power is shared, as it can be through reciprocity and risk taking in collaborative environments, students' power is activated as is their natural intention to learn. The sum total of everyone's input generates far more power for everyone over knowledge than does any individual's attempt to wield power alone. Rather than losing control as a result of sharing power, teachers gain control. While teachers may have more knowledge or different knowledge than their students, in the democratic classroom, teachers' knowledge has greater value because it is an additional source of information for students rather than an imposition on them. This is, above all, not laissez-faire education. Responsibility for learning and teaching is shared. The criticism of progressive education has always been that students control the classroom and create anarchy. In the democratic classroom, however, power and decision making are shared through a process of cointentional education.

Practices Typical of Democratic Classrooms

More likely than not, the democratic classroom would be set up to accommodate small groups, individuals, and, occasionally, the entire class. Teachers' energies would be spent, not so much on performing and evaluating, but on planning for how learning might best occur and on observing how it is going. Selecting materials, structuring learning activities, supporting and extending student decisions on directions for learning, responding to students' meaning-making attempts, and reflecting on their teaching and their students' learning would now be their focus.

The roles that students and teachers play are transformed. Power in the autocratic classroom is most often wielded by a single individual, based on an assumption of authority by that individual, and expressed in a set of implicit and explicit rules. Rules are made independent of the participants. They may even undermine, rather than support, learning objectives. But an authority structure where individual and group responsibility for making decisions about the whys, whats, and hows of learning replaces those imposed by a single, unchanging, detached authoritarian structure releases everyone's power to learn. Instead of a set of inflexible rules, the rules that govern learning in a democratic classroom are generated by the needs of learners in collaboration with the goals of and constraints on their teachers. In this scheme, rules are functional in that they are designed to support and foster learning, and they may change as learning evolves. In other words, power and authority are generated inductively and jointly.

A means for achieving cointentional democratic education is "negotiated curriculum and goal-based assessment" (Boomer, 1982). This philosophy and method of teaching and learning, rediscovered and reconceived in Australia in the 1970s, has echoes of progressive education at the turn of the century. It is built on the view of power and authority, learning and teaching, which we have described before as characteristic of the democratic classroom, and its implementation came as a response to students' articulations about "how they learn best" (Cook, 1982, p. 134). Interviews with teachers and students formed a consistent picture of the conditions and patterns most congenial to learning (pp. 135–136):

1. *Engagement:* Learning should be purposeful, and the learner's own purposes matter more than those of the teacher. Learners need to know *what* and *why* they are learning. Learners want their intentions to mesh with their teachers, so that as much as possible all are thinking along the same lines.

2. *Exploration:* Learners recognize that they have different experiences from one another and so they would like learning to be individualized. Paradoxically, learners need to work together and, therefore, teachers need to open up the range of options and modes of learning.

   The small group is the preferred classroom organization. Learners want to use each other as sounding boards and feel most secure when working with their peers. Learners often feel bored or lost during whole class sessions. Sometimes they already know what's being explained and sometimes their own thinking is so far behind what the teacher is saying that they can't get anything out of the teacher's talk. The opportunity to ask questions and to hypothesize in whole class sessions is severely limited.

   Learners want to be active participants because they understand best when they can inquire, speculate, and hypothesize, rather than copy and regurgitate.

3. *Teacher's Role:* Learners want a facilitator, not a dictator. They want to be challenged but encouraged. They want to take risks, but not feel ashamed if they make errors.

4. *Learner's Role:* Learners need to reflect, both individually and collectively, on their learning, its consequences, and implications. From this reflection, as well as a sharing and presentation of learning, learners can discover new questions, challenges and directions for future learning.

What's so interesting about these points of view is not only that they give validity to the model of the democratic classroom, but that they were generated through democratic discussion. These guidelines are the sorts that we alluded to before when we suggested that learners can create the rules by which they learn best.

In addition, the scheme for learning just outlined is another way of describing what Freire (Shor & Freire, 1987) calls "the gnosiological cycle." Freire defines learning as a two-part process: the first is "producing," in which learners actively build knowledge with one another and for themselves. The second part is "knowing," the process of reflection in which learners examine what they have produced and how they have produced it. For Freire, as for the students and teachers who helped determine the guidelines for negotiating the curriculum, unless both steps in the process are taken by learners, learning has not occurred.

Negotiating the curriculum rests on answering four questions:

- What do I know about X (the topic under study)?
- What do I need to find out about X?
- How can I find out about X?
- How will I show what I learned and/or how will I evaluate my learning?

While considering answers to these questions, the class must also take into account whatever constraints are nonnegotiable. Topics for the year's curriculum may be set by the school or state, specific texts may be required, standardized tests might be mandated and prescribe a focus to the curriculum, and the schedule of marking periods may require a continuous notation of grades. The first step, even before answering the four questions, is for teachers to make these constraints public, and for them and their students to consider their negotiation in light of what is demanded. Negotiating the curriculum sets a climate for learning that places the requirements and the intentions of students and teachers on equal footing.

When contrasted with learning in an autocratic classroom, several differences will emerge. Timing and pacing of learning, which before more or less proceeded in a lock-step fashion, is individualized in the democratic classroom because learning depends on what learners already know and what they have chosen to learn about. Therefore, it can be quicker or slower than assembly-line learning. Motivation proceeds from the inside out as well, and no longer depends either on the teacher's razzle-dazzle or the desire to pass the test. In a classroom where individual learner's needs are met, everyone needn't work on the same things at the same time. Information can be shared and learners can teach each other. Although learners may choose to be evaluated on the basis of some kind of "test," that is no longer the sole criterion for demonstrating learning. A whole range of means of demonstrating competence is now available to the participants.

The teacher's role changes in the democratic classroom along with changes in how learning proceeds. As a result of sharing decision making and recognizing that knowledge resides in the transactions among learners and between learners and materials, students are empowered. Teachers' empowerment rests on their transformation into reflective practitioners. Because they are not making all the decisions beforehand in terms of both process and content, they are forced to respond to these as they arise from the group. This response, their immersion in the role of on-the-spot choice maker and facilitator, is only one step in the process of changing their role. They also need to distance themselves from time to time from the day-to-day classroom activities in order to reflect on what has gone on. This combination of action and reflection, or, as Freire defines it, "praxis" (1970), makes teachers into active learners, professionals who are continually interpreting and reinterpreting context as it unfolds. While it's true that this role is more risky and less certain, it's also true that it's more exciting and purposeful.

Impediments to Democratic Classrooms

Neither the autocratic nor the democratic classroom lives in isolation from the rest of the educational environment. And there's the rub: hardly anything, from teachers beliefs about teaching and learning to the institution's organization, structure, and reason for being, supports the democratic classroom. In fact, the number and kind of impediments to democratic schooling make the possibility of real transformation nearly unattainable. What we learned in the course of our work in Charmont is that embedded in each individual and every system are forces of both change and stasis. One of our goals has been to stir things up enough so that each of these forces must surface. Helping to bring them to consciousness allows us to recognize their existence, even though it might not completely solve the problems. If, however, we do not even recognize the forces of change or stasis, there is little hope of affecting them at all. So let's look briefly at both personal/individual and social/political constraints on transformation.

Personal Constraints

Forces for stasis and change are at work in the structure of an individual teacher's belief system. All human beings build a picture of their worlds, a mental model of reality (Johnson-Laird, 1983), through experience and reflection. As "incipient scientists" (Kelly, 1955), we continually hypothesize about experience and generate a series of interconnected expectations about how things will work the next time around. Some of these hypotheses, what Kelly calls "personal constructs," are permeable, that is, they are open to modification. Others are what he calls impermeable because they are more difficult, and, in some cases, impossible to change, because expectations continually reinforce and reconfirm them. In addition, certain constructs are impermeable because they are superordinate; that is, they subsume numerous other constructs and are, therefore, less easily brought to the surface for reflection and contemplation. Constructs bear a transactional relationship to reality in that they create the reality to which we respond. In mature adults, where constructs have been built over a long time, they begin to mold experiences, where, when they were first developing, experience molded the constructs.

What we have learned from Larry Cuban (1984) and John Goodlad (1984) is that irrespective of historical period or geographic location, American schooling has been largely the same for one hundred years. It is teacher-centered, rote-memorization dominated, and competitive—not so accidentally—the characteristics of the autocratic classroom. Since teachers have learned in these ways, both as students in public school from K–12 and as teachers-in-training, and, further, when they have taught in these ways for over fifteen years, the average experience of today's teachers, then their personal constructs about how things are supposed to be have become static and seemingly impermeable. No real change can occur without examining those constructs that drive decisions about methods and materials.

What we have just described can also be true of students. Students' constructs of teaching and learning are developed in the same ways as those of their teachers: through experience. If students are continually members of an autocratic classroom environment, they come to devalue their own insights, expertise, and intentions as well as those of their peers. They, too, can become formidable obstacles to change. Ironically, when students are given the chance to make decisions over what, how, and why they learn, they often object vehemently to it. They blame teachers for not doing their jobs, for not teaching them. They accuse their teachers of giving up responsibility for *their* learning! Here's how one teacher in this project described her students' reactions to her efforts to create a democratic classroom:

> The class as a whole was dominated by four students, all boys, who articulated early in the second week of school a view of the teacher's role which all but precluded any student ownership or negotiation of the curriculum. Tom, John, Mark, and Paul indicated that my job was to "teach them" and that small groups, peer editing, and any sort of feedback or learning that did not originate from "the Source" were merely symptoms of teacher laziness. I was too lazy to "teach" and so they could not learn, would fail their Regents examinations, and would not get into the Ivy League institutions to which their parents intended to send them. The loud and reiterated objections to brainstorming ("just tell us what to write about"), peer editing ("Alex isn't the teacher. He can't even spell. How can he help me?"), and mirroring ("When are *you* going to read my paper?") made it difficult for those students who were interested in student ownership, conferencing, and working with real readers to speak up, or even to cooperate.

The mechanisms underlying the development of administrators' and parents' beliefs systems about schooling are exactly the same and so they, too, can be impediments to the creation of democratic classrooms.

Institutional Practices as Constraints

Individuals do not teach and learn in isolation. Many of the choices they make are a reflection of the larger social/political structure of schooling. We would like to look at some of what we think are the most important of these to see how they contribute both to change and resistance to change.

A Lack of Autonomy

There is a subtext in the culture of schools based in silence and, sometimes, lies (Fine, 1987). One mechanism for maintaining the status quo is avoiding talk about controversial issues. As long as there are issues that we simply don't discuss or facts that we hide or twist, then we are all complicit in perpetuating the system.

One lie that has had enormous impact all over the state of New York is that a specific formula for writing the persuasive essay on the Regents Competency Test is required. Teachers teach a formula; students learn a formula without acknowledging that the state guidelines suggest nothing whatsoever about how many paragraphs or supporting examples are required in a passing essay. On one level, the lie enables teachers to believe that they are helping their students, but on another level, when the lie matches what teachers already believe and assume about what works, this allows the status quo to be maintained. In fact, this lie is particularly insidious because tests tend to drive the curriculum; therefore, this one belief about the RCT becomes the entire philosophical and practical thrust of the curriculum in composition. Sometimes the simple act of sharing copies of the state guidelines with groups of teachers is enough to expose the lie and to reformulate teachers' expectations. All the lies, unfortunately, that support the fabric of the school system are not so easily revealed or countered.

There are some institutional practices that are impenetrable. These, we discovered, can oftentimes be gotten around. Although it's no longer fashionable to think of teaching as a subversive activity, it is and has always been one. What teachers do behind closed classroom doors, especially when students are happy and successful doing what they are doing, represents a kind of autonomy of which teachers are often not aware. If they're not aware of the potential for autonomy behind their closed doors, teachers will be impeded in their attempts to take risks. An example of teaching as a subversive activity is teachers' resistance to teaching to the test. We have known many courageous teachers who teach writing as a process and do not drill their students for competency tests in writing, trusting that their students will learn to write and to pass the tests, even though there is tremendous pressure on teachers to teach writing as practice for examinations.

A Lack of a Philosophy of Instruction

From work in England and Australia, where for almost twenty years a number of schools have adopted what has come to be known as a "language and learning policy," we've learned about the value of a coherent philosophy or mission for a school. This type of policy is a living document, born out of the experiences and struggles of teachers, fortified by extensive reading and research, and continually growing through critique and reflection.

Such documents have provided us with the critical lens to look at our work here in the United States. Without exception, all the schools we've worked with have lacked a unified sense of purpose and discussion of a school mission. Part of the reason we think schools don't struggle to create a consensus about their mission and philosophy is that Americans value individualism and freedom and fear the power in collective action and reflection. Lacking a mission or philosophy of education, schools are vulnerable to others making educational decisions for them and to changes in educational fashion. They are vulnerable when, for example, states mandate competency tests designed to set minimum standards. Not only do the tests drive the curriculum, leading to the attitude that we must teach to the test, but the minimum standards are almost automatically translated into maximums. There appears to be no reward for achievement that exceeds the standards set and, worse, no questioning of either what the standards are or how they are determined.

Schools are also vulnerable to whatever newfangled notion comes on the market. No new idea ever conflicts with or usurps another. Without a coherent philosophy, it's impossible to assess the relative benefits of different approaches. In many schools, for example, teachers engage in writing workshops, an introduction to "process" writing, while at the same time continuing to use workbooks to teach grammar, punctuation, and spelling. Teachers can't even see that a process approach to writing might have parallels in the teaching of literature, so that literature is frequently taught in these classrooms as if it were a set of facts or a body of information to be memorized.

A high value is placed on eclecticism in American schools. Schools seem to be places where variety in pedagogical "style" is encouraged. Variety seems to be more important than either coherence or compatibility. Changes in schooling are constrained, then, by an open acceptance of many approaches to teaching and learning. Although on the surface this seems democratic and desirable, eclecticism tolerates contradictions and may ultimately impede the effectiveness of all approaches. This kind of attitude discourages discussion, which limits collaboration and the possibility of negotiating and generating purposes for, and philosophies of, teaching and learning. The culture we're describing doesn't allow for a mission to be created and is, at the same time, possible because there is no mission to begin with.

Another consequence of a lack of philosophy is domestication. Novel ideas can be made to look like old ideas. Oftentimes, when a new idea is welcomed into a school after careful consideration, it doesn't look very different from what was already in place. Domestication of new or different ideas helps to mask the fact that a school operates in the absence of a mission. Domestication is a strategy for appearing to conform to public pressure while at the same time not really changing anything.

This vulnerability to educational fads also leads to cynicism. On more occasions than we care to remember, our initial in-service workshops have been greeted with "it's you and your ideas this year; it was somebody else last year; and it will be someone else again next year; and besides that if we just wait long enough whatever we are already doing will come back into style, so there's no need to change anything now."

A Lack of Intellectualism

Eclecticism and subjugation to outside authority are partially responsible for institutionalized anti-intellectualism. Eclecticism shortcircuits inquiry, whereas subjugation denies inquiry. There are other ways in which the school culture works against intellectual critique and inquiry.

The structure of the school day is one impediment to creating an intellectual environment. From our work in schools, we know that teachers are not given any time in their school day to talk together, preventing opportunities for continued intellectual exchange and professional growth, thus limiting the possibility for change. By not giving any time for teachers to collaborate on intellectual issues, schools are implying that teachers' ideas are not important to the functioning of the school. Teachers are supposed to carry out orders dictated to them, rather than set agendas for their own work.

The fragmentation of the school day affects the curriculum and student learning as well. It is impossible to support inquiry and critique when each investigation must be limited to a forty-minute period or a six-week marking period. Depth is replaced by coverage and coverage implies casting a blanket over the surface of a discipline or field. There is simply no time to delve beneath the surface.

Neither the scheduling of the day nor teachers' attitudes about sharing and probing together support inquiry and risk taking. In fact, most teachers we have worked with are both afraid and defensive about letting their colleagues into their classrooms to see what's going on or sharing their doubts and questions openly. Their isolation from one another reconfirms the myth of their expertise while undermining their oftentimes heartfelt desire to learn and grow. This myth has been institutionalized and is responsible for repressing intellectualism in the schools. Underlying this attitude is the belief that experts operate in isolation, don't need to seek or get help, or want input and advice from those they respect. If you're an expert, there is little for you to learn. Risk taking is not valued either because those who take risks, those who learn from trial and error, are considered to be novices, whereas those who continue to do the same thing, no matter who their audience or what the context, are considered the experienced, thus expert, teachers.

A Lack of Supportive Institutional Practices

We have been in many schools around the country and have found enormous similarities among them. A number of institutional practices have become so familiar that we have lost sight of the fact that they are forces for stasis. The central role of the textbook, for example, as the chief means of information giving and getting is all pervasive. Like the tests that drive curricula, textbooks may be either atheoretical or antithetical to some of a teacher's beliefs. Since reflection and philosophy are absent from the typical institution, both the notion that textbooks are an inadequate, and perhaps evil, means of learning and that they may contradict accepted theory goes unnoticed and uncriticized. But as long as they play a pivotal role in teaching and learning, and to the extent that they support features of autocratic teaching and learning, textbooks are a force for constancy.

Whether publicly proclaimed or implicitly enacted, tracking is a fact of life in American schools (Oakes, 1985). It expresses itself in segregated classes as well as in homogeneous groupings. It implicitly promotes racism, sexism, and classism. Although the stated purpose of tracking is to enhance learning, we are never surprised to find children of color in the majority of the lower tracks, unruly boys in special ed, few girls in advanced math and science classes, and very often the poorest children in noncollege-bound courses. The effect of tracking on preventing change within the system is undeniable. It rationalizes the use of tests and textbooks, prevents collaborative learning amongst students, supports competition, reinforces curricula based on the lowest common denominator, and saves innovative teaching for the ones who probably need it the least, the highest track or accelerated classes. In other words, Pygmalions are members of every classroom, struggling to be released from the self-fulfilling prophesy that is tracking. Above and beyond these, the most devastating effect of tracking is its denial of democratic education, a denial of all those attributes we described earlier in this chapter that characterize the democratic classroom (Bastian, et al., 1988).

Perhaps the most invisible force for stasis is the forty-minute period. Talk to any teacher anywhere and you will discover that time is tyranny. Certainly none of us, no matter which subject or grade level we teach, has enough time to accomplish what we wish to. Trying to build continuity, a sense of community, deep involvement in work, and sensitivity to the needs of individual students is impeded by the ubiquitous bell. But almost more than any other reason for not attempting alternative models for teaching and learning is time. The familiar reactions to a new idea, such as "it takes too much time; when will I have time to teach them the skills; it's more efficient to just give them the information; and if I help them learn how to do things, when will I have time to teach them the content," point to the strength of this institutional practice to prevent change, at least change to a democratic classroom.

A Lack of Democratic Decision Making

The structure of power we outlined in our discussion of the autocratic classroom is mirrored in the institutional hierarchy. On the lowest rung are the students, paradoxically, the ones closest to the learning act. Next are teachers, whom we might describe as civil servants, carrying out the wills of those on the rungs above them. Their place in the hierarchy makes teachers powerless in decisions about curriculum, staff development, building management, in short, all of the factors that figure most prominently in a teacher's day-to-day experience.

Administrators are, by and large, power brokers and managers, not educational leaders or innovators. Even though they come from the classroom, they quickly forget their roots in deference to the whims of superintendents, parents, and boards of education. In New Jersey, for example, principals don't even need a teaching license anymore to become administrators. Superintendents, seemingly on the top rung, are also subject to outside power wielded by parents, boards of education, and unions. Yet, within the context of the daily school operation, they are considered by everyone else as rulers of the roost. But because, in reality, they are subject to outside control, they seek the golden mean, not rocking any boats, and in attempting to satisfy, mollify, and temper everyone, end up innovating little. In this sort of hierarchy, like a bureaucracy, there is infinite regress: we never can be sure of who has the power, where the ladder stops. The sum total of this hierarchical structure is the disempowerment of teachers and students, and there is nothing that blocks change as effectively as the perception that the reins of power are in the hands of others, others with whom one has little contact, respect from or for, and whose decisions are arbitrary, punitive, and atheoretical.

The issues and people involved in reforming the school culture and changing the way teaching and learning are conducted are complex. Part of the complexity lies in the fact that the individual and institutional components are part of an ecological system in which it is difficult to determine who is affecting what. While all of this makes reform more complex, it also lends support to the view that changes in individual teachers will simultaneously affect students, administrators, and institutional practices. And, finally, such a view places complexity at the heart of teaching and learning. Even though complexity makes the job harder, to simplify makes it harder still. We have for too long tried to make teaching simple and easy, to find the one answer and the quick fix. We're suggesting that in all of these complexities inheres a dignity, a professionalism, and a mission for education. So whereas transformation may appear to be difficult to attain once complexity is acknowledged, the effort to change is both more significant and more serious and the chance for reform more challenging, and, therefore, more exciting.

Chapter Two

Philosophy and Structure of the In-Service Program

The kinds of expectations we brought with us to Charmont in September, 1985, had already been modified by the goals and expectations of the school district itself as well as our own continuing reflections on our in-service work. While it's true that both the district's and our goals continued to develop over the three years of the project, it's also true that a lot of rethinking had gone on before we even began. What follows is a brief history of events in Charmont that laid the groundwork for this project and our responses to the stated needs of the district.

The educational climate in the state of New York in 1985, especially in the area of composition, was one of readiness for change. The Regents Competency Examination in Writing and the Fifth Grade Writing Assessment, both newly instituted, shortened dramatically the typical lag of fifty years between educational research and classroom application. At that time, research and publication in composition suggested that teachers adopt a new pedagogy, one that focused on writing as a process rather than on the common approach to teaching writing as isolated skills. The new fifth-grade test, for example, demanded that students display knowledge of audience and purpose, drafting, revising, and editing. Both tests required that the teaching and learning of writing change, creating anxiety for teachers. Further, the publication of test

37

results created more anxiety for teachers and school districts by exposing class-rooms to public scrutiny.

Our in-service program was foreshadowed by a series of events that occurred in Charmont from 1977 to 1984. Charmont began its own soul search-ing with a Middle States' assessment in 1977. As a result of this assessment, which found that "a sequential composition and grammar program must be in-stituted in grades 9–12," a K–12 instructional plan in English was developed by the district. The following year, the Superintendent requested an evaluation of the K-12 English program by the New York State Education Department. These two assessments spurred a series of activities: local workshops that exposed the faculty to different approaches to the teaching of writing, such as the National Writing Project, visits to other school districts to examine writing programs, and an in-house needs' assessment in each of the three schools in Charmont. In addition, three teachers were sent to a workshop to learn about the Weehaw-ken Writing Program and to bring materials and strategies back to their schools to share with colleagues. These activities spanned the period 1977 to 1984.

Still feeling dissatisfied with progress toward building a sequential writ-ing program, the district hired two nationally recognized figures in English education to examine the writing program. Their report, The Dunning Report (Maloney & Dunning, 1984), made a series of recommendations for improv-ing, still further, instruction in writing. Chief among these was the suggestion to seek out and hire an outside consultant who would spend at least "thirty days over the course of the year" leading departmental development of a sequential writing program and following up on this work through classroom visitations. The report proposed developing writing across the curriculum by:

> arranging with appropriate non-English teachers to agree upon two "starred" papers per semester, or papers jointly assigned by English and other teachers, that will be evaluated for content and for "English"—not only such surface features as spelling, diction, and mechanics, but for how the papers are organized, what they say, and for the effectiveness and style with which they say it. (p. 7)

In his proposal to the superintendent for implementing a program that would reflect the "variety of initiatives taken to address concerns in the area of teaching writing and language arts," Mr. Fallon, the high school principal, offered the following assessment of past efforts. He wrote a memo in Septem-ber, 1984:

> My recommendation for the future of language arts, and particularly writ-ing instruction, in the district, then, is based upon a perception that our past efforts have been handicapped by a desire for solutions that were too immediate and too simple to be permanently effective.

Fallon's proposal suggested a two- to three-year project, release time for teachers to attend in-service workshops, staff involvement in the selection of a consultant, and a reorganization in the middle and high schools to allow English teachers only four class assignments per day and a maximum of eighty students. To a large extent, it is Fallon's proposal that structured the project we were hired to coordinate.

We think the combination of external and internal pressures for change in the teaching of writing along with the history of trial-and-error attempts at change is fairly typical of districts that eventually hire outside consultants to assist in this process. What might, perhaps, distinguish Charmont was recognition that there was a problem, discussion on all levels, and, eventually, consensus about the solution from all parts of the educational community: teachers, administrators, and the school board. In addition, the Charmont District was aware that the process would be long-term, and they made a commitment to allocate resources accordingly.

By the time we arrived in September, 1985, we had already discussed and negotiated some revisions in overall structure and goals for the project. This was, it turned out, not going to be a writing project for English and language arts teachers. At our interviews, it became clear that there was real concern for developing students' writing abilities generally, not just for creating a curriculum guide and some appropriate strategies for teaching writing. And so the teachers and administrators who interviewed us quickly recognized that their deeper goal could be most effectively met by a writing across the curriculum program.

At one interview, we discussed our discomfort with what they were calling a sequential K–12 writing curriculum. Aside from the fact that curriculum guides are notorious dust collectors, clearly evidenced in Charmont by the three shelves filled with such guides, they also focus too much on output and demonstrations of grade-level mastery. By pointing out the dusty tomes, our interviewers demonstrated the uselessness of such guides. At the same time, they made it clear that they didn't have alternatives for guiding the development of curriculum. If the school district wanted a unified program for students, we believed this could be best achieved by creating a philosophy of instruction for writing. A philosophy of instruction, in contrast to a curriculum for writing, would allow the greatest amount of flexibility and innovation for teachers and support the process of developing shared principles and intentions. We called this philosophy and framework a "language policy," after work done in a similar vein in England and Australia.

Immersion and Distancing: The In-Service Philosophy

Our major premise is that an in-service project should contain a unified set of guiding beliefs. We have chosen the principles underlying a democratic classroom to be our set of guiding beliefs because this kind of organization allows for the greatest amount of individual choice and collaborative decision making. Democracy in in-service programs promotes negotiation for building shared purposes, shared meanings, and shared intentions. Dewey (1938) asks us to consider these questions:

> Can we find any reason that does not ultimately come down to the belief that democratic social arrangements promote a better quality of human experience, one which is more widely accessible and enjoyed, than do non-democratic and anti-democratic forms of social life? Does not the principle of regard for individual freedom and for decency and kindliness of human relations come back in the end to the conviction that these things are tributary to a higher quality of experience on the part of a greater number than are methods of repression and coercion or force? Is it not the reason for our preference that we believe that mutual consultation and convictions reached through persuasion, make possible a better quality of experience than can otherwise be provided on any wide scale? (p. 34)

We find ourselves continually on the horns of a dilemma. While we have a philosophy, while we have a program, while we have our own intentions and purposes, we continually seek to encourage as much participation, as much freedom, and as much room for authenticity, willingness, and open-mindedness as we can. We answer all of Dewey's questions in the affirmative: we cannot think of any organization other than a democracy that can achieve mutually satisfying goals for all participants.

Uncovering Beliefs: A First Step toward Change

At the end of his study of the effects of technology on teaching practice, Larry Cuban (1986) sounds a warning to educational policy makers interested in modifying classroom practice. He writes:

> Teacher repertoires, both resilient and efficient, have been shaped by the crucible of experience and the culture of teaching. Policy makers need to understand that altering pedagogy requires a change in what teachers believe. Getting professionals to unlearn in order to learn, while certainly not impossible, is closer in magnitude of difficulty to performing a double bypass heart operation than to hammering a nail. (p. 109)

As Cuban suggests, revising practice is a matter of changing beliefs. "Getting professionals to unlearn in order to learn" has been the slogan that has reverberated in our own practice and purposes for the last several years. Cuban

(1984) demonstrates quite convincingly that "the crucible of experience and the culture of teaching" has been formed and perpetuated for one hundred years. This fact makes the task of changing beliefs even more daunting. The goals, then, are to help teachers unlearn in order to learn, to assist them in experiencing new ways of teaching and learning, in reformulating their beliefs, and from these reconstruing and, eventually, inventing an alternative culture.

By assisting teachers in experiencing new ways of learning and teaching, we might very well be able to accomplish the first goal—to unlearn in order to learn—but not with the intention that teachers strip themselves of all prior learning or make their minds a blank slate. This is both impossible and undesirable. Genuine learning or change comes from questioning or reassessing our existing beliefs about the world. Change can occur through having experiences that present and represent alternative systems of beliefs and trying to find a place for new experience to fit into already held beliefs.

It is clear from all we know about how the human mind works (see, for example, Britton, 1970; Johnson-Laird, 1983; Salmon, 1985; Smith, 1975; Sperber & Wilson, 1986) that the only way to learn something is to make connections to what we already know, even if what we know seems to contradict the new information. We think this is the key to unlearning, too. No amount of brainwashing, or conversion in the religious sense, or, even, new methods and materials will do the job, because all of these ways deny or devalue the power of prior experience and the existence of an already formed and formidable mental picture of how the world does and should operate. Getting at that picture, exposing it to a different light, sets the process of unlearning to learn in motion.

Because of the nature of teaching—it is unpredictable, individual, and chimerical—we might be tempted into thinking that teachers' mental models of teaching and learning and schooling are less fixed or less rigid than other professionals. Consider what Stephen North (1987) has to say about teacher knowledge, which he defines as "practitioner's lore." He writes that practitioner's lore

> is driven, first, by a pragmatic logic: It is concerned with what has worked, is working, or might work in teaching, doing, or learning. . . . Second, its structure is essentially experiential. That is, the traditions, practices, and beliefs of which it is constituted are best understood as being organized within an experience-based framework: I will create my version of lore [knowledge] out of what has worked or might work— either in my own experience or in that of others—and I will understand and order it in terms of the circumstances under which it did so. (p. 23)

The clear implications from North's point of view are that teachers' knowledge is unconsciously systematic, comprehensive, concrete, and built out of a powerfully confirming set of experiences. The in-service education implication, which comes from both Cuban and North, is that one way to enrich teachers' knowledge is to create another set of experiences from which new experiences of learning, new forms of teaching, new knowledge, new world views, and a new culture might be built.

We recognize a real dilemma in what we do. After all, we have a set of beliefs that we are pretty much wedded to at this point, and for which our in-service program becomes an argument. How can we simultaneously be true to our own beliefs, engage in reflection ourselves, encourage our in-service participants to question and reflect on their beliefs, and not control the direction that the participants' self-reflection process takes? And the answer isn't all that simple.

Practitioners have long been cynical about the expertise of theorists and researchers. Much of this cynicism, to be honest, has been valid, since a great deal of educational research has not been grounded in the context of teaching and learning and has held little relationship to the day-to-day realities of the classroom. Much of it, too, has been contained in an attitude that practitioner knowledge is always inferior to the knowledge of the so-called experts. And so teachers are accustomed, and rightly so, to rejecting input from those outside their contexts. Some in-service education programs that are particularly sensitive to this have eliminated any role for outside expertise. The model of teachers teaching teachers is one result of this attempt to dignify the knowledge of practitioners and to release them from the oppression that so often accompanies expertise.

Oppression by experts can take another form. Teachers have been encouraged to treat with awe and unquestioning respect ideas that issue from the "ivory tower." They debase their own knowledge and tend to revere knowledge produced by academics. Coupled with the belief that knowledge can be simply transmitted from expert to novice, this sort of rejection appears as unquestioning deference to the views of outside experts. So, not only must in-service educators work to support teachers in the knowledge they bring to in-service programs, but they must work equally hard to support challenge to their own authority and beliefs.

Problem Posing: Another Step toward Change

Our attempts to create a democratic classroom as the context for in-service education are designed to minimize oppression, support critique, and reduce inequities in authority and power. The best vehicle for achieving our goals in in-service work is to help teachers to become problem posers (Freire, 1970). Problem posing is a direct rejection of the customary professional development emphasis on problem solving. Problem posing is not simply what we do prior to solving a problem. Instead, problem posing rests on an entirely different conception of what a practitioner knows and how she knows. From an inquiry stance, the act of framing a problem generates potential solutions in the very act of framing. Problem posing is, in itself, a potential way into new thinking and learning. By becoming problem posers, learners may reformulate their beliefs and see the role that their own questions and problems play in generating new knowledge for themselves.

We want to contrast problem posing with problem solving, the more traditional approach to learning. Problem solvers assume that constancy, predictability, and stability are categorical features of the context. The goals or ends they wish to achieve are unvarying and their questions center on the means to achieve prescribed ends. And so the process in which a practitioner engages in this model requires finding solutions to preset problems. In contrast to this circumscribed and circumscribing situation, the problem poser assumes that what is typical is "uncertainty, instability, uniqueness, and value conflict" (Schön, 1983, p. 49). Given these categorical features, knowledge is continually being generated by the practitioner. There are no preset problems, only "seeing as" and "doing as," that is, intuiting similarities to other practice situations and acting on the basis of what is familiar in the unique situation and reflecting-in-action on what is different and what is possible (Schön, 1983, pp. 138–139).

Many teachers we have worked with have tried to solve the problem of students' lack of motivation to write. They have identified the problem as one of students' resistance to writing. Very often the solution they decide on is to construct more interesting writing assignments. When these new topics don't result in greater student motivation, these teachers find themselves back where they started. Once they begin to open up the issue with their students, to examine together what the impediments are to enjoying writing, they discover that frequently students wish to choose their own topics and often students will not agree among themselves on a single topic. Allowing the situation to inform them, recognizing uniqueness, and responding to what students are trying to tell them by their actions, rather than assuming what students need, teachers in this problem-posing mode often find answers to new questions.

The relationship between the inquirer or problem poser and the situation is a transactional one. Practitioners do not merely act upon the situation, but allow the situation to talk to them about the effects of that action, and, as a result, both the problem poser and the problem are changed.

The route to problem posing begins with uncovering and examining those tacit and implicit beliefs, attitudes, and assumptions that drive our practice. In other words, we examine and reflect on the often more revealing instantiation of our beliefs—our actions. We allow our actions to speak to us of what we know. Examining and reflecting on any one or a combination of beliefs and actions has the potential to set a question in motion. Learners are now in the position to modify, extend, explore, or discard what may have been unconsciously guiding their decision making and guiding the situation as well. Practitioners, then, are attempting to do two things at once in the attempt to set, solve, and reflect on a problem: they are seeking both "to understand the situation and to change it" (Schön, 1983, p. 134). Reflective practitioners can enter into professional conversation with others' theories, plans, or research. They can learn how to construct a philosophy of teaching and learning.

By uniting inquiry with action and emphasizing problem posing over problem solving, alternative cultures of schooling are being created. Where before conformity, tradition, and predictability reigned, reinforcing the notion of teacher as expert, now a culture that supports questioning, critiquing, and transforming reinforces the notion of teacher as reflective practitioner. Our real interest is in helping teachers develop a reflective stance, not demanding that their beliefs conform to ours, although we cannot deny that we are also seeking, through reflection-in-action, a change in beliefs, theirs and ours. And so we see problem posing as a way out of the dangers and dilemmas we discussed earlier.

Immersion and Distancing: Completing the Change Cycle

The most important guiding principle in the way we think about how in-service workshops ought to proceed is that the workshops must be demonstrations of the best teaching practices and, for us, this means that they must take into account all the principles of teaching and learning that we described as democratic. What our in-service philosophy of immersion and distancing (Lester & Onore, 1985) requires is time for demonstration, exploration, enactment, and critique.

Many in-service projects have succeeded in getting teachers to be writers, readers, responders, and editors, to engage in the immersion side of learning. But this is only the "producing" event in the learning process (Shor and Freire, 1987). To the extent that the impact of these in-service programs has been limited, this limitation, we believe, centers on the absence of opportunities for distancing or reflection and, therefore, for enacting the second event in the learning cycle, "knowing." Learning and changing are short-circuited because they don't involve learners in distancing—knowing what, how, and that they know. To engage fully in distancing requires a combination of personal reflection, community reflection, and connection making to ideas generated by practitioners and theorists outside the immediate context. Without the opportunity to reflect through distancing, it's much too easy to accumulate a storehouse of conflicting lessons, ones that mismatch theoretically either with one another or with one's beliefs.

Reflection, itself, cannot occur unless there is something to reflect on. Certainly, learners should reflect on immersion activities. But if learners do not also reflect on why they are learning in the ways they do through these activities, then the beliefs and assumptions that underlie and give rationale to activities are never exposed. Since these immersion activities are demonstrations of alternative ways to teach and learn, ones that we hope teachers will try out in their own classrooms, it's essential to reflect on them in order to make those connections to the classroom, not just on the level of a technique or strategy, but with an understanding of why any activity works in the ways that it does.

The circle that's created by action and reflection needs to be expanded beyond the immersion activities. One way to do that is to bring in additional sources of knowledge to build on. In other words, while the act of looking at and assessing oneself is central to the knowledge-building process, it is not complete without looking also at fresh sources of information, assessing that information, and uncovering how and whether those sources complement, undermine, or extend one's own knowledge system. There is room, then, for thorough examination of the literature in the field, for interactions with people who are not automatic members of the community and so represent a point of view derived from a different context, and perhaps, most importantly, for collective critical inquiry and reflection.

Immersion and distancing are democratic means to a democratic classroom. Learners construct their own meanings, share those meanings, and build collaborative meanings within the group. In other words, each participant learns from every other participant. Power is shared within the group, since everyone has a chance for equal input and there are no set ends. What would appear to be disruptive resistance in an autocratic setting becomes healthy challenge to perceived expertise. And so this process of learning, which must involve unlearning, and may further involve creating a whole new set of constructs of teaching and learning, can be set in motion by immersion, but will stop short of producing transformation and fail to have a long-term lasting effect if not accompanied by distancing.

Immersion and Distancing: The In-Service Structure

The Charmont in-service program that we are about to describe is, by its very nature, nonreplicable. Although we entered the project having specified goals with the district and having planned certain kinds of activities and readings, we were continually rethinking and changing the structure and content as a result of the teachers' needs and the district's evolving goals. In this sense, this project, like any other that is developed collaboratively with a school district, cannot be replicated. But the spirit of the project, the fact that it was collaborative and, we hope, democratic, can be reproduced elsewhere.

Charmont supported an unusual amount of contact between us and the teachers, as well as among teachers in our absence. This was facilitated by the fact that Charmont is a very small school district and above average in budgetary resources. The district is composed of three schools, Charmont Elementary, Middle, and High Schools. The total student body has decreased during the last fifteen years, down to approximately one thousand students. There are about 135 full- and part-time faculty and staff members.

Although the district committed itself, from the start, to at least a three-year program, it was never anyone's intention to involve the entire faculty and staff. Underlying this was our desire to turn over professional development leadership to the faculty itself and hope that the teachers who would participate in the project would be responsible for collaborating with their colleagues who had not participated. Therefore, we chose to limit participation to groups of no more than fifteen members. Our guidelines for selecting fifteen volunteers each year consisted of having an administrator from one of the schools, one member of the Board of Education, and a representative from each grade level, 1–8, and teachers of different subjects areas in grades 9–12. For convenience, we designated the first group of teachers as Team A, the second as Team B, and the third as Team C. Team A members were participants, therefore, for three years, Team B for two, and Team C for one.

We demanded, and the school district agreed to the demand, that all workshops would be full days and that substitute teachers would be provided to release teachers from their classroom responsibilities. To the extent possible, the same substitute teachers were used each time the teachers attended a workshop. When difficulties arose finding the number of substitutes required (this only occurred during the third year and was limited to follow-up sessions with Teams A and B), we compromised by holding half-day sessions for Teams A and B on the same day. We held sixteen sessions with Team A during the school year. Team B began with an intensive one-week program during the summer and twelve full-day workshops during the year. In response to concerns expressed by the teachers that even twelve days out of their classrooms were too many, we reduced the number of full days for Team C to 10.

In addition, we visited each member of Teams A and B in their classrooms at least four times over the school year and held individual conferences with each of them after the visitation. The teacher/advisors were responsible for visitations with Team C during the third year of the program, but like us, they also visited A and B Team members as well.

Four Cycles of In-Service

Although the number of workshops varied from year to year, the order of arrangement did not: Cycle 1, Language and Learning; Cycle 2, Fluency; Cycle 3, Clarity; Cycle 4, Correctness and Evaluation, the last three cycles based on the developmental model of writing described in Mayher, Lester, and

Pradl (1983). In articulating the rationale for this organization, it bears repeating here, briefly, why we chose learning, rather than writing, as the place to begin. Our goal was only subsidiarily to develop the writing abilities of students. We were much more concerned with developing students' thinking and ability to learn how to learn in the context of a particular discipline. As a result, we deliberately focused participants' attention on learning, because without altering what they believed learning was, we didn't think it was possible to use writing in a productive way in any discipline, nor was it possible to teach writing effectively in English and language arts. We wanted to go beyond increasing the amount of writing students do across the curriculum and explore what, how, why, and who writing is for.

By exploring these last questions, we were attempting to uncover beliefs about knowledge. We came to understand, for example, that if writing was merely plugged into a teacher's already established ways of teaching and into a concept of knowledge as given and received truths, then writing would serve only to test students' abilities to memorize and regurgitate the teacher's knowledge. And, of course, once we came to see that we needed to tap teachers' beliefs about knowledge, we also came to see that we were exploring redefinitions of authority relationships in the classroom. The next logical step was to connect all of these to a vision of democratic schooling. The goal, then, was to help teachers and their students to use language as a way to question, critique, explore, and analyze their own learning and the culture of schooling in which they learn and teach.

With learning as the umbrella concept, we are able, then, to look at and study how people learn, whether it's through talking, reading, writing, and/or listening. We have discovered, for example, that talk has an enormous role to play in both learning a subject and developing writing abilities. We have also learned that it is the most hidden, repressed, and feared language mode in school. As a result, the first cycle focuses on activities that engage participants in talking to learn and examining the role of talk in learning. Without directing our attention to learning, it wouldn't be possible to look at all of the language modes and a range of language functions that are involved in learning. In addition, the goal in the first cycle was to help teachers look at learning and try to understand how their students' learning can guide their teaching.

The remaining three cycles, fluency, clarity, and correctness/evaluation also reflect a movement from the top down. Fluency might be described as comfort with language and the ability of learners to say what they wish to say in talk or writing. Clarity moves learners from writing mostly for themselves to considering an audience and explicit purpose for the writing or talking. Here language is shaped in order to share. Correctness and evaluation involve everything from the cosmetic aspects of texts to writers' or speakers' assessments of their own and others' work. It involves more public sharing of language and has the goal of ensuring that the text can stand on its own. We see fluency, clarity, and correctness/evaluation as having equal power for describing how we come to know anything. Learning in all subject areas requires time for risk taking and exploration; time for attempting to share and receive feedback on meanings and interpretations; and time to assess what has been learned and to be more precise in one's understandings.

This model is based on the notion that one grasps wholes and creates generalizations and hypotheses that are tested against specific instances. Further, it stands on the theory that meaning is made from large chunks, not discrete bits. Successive approximations and successive refinements define for us the groping from apprentice to master. The progression from fluency to evaluation represents a living through of Vygotsky's theory of the "zone of proximal development" (1962), where learners explore a territory on the borders of their understandings in the course of growing toward precision.

Immersion and Distancing: The Practice

We begin with the assumption that the teacher/participants in the inservice are learners first and teacher/reflectors second. As a consequence of this assumption, then, teacher/participants engage in a variety of learning activities. They immerse themselves in one or more activities that are designed to illustrate a concept. One such demonstration might involve teachers in reading a very difficult passage from a field with which they have little familiarity. We might deliberately prevent them from talking or writing about what they are reading, and give them an objective test to discover whether or not they have read the material. We would then contrast this experience with guided writing and talking about the passage. Such immersion activities are designed to enable teacher/learners to develop a variety of conceptual understandings: they might discover that testing does not necessarily prove whether or not a learner has read the material; that prior knowledge of texts as well as content plays a role in making meaning; that shared understandings generated through talk contribute to enriching each individual's meaning making; and possibly that writing supports learning and understanding.

Distancing or reflection is then accomplished through talking and writing about what and how we have learned. We can't predict how many or which of the concepts will be grasped, but we do know that stepping back from the activity provides the learner with the potential to conceptualize. Distancing also involves one more round of immersion in that from these conceptual understandings, teachers are then given an opportunity to design their own learning activities for use in their classrooms. This sequence continues throughout the four cycles, although the responsibility for designing and implementing the immersion and distancing activities gradually shifts from us to them.

Another way we encourage distancing is to ask participants to write us a letter at the end of each session reflecting on the day's experiences. These letters serve to help the participants integrate the various experiences they have had during the day as well as to connect what they have done with what they have read. They also serve to give the workshop leaders an ongoing evaluation of the program.

A Typical Cycle

In order to clarify how immersion and distancing look when they are translated into a concrete workshop situation, we are going to describe the series of activities that comprise a typical in-service cycle. Our examples come from a composite picture of what we've done during the language and learning cycle in Charmont.

The cycle runs for four full days, spanning approximately two months. The first and third days are immersion and distancing; the second and fourth days are negotiation and action research. Two illustrations of immersion and distancing activities for days one and three are "A Time When You Learned Something" and "A Student's Nightmare."

We begin the first day by asking teachers to write a story about a time they learned something new, either in or out of school, either a positive or negative experience. Stories are shared in small groups and participants are instructed to look for patterns across the stories. The group records the patterns discovered on chart paper, hangs the paper on the wall and then we all look at each group's work to discover patterns across groups. (An example of one group's work appears in Chapter 4, page 102.) We guide the development of a composite list that represents a synthesis of the thinking of the entire group. This composite list, which is called "How We Learn Best," becomes the seed for a language and learning policy.

The first activity for "A Student's Nightmare" involves having the teachers read a five-page excerpt from Noam Chomsky's *Aspects of the Theory of Syntax* (1965). They are not allowed to talk or write while they're reading. We then give them a multiple-choice, true-false quiz on the reading, introducing it by saying that "We want to make sure you read the piece." Then we ask them to reread the excerpt, but this time we encourage them to take notes, to write summaries and questions, and to respond to the article in writing in any way they see fit. This writing is then shared in small groups. (A partial transcript of one group's discussion of the article appears in Chapter 3, pages 78–80.) Finally, teachers are asked either to write a letter to a friend about what they learned about Chomsky or to write to the rest of the group about what they did and did not understand about Chomsky.

After all immersion activities, we ask teachers to distance themselves by writing about "How and What You Learned." These reflections then serve as the basis for a whole group discussion of learning, of language and learning, and implications for teaching. The activities are also supported by outside reading. In this cycle, we might ask the participants to read Torbe and Medway's *The Climate for Learning* (1981), Judith Lindfors', "How Children Learn or How Teachers Teach? A Profound Confusion" (1984), and Harste, Woodward, and Burke's *Language Stories and Literacy Lessons* (1984).

On the second day of the cycle, we generate action research through negotiating the curriculum. We ask teachers to write about "What You Already Know About Language and Learning" and "What You Would Like or Need to Find Out About Language and Learning." After sharing these, we develop goals for whole group learning and begin planning for ways to investigate questions that drive individual teacher's action research. By the end of the day, teachers have tentative plans for their research and all of us have directions for where we will go next. (One teacher's action research for the first cycle is described in Chapter 4, pages 107–111, and a transcription of a negotiating session appears in Chapter 7, pages 173–174.) Readings done prior to this session might include Garth Boomer's *Negotiating the Curriculum: A Teacher-Student Partnership* (1982) and Dixie Goswami's "Teachers as Researchers" (1984). Part of what we do on the third day derives from the questions raised during the negotiation session on day two and includes teachers deciding on, designing, and refining their action research.

The last day of each cycle focuses primarily on teachers sharing their action research. Oftentimes, as you'll see in Chapter 4, each piece of action research raises as many questions as it answers, and so can become the research that a teacher engages in throughout the entire time she's in the project. The topic for the next cycle is introduced and we begin negotiating what we know and need to know in preparation for that cycle. Again, throughout the second and fourth days, teachers are asked to reflect on their learning with these reflections shared and discussed with the entire group. At the end of each cycle, we ask teachers to evaluate the cycle by rating all of the activities and the readings.

Reading/Learning Logs

For each cycle, materials have been chosen for reading and response. The materials are linked to the focus of each cycle and represent work of theorists, researchers, and other practitioners of language and learning. Many of the activities in which participants engage during the cycles are direct reflections of the ideas presented in these works. While initially we provide a nonnegotiable reading list, later the participants seek out relevant readings and bring them in to share with the rest of the group.

The readings represent another source of knowledge and greatly aid in the process of helping teachers become theory builders and philosophers. The readings also provide two seemingly contradictory functions. On the one hand, they comfort teachers by allowing them to see students like their own responding to language across the curriculum and teachers and theorists like themselves struggling with the complexities involved in language and learning. Simultaneously, the readings often generate conflict and anxiety as they have been chosen, in many cases, to present an alternative culture of teaching and learning from the one that teacher participants are most familiar with. These readings serve the goal of helping teachers invent their own alternative culture of schooling.

In order to help resolve the tensions created and identify more fully with the experiences described in the readings, we ask that teachers respond in writing to what they are reading. Tensions are not resolved and identification is not achieved simply by writing in a log. The log is conceived of as a dialogue between the writer and a reader. Oftentimes, it is a reader's response that may first increase the tension by probing the writer's ideas through questions, alternative interpretations, and sharing personal experiences. Responses can also help resolve tensions through these same vehicles. Identification can best be achieved, we have found, when readers help writers come to terms with their own personal learning experiences that have been captured by what readers have read. As Roger Shuy (1987) has recently pointed out, there is a very long history of dialogue supporting learning. Quoting Plato, in part, Shuy writes, "Dialogue is, indeed, 'written on the soul of the learner' and it 'goes together' with knowledge" (p. 896).

These learning log responses, which are shared both in small and large groups, serve as the opening activity for each workshop. Issues generated during discussion form the centerpiece for whole group discussion of the theories and concepts they reflect. At the beginning of the in-service, learning logs are submitted to one or two readers, usually the workshop leaders, for written feedback. At some point toward the end of Cycle 1, we ask the participants to exchange logs with one another, to respond in writing to their partner's log, and then to engage in small group discussion. During the third year, the teacher/advisors became primary respondents to Team C's learning logs.

We construe our written dialogue as models for teacher response and, therefore, for the first few times that learning logs are written, the workshop leaders take on the task of responding to them. Our intention is to encourage teachers to begin asking their students to keep learning logs and to use our responses to their logs as guideposts to what they could do.

The teachers who participated in the first year helped us see a limitation in the workshop leader/participant dialogue. They demanded a role in the process as well. We, therefore, initiated a shift from leader-only response to peer response, with participants exchanging logs with a partner, responding in writing to their partner's log, and then discussing the readings in small groups. The participants helped us recognize that we needed to relinquish our role as sole reader and responder to their learning logs, and pushed our notions of control and authority toward more democratic thinking. They also were expressing their growing ownership over their own processes of learning. The exchanging of learning logs became one more instance of collaboration, one more opportunity to share power with the participants and to enact democratic principles.

With Teams A and B during follow-up sessions after their initial year of participation, we asked that they bring their learning log responses with them for reflection. Participants reread and reviewed their own writing, attempting to discover something about their own patterns of growth, their focuses, and driving questions.

Visitations and Conferences

We can't teach people we don't know. The visit and post-visit conference help us to establish a personal relationship, to share who we are, to learn about who the teachers are, and to set friendships in motion. It's not unusual during conferences to learn about children, husbands/wives, new houses, former jobs, family problems, and a host of things that makes us all human. It's the whole person who is in the classroom teaching, who comes to the in-service workshops, and who is attempting to explore and change. While we, perhaps, cannot document the role that's played by personal relationships with individual teachers, we believe firmly that the spillover from the one-to-one contact on visitation days to the less individual setting on workshop days accounts for the trust and mutual respect that underlie all of the learning and all of the risks that we all are willing to take.

A regular feature of the four-cycle in-service program was the visits we made to the teacher/participants' classrooms. We view our visits as providing another set of eyes with which to view the context. Too often the impact of in-service projects is limited because leaders aren't given the time or do not take the time to share the teachers' worlds. Visits certainly helped us to understand who the children were and the kind of classroom environment the teacher had established. They provided the opportunity for teacher/participants to try out new ideas and to use us as support for implementing a new strategy. Because we view the classroom as a dynamic setting, our visits provided a means of spontaneously shaping appropriate responses that are sensitive to whatever may arise. Our presence in the day-to-day lives of the teachers we worked with helped us to be co-researchers with them as they began to explore.

Teachers chose the focus for our lenses by suggesting to us what we should look for and how we could help. They shared the questions they had posed, so that we could, through our set of eyes, give them additional ways of seeing what their contexts were saying. Teachers encouraged us to talk with their students and to participate in whatever activities were going on, again as a way of providing an additional resource for their investigations. We recognize that some teachers "performed" for us on those days we visited, but the possibility that they might discover something new even in a somewhat per- functory attempt to please us always existed. The relationship between the individual teacher and the visitor governs, to a large extent, the nature of the visitation. Although we attempted to establish a collaborative relationship, there were teachers who continued to be overly anxious about these visits, to interpret them as evaluative rather than cooperative, and so the impact of the visit was reduced.

The most exciting part of the visit often tended to be the post-visit con- ference, where teachers and visitor got to share what they had done and seen. This was also an opportunity to reflect collaboratively, to share the variety of pictures that were captured by the different lenses, to evaluate the sometimes conflicting interpretations. Both in the classroom and during conferences, we were able to be co-researchers with the teachers we visited. Adding our perspec- tive to theirs could result in dissonance. At these times, our conferences posed challenges to the teachers to reconceptualize what had gone on and why. In other words, the conference is a time to explore the thinking behind the action. Oftentimes, conferences led teachers to further investigations and inquiries.

Democracy in In-Service Education

As problem posers and teacher/learners ourselves, we were concerned, as we read our in-service situation and as it talked back to us, that the success and longevity of language across the curriculum would depend on the force of our presence, on the loyalty that individual teachers felt they owed us, and on our charisma. We felt that in helping teachers unlearn in order to bring about new learning, to experience new kinds of teaching and learning, to reformulate their beliefs, and to create an alternative school culture, we would need to be particularly sensitive to the authority structure we were both implicitly and explicitly building in the in-service workshops and visitations. The problem, as we framed it, was: How can teachers take responsibility for their own con- tinued inquires and reflections? How could teachers come to own and to direct their learning? How can we make our own practice more reflective of our beliefs, particularly as they applied to democratic classrooms? The following sections, "Negotiating the Curriculum for the In-Service," "Action Research," "Advisors," and "Language Policy," describe our attempts to develop answers to these questions.

Negotiating the Curriculum for the In-Service

In an attempt to strengthen and give credence to the participants' owner- ship over their own learning, a precursor to long-term change, and in aiming to practice what we had been preaching, we looked to a model developed and under experimentation in Australia. "Negotiating the curriculum" was described extensively in Chapter 1, and the principles that we wrote about there are those we applied to the in-service program itself. We began in very small ways to share decision making about the content and process of the in-service workshops with the teacher/participants during the first year of the program by beginning with the four questions that serve as the basis for negotiating.

Increasingly, we have shared the range and depth of teacher input into the project. While we negotiated the curriculum for only one of the cycles during the first year, by the second year, some part of each cycle was determined by the teachers' knowledge, questions, and intentions. By the third year of the program, teachers were making decisions ranging from which readings to include to who would be responsible for which kinds of activities. Through negotiation, participating teachers were able to pose their own problems, set their own directions for learning, and develop their own ways of investigating their questions. Sharing their findings contributed to building knowledge collectively, so that each individual teacher's knowledge could be connected to and enriched by everyone else's. A teacher's individual inquiries were integrated into the in-service workshops, not tacked on to an agenda. Whatever initial intentions the workshop leaders had for goals and directions were continually modified and reconstructed. In this way, teachers could come to see that their intentions to learn were not extraneous to the work of the group, but that the work of the group could be centered on whatever were the authentic concerns of its members. This makes negotiating the curriculum a means to "cointentional education" (Freire, 1970), which is at the heart of democratic schooling.

The first time teachers stayed past the 3:00 P.M. close of a workshop to continue their explorations and their planning for the next workshop, we knew that ownership and responsibility were shifting away from us and on to the teachers themselves. What negotiating the curriculum for the in-service has allowed us to do is to find areas of overlap between our intentions to teach and the intentions of the teachers to learn. So, whereas, as is the case in any negotiated curriculum, in fact in any democratic classroom, some issues may fall outside of the shared intentions, allowing the agenda to be set mutually is more important then covering every area that we deem necessary and appropriate. We know in our hearts, and much better now in our minds, that even if we were to cover all the material, that learners who are not given authority over their own learning will withhold and opt out, and so will not, even under a strict adherence to content, learn it all. And so the problem-posing process that we wish to engender in teachers in their role as practitioners is the same process we must enact with teachers in their role as learners and in our role as teachers.

Action Research

Problem posing must be extended outside the boundaries of the workshop setting and into the classroom if it is to become a natural way of thinking and acting. We've tried to indicate that we see the workshop climate as being somewhat safe and secure for risk taking and experimenting. While we recognize that a teacher's classroom is an inherently more risky environment for problem posing, we are acutely aware that teachers' intentions to pose problems cannot stop at the workshop door. Yet, how do we help teachers take the chances that problem posing in the classroom involves? Classroom inquiry must be purposeful. Negotiating the curriculum sets in motion a context in which each individual teacher's inquiries are essential for group knowledge building. Through negotiation, teachers come to see and value and need their own input and the input of their peers. The need to know, the need to share, and the need to construct knowledge collaboratively find their ultimate realization in action research. It is action research that documents and supplies data for their knowledge building. The classroom, then, becomes the richest source of learning, students become coparticipants in building a teacher's knowledge, and teachers contribute to ongoing problem posing in the workshops. Our investment in action research is as high as it is because change is inherent in inquiry. Action research enables a teacher to act and reflect-in-action in order "to understand the situation and to change it" (Schön, 1983 p. 134). We want to acknowledge our debt to others who have actively supported the classroom teacher as researcher during the last several years: see, for example, Brause and Mayher's column in *Language Arts* called "Learning Through Teaching" (1983–1986), Gere (1985), Goswami (1984), Goswami and Stillman (1987), and Mohr and MacLean (1987).

Classroom research investigations were conducted regularly as part of the four cycles of the program. Some of these were individual; others were collaborative. Oftentimes, one question or set of questions guided a series of inquiries. At other times, the participants conducted a number of small-scale, discrete inquiries on a cycle topic. One of our goals in encouraging teachers to become researchers was to raise the level of close observation by teachers of individual or small groups of students as a way of helping them learn about how their students learn. The research stance allows teachers to notice what may have been part of their context all along. By adopting the researcher point of view, teachers see their contexts both from the perspective of what is familiar, as well as seeing what is different or novel. Observing and noticing, then, are springboards for understanding and changing. Although we recognize that much of the literature about teacher/researchers has attempted to raise the professional status of teachers by encouraging them to publish their classroom research findings, our emphasis has focused more on the use of classroom research as a means of changing classroom theory and practice.

For us, a true professional is someone who continually learns on the job. The whole notion of reflection-in-action suggests that when teachers are researchers, they are not just adding on to the role that they are required to play. Rather, they are recognizing that practitioners are natural inquirers into their worlds.

Advisors

During the first year, teachers from Team A began to initiate discussions during workshops about the future of the project. They were concerned that once the district's contract with us was terminated, the program would fall apart. All of us regularly began to brainstorm ways that the teachers could carry on their work and support one another. One idea, which we experimented with during the second year, was a buddy system. Team A members paired themselves with Team B members by school or subject area in order to provide a collaborative, onsite relationship. All recognized that there was a need for more spontaneous, more ongoing contact among the participants, that is, above and beyond what would happen during the scheduled in-service workshops. Team A teachers recognized they had a great deal of experience they could share with their colleagues new to the program.

Even though Team A endorsed this idea, by midyear, it was apparent that the system wasn't working. Teachers were not finding the time or making the time to see each other. We continued to brainstorm other ways to work together and we all recognized that an institutional change had to be made in order to accommodate real peer collaboration. (See Chapter 7 for a more detailed discussion of the buddy system.)

We were familiar with a teacher/advisor model developed by Lilian Weber at the City College Workshop Center for Open Education (Albert & Dropkin, 1975) and suggested that it be adapted for use in Charmont. None of us wanted to establish another administrative position within the district, which was one option that the district seemed interested in. We all felt that the advisors needed to be classroom teachers simultaneously. At the end of the second year, teachers volunteered for the position of teacher/advisor. We worked with them to negotiate released time, roles, and responsibilities for the teacher/advisors with the school superintendent and building principals. The four teacher/advisors who volunteered were released from 20% of their load. In the elementary school, each of the two advisors was released from her classroom responsibility for two half days a week; classes were covered by a regular substitute teacher. In the high school, each of the advisors taught four, rather than five, classes a day.

The teacher/advisors met with us during the summer before the third year and regularly throughout the school year. We mapped out plans for the year and individual responsibilities. One of the interesting things that occurred was that the advisors formulated their roles very differently from what we had envisioned. Most especially, they took on more responsibility for the running of the project than we had expected. They evaluated the readings we had done during the previous two years and selected the ones they felt worked best. They reviewed all of the workshop materials and chose the ones that had been most effective from their point of view and decided to create new activities based on their experiences in their classrooms. They developed workshop schedules and ran those workshops they developed. They started newsletters in both the elementary and secondary schools as a way of sharing classroom research inquiries, strategies, and student work. They instituted regular monthly meetings, which are open to all faculty and in which the entire group sets the agenda and determines the focus for their discussions.

The advisors decided that classroom visitations should not be conducted by us. Instead, they chose to establish an informal schedule of visits encouraging interclass visitations. Because they had time in their workday, they volunteered to cover classes for other teachers, freeing them to visit colleagues' classes. They chose to read and respond to the third-year teachers' learning logs, while continuing to read and write their own logs to exchange with them. All in all, the results of implementing the advisor role have been the most unplanned for, yet most thrilling, part of this in-service program. The advisors have received an unprecedented amount of support from their colleagues as well as from the administration. And this certainly accounts for much of what has occurred. Nonetheless, the sheer commitment and energy that the advisors have invested in their new roles is awe-inspiring and a tribute to the whole idea of taking ownership over one's learning.

Changes in the In-Service Structure

Table 2–1 on the following page makes it easier to see the evolution of the structure of the in-service program. Changes resulted from ongoing conversations and evaluations with all the participants.

A Language Policy

Our intentions in introducing the notion of a language policy were numerous. When we were invited to conduct the in-service project on writing across the curriculum, we were asked to develop an articulated K–12 writing curriculum for the school district. Fearing that no matter how collaborative the writing of such a curriculum might be, it would nonetheless suffer from all of the problems typically associated with curriculum guides, we refused to focus our work in that way. Moreover, we view a language policy as containing a philosophy of instruction, rather than a cookbook of activities or a statement of scope and sequence. In addition, our views about writing are such that we believe that no prescribed curriculum can reflect adequately the dynamic nature of teaching and learning it. We proposed instead to develop a language policy based on work done in England.

One of the central recommendations of the Bullock Report (Bullock, 1975), a major study on language in British schools conducted by the Committee of Inquiry of the Department of Education and Science, is that schools develop a policy for language across the curriculum. This policy would establish a set of guiding principles for developing learning in all subject areas by

Table 2–1
Evolution of the Structure of the In-Service Program

YEAR ONE	YEAR TWO	YEAR THREE
Cycle 1	*Cycle 1*	*Cycle 1*
Workshop Activities (Consultants)	Workshop Activities (Consultants)	Workshop Activities **(Advisors)**
Workshop Readings (Consultants)	Workshop Readings (Consultants)	Workshop Readings **(Advisors)**
Response to Learning Logs (Consultants)	Response to Learning Logs (Consultants)	Response to Learning Logs **(Advisors)**
Visitations (Consultants)	Visitations (Consultants)	Visitations **(Advisors)**
Action Research (Negotiated)	Action Research (Negotiated)	Action Research (Negotiated)
		Negotiating the Curriculum
Cycle 2	*Cycle 2*	*Cycle 2*
Workshop Activities (Consultants)	Workshop Activities (Consultants)	Workshop Activities **(Advisors)**
Workshop Readings (Consultants)	Workshop Readings **(Teachers & Consultants)**	Workshop Readings **(Teachers & Advisors)**
Response to Learning Logs **(Teachers & Consultants)**	Response to Learning Logs **(Teachers & Consultants)**	Response to Learning Logs **(Teachers & Advisors)**
Visitations (Consultants)	Visitations (Consultants)	Visitations **(Teachers & Advisors)**
Action Research (Negotiated)	Action Research (Negotiated)	Action Research (Negotiated)
		Negotiating the Curriculum
Cycle 3	*Cycle 3*	*Cycle 3*
Workshop Activities (Consultants)	Workshop Activities (Consultants)	Workshop Activities **(Advisors)**
Workshop Readings **(Teachers & Consultants)**	Workshop Readings **(Teachers & Consultants)**	Workshop Readings **(Teachers & Advisors)**
Response to Learning Logs **(Teachers & Consultants)**	Response to Learning Logs **(Teachers & Consultants)**	Response to Learning Logs **(Teachers & Advisors)**

YEAR ONE	YEAR TWO	YEAR THREE
Visitations (Consultants)	Visitations (Consultants)	Visitations **(Teachers & Advisors)**
Action Research (Negotiated)	Action Research (Negotiated)	Action Research (Negotiated)
		Negotiating the Curriculum
Cycle 4	*Cycle 4*	*Cycle 4*
Workshop Activities (Consultants)	Workshop Activities (Consultants)	Workshop Activities **(Advisors)**
Workshop Readings **(Teachers & Consultants)**	Workshop Readings **(Teachers & Consultants)**	Workshop Readings **(Teachers & Advisors)**
Response to Learning Logs **(Teachers & Consultants)**	Response to Learning Logs **(Teachers)**	Response to Learning Logs **(Teachers & Advisors)**
Visitations (Consultants)	Visitations (Consultants)	Visitations **(Teachers & Advisors)**
Action Research (Negotiated)	Action Research (Negotiated)	Action Research (Negotiated)
	Negotiating the Curriculum	**Negotiating the Curriculum**

Note: **Boldface type indicates a change in responsibility for the activity.**

promoting purposeful, active language use in all four modes. The principles would grow out of and continue to evolve from classroom practice and experiences with language-in-use alongside continuing investigations into the theoretical and research findings of the role of language in learning. A number of secondary schools in England took this recommendation seriously enough to create language policies during the period immediately following the publication of the Bullock Report.

In order to prevent a language policy from becoming just another dust gathering curriculum guide, Mike Torbe (1976) reinterprets the Bullock recommendation by seeing a language policy as a living document:

A language policy is not merely a document, though document may form part of the total approach. Nor is it something which can be completed in a set time, and is then finished with. It is a series of strategies, in the classroom and the whole school, and a *process* —of discussion, of asking questions, finding answers to those questions. Once begun, the process continues permanently (p. 10).

Torbe's notion is that a language policy be open to continual questioning, revision, addition, and modification in light of teachers' and students' emerging theories and activities. For Torbe, a language policy is always a draft, drawing its strength from the fact that it is not a set of prescribed and prescribing daily activities that aren't sensitive to the dynamics of a given school: "It [a language policy] must relate to the specific problems and approaches of that school, and it draws impetus from the kinds of questions the staff themselves ask about teaching and learning" (p. 6).

We hoped that a language policy would stimulate collaborative sharing and discussion both inside the in-service group as well as between the teacher/participants and their colleagues in their individual schools. We also wanted the writing that the participants engaged in as part of their workshop activities to include not only personal writing to be shared within the group, but also writing that would embody Freire's notion of praxis, that is, work based in action and intended to promote action, reflection, and change. Such writing, by its very nature, is published, and so this became a natural and purposeful forum.

As you will see in Chapter 6 where we present a transcription of Team C discussing the language policy, the nature of that conversation signals a marked change in school culture. Not only are teachers attempting to create a mission for their schools (a striking contrast to typical teacher school talk), but they are also confronting the role that the institution and that the normal definitions of what constitutes a teacher's purview play. On the simplest level, the language policy engendered discussions among teachers from first through twelfth grade and across curriculum lines. This, in itself, given commonsense school divisions, is revolutionary. Teachers are breaking down barriers and, as a result, changing the culture in which they teach and their students learn. The quality of life for these teachers is transformed in the very act of having conversations about issues that they have deemed essential to them.

During the first year of the program, participants began to set down on paper their theories, based on practice and immersion, about the relationships between writing and learning. They drafted, shared, and revised their individual and small-group statements about these relationships. A full draft of the policy was completed by the end of the first year, which served as the focus for a one-week summer seminar, during which time the document was revised and entirely redrafted. In the process of revision during the summer, the participants focused much of their discussion on who the audience for this draft would be. They decided that this first full draft should be shared with Team B alone. In spite of pressure from the district superintendent, the group did not yet feel comfortable sharing the document with either the Board of Education or the rest of the district faculty.

Team B participants read and responded to the draft, based on their learning about writing and learning, and made suggestions about wording, organization, and tone. They decided to add a section to the document and sent the new section on correctness and evaluation along with all of their comments back to Team A. This group then fine-tuned the policy, getting it ready for public sharing with the Board of Education and the community during the final board meeting at the end of the second year. Part of the focus of discussion at each group's deliberations centered on what to call the document. Hardly anyone was comfortable calling the document a policy, since they believed this designation reflected another imposition of beliefs and attitudes by one group onto another, an institutional practice common to schools. Agreement was finally reached by Team C to title the paper, "Learning Through Language Across the Curriculum, K–12," reflecting the feeling that contributions would continue to be sought, discussions would remain ongoing, and changes welcomed and encouraged.

The "working paper," as the teachers have described it, has been a consistent agenda item at the after-school ABC Team meetings. Discussion has centered on how to continue to share the working paper with colleagues, how to use it in conjunction with hiring new teachers and administrators, and what sorts of actions the Board of Education might be urged to take in order to implement the philosophy contained in the paper. "Learning Through Language" has also continued to transform conversations in the teachers' lounge. Workshop participants at the high school meet every two weeks at lunch for informal discussions, and it is here where the working paper continues to live.

We hope that it's clear from this description that the in-service program we have developed thus far is not static, that, in fact, it continued to change even as it became more institutionalized. We had to learn to pay careful attention to what the participants and the context were saying to us. The descriptions we have provided of the in-service program are not contained in any package. Many of the activities evolved for us because of the participating teachers' interests and questions. We had to become reflectors-in-action, in short, real learners ourselves. Our role, as we came to define it, was to act as catalysts and facilitators. In this chapter, we have attempted to demonstrate how and in what ways we responded to the teachers' emerging needs. In the chapters that follow, you will see what the teachers did in response to the activities we've described in this chapter as a result of their participation in the in-service project. All we can claim responsibility for is setting a process in motion. This is not to underplay the importance of our role or the hard work it entails. But the direction, intensity, and continuance of the project were controlled by the teachers. We became thoroughly dispensable. The teachers discovered what was possible and how to transform possibility into reality.

Part II

The Teachers

A Methodological Introduction

What do we talk about when we talk about research? How do we talk when we talk about research? We want to try and answer these questions before turning to the stories we'll share about the people and the place from which our research grew. Beginning this introduction with questions is intended to signal that, in fact, a good deal of the talking, thinking, and writing we do centers on posing questions. Because we think questions are so important, because the questions we ask always already imply answers, because questions are what sets research in motion, and because questions are the soul of teaching and learning, we'll focus on them in order to make clear how our thinking evolved and how this evolution is reflected in our research.

Let's add another question to our growing list. It's a question that we just discovered was the one we were asking all along, the one that informed all of the other questions we asked, but, paradoxically, the one that we have only just now been able to formulate. We recognize this as part of the process as well. That is, that we don't always know what we are looking for until we find it. This question is raised by Howard Margolis in *Patterns, Thinking, and Cognition: A Theory of Judgment* (1987):

> Questions about learning will be misposed if the problem is taken merely as, "How did a person learn B?" For adult learners especially, the question should be, "How did he learn B, given the habits of mind (the entrenched networks) on hand when he faced the problem?" (p. 126)

Margolis's question applies not only to the teachers whose stories we will tell, but to our learning. Our "habits of mind," the questions we posed, and the ways we investigated those questions are our methodology. We want to explore how we went about looking at the teachers we worked with, looking at ourselves and the context, and making judgments and interpretations. All of these constitute the stories we will tell. Defining learning as changing prompts us to reformulate Margolis's question into our own: *How do teachers change, given their habits of mind, when they pose problems for themselves?*

How Did We Research?

In literary criticism, the question of a narrator's reliability—do we as readers trust the narrator's point of view?—is central to the interpretation process. In our research, we are just as much a part of the context we are describing as any of the other characters in the story, and so interpretation of our findings rests as much on judgments of our trustworthiness as narrators as it does on the characters and events in the stories. Our task, then, is to open up our processes of puzzling out and through our data so that judgments of our trustworthiness can be made.

Trustworthiness does not imply a lack of rigor, a lack of seriousness or an absence of accountability. (See Guber & Lincoln, 1985; and Ely, 1984, for further discussion on "trustworthiness" in research methodology.) You should be able to make judgments about whether or not you trust us based on your answers to the following questions: Have we provided sufficient data to support our interpretations? Are the interpretations compatible with and grounded in an overarching theoretical framework? And perhaps most crucially, have we tested our interpretations against the data and against the other participants' interpretations? Part of what we will do is to share chunks of our data with you so that you will be able to answer these questions and make judgments of your own. In contrast to research that depends on reliability and validity to give generalizability and authority to its truth claims, the research we present here grows out of an entirely different epistemological framework. We are not seeking truth, the underlying goal of research that relies on reliability and validity. Rather, our research is based on a constructivist notion that research seeks to make meaning, and knowledge is built collaboratively, reflectively, and transactionally and so must be evaluated on its trustworthiness.

From our present-day perspective, the drive to Charmont in the fall of 1985 launched us on a journey that opened up vistas we couldn't have imagined. James Britton has suggested that exploratory talking and writing are like pushing a boat out from the shore, not knowing where it will land, but confident that it will safely arrive at the shore again. What we thought we were doing was setting off on a new in-service project on language across the curriculum. And like teachers everywhere, we trusted that we would learn something from our experience. And like the boat that will actually make it to shore, because it's watertight, we had hypotheses, theories, expectations, and dreams about what would happen. Starting with these, which included what we knew and believed about the relationship between language and learning; about how people learn; about what teachers need to do in order to change themselves, their students, and their schools; about what a democratic classroom might look like; and about what potential there might be for learning in school, our earliest questions and interpretations were inevitably framed. In addition, we were learning to reflect on our work with teachers, to question our practices, and to critique the choices that we made. The return rides from Charmont to our homes in the city were always filled with conversations about the day: What happened? Why did it happen? How did it happen? Certainly, it would have been possible for each of us to have answered these questions by ourselves, but one of the advantages of our partnership, of team teaching, is that we are continually able to share and reinterpret our individual interpretations, thus building collective and social meanings from our experience, a process, by the way, that continues even as we construct this sentence.

Suggesting that we started out with a framework does not imply that the framework was rigid. By talking and reflecting together on the day, we continued our theory building and, as a result, reconstrued our practice and changed what we did. We were involved in a kind of naturalistic and spontaneous inquiry that automatically located us simultaneously in the positions of participants and observers. However, we did not become systematic observers until we were six months into the in-service project, when we finally posed researchable questions and began to consider more formal ways of analyzing what was occurring.

At some moment at the midpoint of the first year, we recognized that our spontaneous responses to the teachers' learning logs, while fruitful in and of themselves, could be enhanced if we photocopied those logs in order to be able to reflect on them more carefully and systematically. Thus, our first data base was born. Although it may have been sufficient for us to use our more careful reflections on these logs as ways of improving our teaching and the learning in the workshops, these logs began to speak to us in very powerful ways about the people behind the texts and the rich explorations and struggles that they were involved in. Thus, the research idea was born. That research idea was based on the question: What model of in-service education is most successful? Although we had created a model inductively, which we called "immersion and distancing," out of our previous in-service work and had even published an article describing it (Lester & Onore, 1985), once we posed this research question, we began to see our experience in Charmont as an opportunity to explore and refine the model.

Giving birth to the concept of researching our practice led us to collecting additional data. The data, which serve as the bases for analysis and interpretation in the next five chapters, ended up including:

- learning logs
- reflective responses to the workshop day
- transcripts of small-group and whole-group discussions
- interviews with teachers
- field notes on classroom visitations and post-visit conferences
- evaluations of the workshops
- self-evaluations
- writing tasks from the workshops
- teachers' action research reports
- transcripts of students' discussions and students' writings
- faculty writing survey
- our workshop notes

- our field notes on meetings with faculty, administrators, and students outside the workshops
- documents and artifacts from the school district, such as memos, reports, curricula, and report cards

These data presented us with a mountain of paper, especially considering that each year more teachers participated, culminating by the end of the third year with data from forty-five separate individuals.

The method we used to analyze our data may appear wildly asystematic, to some eyes messy, to others organic, but nonetheless nonlinear. We prefer to call it transactional or dialectical, emphasizing the back-and-forth nature of our construction process. We continually moved between analyzing and theorizing. We read and responded to the data, talked, and shared. We wrote, created tentative hypotheses, returned to the data, reinterpreted the data, hypothesized some more, talked, read, and wrote, thus reconstruing the hypotheses, the data, and, interestingly, the materials we were reading. (A similar model for generating hypotheses in descriptive studies can be found in Brause & Mayher, 1982.)

Because language itself in its visible forms is linear, our list of sources for data tends to create the impression that these activities occurred in some sequence, but it is probably more accurate to say that many of the activities occurred almost simultaneously, overlapping so much that it is difficult to say what gave rise to what. What follows will serve as both an illustration of our constructive process as well as a description of how the chapters that follow came to be.

There's a Method to Our Madness

At the end of the first year, we had accumulated all of the data that we listed above for fifteen participants. We began with the learning logs, which we read over several times until we began to see patterns in the learning of an individual teacher over the course of the year. We shared with one another the patterns we saw in the context of our present state of knowledge, negotiated the meanings that were emerging, and returned to the logs to make selections that represented the tentative themes we had created. These patterns ranged from a teacher's concern for correctness to the role of seeing oneself as a learner in the growth process. From these selections, we wrote individual portraits of each of the fifteen participants. These portraits became a new source of data for us, open to reevaluation and reconstrual. By writing them as narratives, we were impelled to find connections within the patterns, in other words, to create organizing ideas. These organizing ideas spurred on questions about how we could account for what we saw emerging within each portrait. Moreover, by placing one portrait alongside of another, we wanted also to discover what might account for differences and similarities among individuals.

In trying to account for the effects of the in-service program on the patterns we saw, we began theorizing. Our theorizing led us to read and reread professional literature on a variety of topics. We mention rereading because having identified certain patterns and raised new questions about them, we needed to go back to some literature we thought we had been very familiar with already, knowing full well that in light of our new inquiries, the old literature would also become new. Rereading some of the professional literature turned out to be one of the crucial insights we came to about learning. Once we had identified certain patterns in teachers' logs and portraits, a new set of questions arose. Our identification of patterns and our search for answers to the new questions they posed actually transformed our thinking. Torbe and Medway's *The Climate for Learning* (1981), for example, which we had read many times already, when read again with our new frame of mind revealed a rich new meaning to us that we had not even seen before because we weren't looking for it. We probably couldn't have seen before how student and teacher talk reveal how knowledge is viewed in the classroom—the new meaning we interpreted from *The Climate for Learning*—because our own thinking about how knowledge is generated in school hadn't yet been formulated. What we learned about learning from this was that when learners' knowledge changes so does the knowledge that they are seeking. You can, indeed, return to an old favorite book and find new meanings in it.

But we also searched for new ideas. Our search took us to other literature on writing, on writing and learning, on language and learning, on learning, on reading, on teaching, on schooling, on research, on in-service. We took notes on our reading, shared those notes, discussed the ideas, and returned to both the portraits and the original data.

The working title of our research at this point was "Immersion and Distancing: A Case Study in In-Service Education." This title reflects the focus of our original search to understand how in-service might work best. The work described in the previous paragraph was a reenvisioning of what we really wanted to know about. All of a sudden, we became more interested in the change process than we were in the in-service model itself. Our revised working title became "Transformation and Stasis: A Case Study in In-Service Education." The title indicates that some of what we were discovering was that some teachers seemed to have changed and others had not. Before we knew it, our guiding question was: *What factors contribute to or inhibit teacher change?* While all of this was going on, we were continuing to conduct the in-service workshops with a new group of participants and to collect data from our work with them as well as additional data from the original group. Of course, given all the thinking, writing, reading, talking, and reflecting we had done on the data from the first year, the in-service project during the second year was also transformed.

As a result of refocusing our research question, we provided different writing and reading activities in the workshops, focusing the teachers' attention much more on themselves as learners, on the relationship between teaching and learning, and on alternative power and authority relationships within the workshop and classroom settings. By providing these new resources, we inevitably were changing the nature of what the teachers wrote in response to these new resources. Although we were still collecting learning logs, the logs themselves were written responses to new readings. The new readings, many of them now having to do more with teaching and learning, stimulated the teachers to write and respond somewhat differently from earlier log responses to readings that focused mostly on writing. Since we were shifting our focus in the workshops more and more to one on language and learning, we were getting more explicit and deeper insights on learning and teaching in the responses teachers wrote. And, of course, by changing the resources, we changed what and how we could learn from them.

At this point, we felt we really needed to start writing. We were not yet ready to write about the teachers, but we did want to begin to put down the theories that seemed to drive our practice, and since we'd already written something on the in-service model, we felt we could start expanding on that, too. One thing that the in-service workshops gave us during the second year was a new set of priorities. Where we once had focused on the teaching of writing, we began to see, thanks to Judith Lindfors (1984), that in order to understand how to teach writing and to change how one teaches writing, we needed to understand how students learn. The importance of this idea didn't really become clear to us, even though we were playing with the idea in the workshops themselves, until we sat down to make our own theories explicit. In talking through our individual understandings of our theories, and negotiating shared understandings, we also began to recognize that a focus on learning would have its most significant impact on what classrooms look like. The more we explored this notion, the more we became committed to new roles and relationships for teachers and students. The more we explored, the more we recognized that there would be differences between classrooms where teachers focused on learning rather than teaching.

During the process of writing the chapter on democratic schooling, we returned again to the professional literature, since we now had an additional area to explore, namely, radical educational theory. This reading, combined with the actual writing, gave rise to our expanding from a narrow focus on the teaching of writing to a much wider lens that allowed us to look at how classrooms are organized and what those organizations say about the kinds of learning that can and cannot take place. All of this led us, inevitably, back to the data.

And here's what we did. The patterns and themes we had uncovered became emblems for us of entire structures of attitudes and beliefs on the part of teachers. We were beginning to see that teachers operated on a day-to-day basis through the mediation of a worldview, and we wondered if we could name those worldviews and reinterpret what the teachers said and wrote in light of this structure of beliefs. Our term for the structures, which we borrowed from George Kelly (1955), was "constructs." We didn't yet have names for the constructs we saw operating in the teachers' thinking and acting, but we were able to begin to construct categories by sorting teachers' statements into groups. This process of data reanalysis turned our attention once again to the chapter on democratic schooling. We worked with our own theories inductively, allowing them to tell us what we might call the categories that were emerging. We saw in our own writing that we seemed to cluster certain kinds of ideas. For example, we had a cluster that centered on the differences between teaching and learning, a cluster on transmission and interpretive teaching, a cluster on the role of a teacher as coach or examiner, and a cluster on collaboration and competition.

When we went back to the old data once again and explored new data as they were coming in, we used the clusters we had constructed to guide another analysis. The categories themselves and what we would call them became much clearer as we did this. Before long, we had not only names for the categories, but even a hierarchy for categories. Playing with the categories and their relationships to one another helped us to see that the emphases, both stated and implied in the chapter on democratic schooling, didn't work for us anymore. We began to revise that chapter to reflect our newfound theory. And we changed the working title again. We were loathe, despite a great deal of criticism, to admit that "transformation and stasis" and "immersion and distancing" were both big mouthfuls and jargony, because at the moment, they seemed to capture what we were trying to say. Now that we were saying something different, we could relinquish our obstinacy and the new working title became: "Change and Resistance to Change: A Case Study in In-Service Education."

Zeroing in on Our Theoretical Framework

Once we had sorted these patterns into categories, we recognized that each category implied a dichotomy and we wondered what kind of relationship each category had to another. Uncovering the dichotomous nature of the categories, as well as the potential for a hierarchical organization of them, led us directly into Kelly's theory of personal constructs. Kelly's work has been used in the field of education precisely because learning, that is, growing and changing, has a central place in Kelly's theory. (See, for example, C. T. P. Diamond, 1982, 1985.) In fact, the theory itself is a theory of learning in the sense that it claims that all human beings, like scientists, are constantly questioning, testing, hypothesizing, and reformulating their worlds. And further, because of that, the worlds that are created are worlds *we* create, both individually and collectively, not worlds that exist independent of us. The constructivist nature of Kelly's theory has great appeal for us because it places the active, meaning making of teachers at the center of their world making.

We would like to sketch briefly an overview of Kelly's personal construct theory by summarizing its essential features. A construct is a belief, built on accumulated experience, that establishes the expectations a person brings to events, and, therefore, "channelizes" what that person finds in those events. In other words, beliefs shape the interpretation of an event. As Bannister and Fransella (1971) state,

> This implies many things—it implies that man is not reacting to the past so much as reaching out for the future; it applies that a man checks how much sense he has made of the world by seeing how well his "sense" enables him to anticipate it; and it implies that a particular man is the kind of sense he makes of the world. (p. 19)

Kelly asks us to acknowledge that one's personal construct system be viewed in hierarchical ways. Certain of the constructs, therefore, hold sway and subsume others. As a result, it is not theoretically possible to change a single construct without simultaneously affecting others. This does not imply, however, that human beings can't also live with contradictions between constructs, but only that they don't necessarily recognize the contradictions. Each construct implies its opposite, even if a person cannot name or say what the negative formulation of the belief is. Constructs are context sensitive, so that within any context, a person will anticipate both confirmations and disconfirmations of the construct. Kelly also makes a distinction between what he calls "permeable" constructs and "impermeable" constructs. This distinction reveals that some constructs are more open to change and reconstrual than others, or even that some constructs contain within them a greater possibility for elaboration and extension than others.

While constructs are personal, psychological realities, they have a social dimension as well. As Phillida Salmon (1988) states,

> Though each of us inhabits a unique experiential world, psychological meanings must, if they are to be viable, be built together with others. The human enterprise depends on a shared social reality. The sense we make of our lives must also make some sense to others. And since human realities are, first and foremost, *social* realities, personal meanings have their essential currency in relations between people, rather than within some private, individual world. (p. 22)

Salmon and Bannister and Fransella helped us to see that, even though we were analyzing teachers' personal constructs, and thus focusing in on individuals' attempts to change, inevitably, the constructive nature of personal constructs is built in and through our transactions with a larger social context. As a result, we were able to begin to formulate a transactional theory about the relationship between the individual and the larger social context. This broadened our perspective even further, so that we were looking at the data not just on a teacher's personal construct level, but on how those constructs came to be and came to change as a result of teachers' transactions with the larger social context that surrounds them.

Having discovered a theoretical framework for analyzing our data, we were able to reformulate, once again, the fundamental and guiding question for our research. For Bannister and Fransella, the fundamental question is: "Why is it that two people in exactly the same situation behave in different ways?" This question resonates with both Margolis's question that began this introduction, as well as our reformulation of it: *How do teachers change, given their habits of mind, when they pose problems for themselves?* The answer that Bannister and Fransella provide is, "Of course . . . they are not in the 'same' situation. Each of us sees our situation through the 'goggles' of our personal construct system" (p. 22). One of the purposes, then, of our research is to see how fully their answer accounts for our discoveries.

Formulating Our Hypothesis

We applied what we had learned from personal construct theory to both participant portraits and learning logs. This allowed us to be able to assert that a view of the world of teaching and learning is created by the confluence of the constructs. First, we tried to name the constructs and here's what we came up with:

1. Knowledge is constructed by human beings/Knowledge exists independent of knowers.
2. Language is a mode for learning/Language is a mode for testing learning.
3. Teachers are coaches and facilitators/Teachers are evaluators and examiners.
4. Learning is collaborative/Learning is individual and competitive.
5. Teachers are learners/Teachers are experts.
6. Meanings are negotiated by teachers and students/Meanings are fixed and transmitted to students.
7. Teachers are reflective practitioners/Teachers are technicians.

We were still unsure of how or in what ways these constructs related to each other. In fact, we worked through their relationship in a variety of ways. We wrote about how the constructs were connected. We drew diagrams, attempting to represent the relationships visually. We looked back at the logs and portraits, searching for keys to the organizations that teachers gave to their personal construct systems. Eventually, using our language to learn paid off. We began to see and believe that one of the constructs seemed to predict all of the others, and so it emerged as the core construct, the one that defines the nature of knowledge: Knowledge is constructed by human beings/Knowledge exists independent of knowers. In turn, the core construct shapes the satellite constructs that are the remaining six just listed. We chose the term satellite because of the diagrams we drew. Our use of the term satellite is similar to Kelly's use of "subsidiary."

We listened with new ears to what the teachers were telling us, discovering along the way that there were assumptions we could identify that seemed to undergird what they said and how they worked with their students. What was happening was that the constructs we had identified on paper were coming to life, and, thus, verifying our analyses. We can do no more than speculate about how any teacher's personal construct system came into being or why. We know that we shape our theories of knowledge on the accumulated experience of living as well as of being students for many years. We know, too, that the culture of schools exerts a powerful influence, and that our own Western culture tells us, in many ways, what teachers are. As Mayher (1990) argues, we have a "commonsense" view of schooling, built out of one hundred years worth of traditions of teaching and learning in the United States. Such a commonsense view, which ranges from assessing students' learning only by testing them to seeing talking in school as a disruption rather than using it as a means of learning, has contributed to shaping teachers' constructs of teaching and learning as well. Even our literature signals such stereotypes.

It is no wonder then that we changed our title one more time to capture our new learning. The title, "Learning Change," suggests our hypothesis that teachers' personal construct systems account for the kinds and extents of change that are possible. In recognizing and recapturing their construct systems, teachers learn about change, how to change, and what change is while at the same time changing their learning. We also began to recognize that there was another large piece to the picture. And so we began to hypothesize that institutional practices and institutional culture also account for the kinds and extents of change that teachers learn to do and institutions learn to respond to. Our final formulation of our guiding question thus became, *What are the factors, both individual and institutional, that promote and enhance or inhibit and stifle change?*

Selecting the Teachers for Close Study

Choosing from among the forty-five participants in the project was a challenging and complex task. But once our hypothesis was in place, we decided to find individuals who best illustrated how the constructs work in their teaching and learning. By doing so, we could learn how the constructs themselves either limit or contribute to the changes that took place. Our first step was to return to the logs. We took advantage of a number of opportunities to present our work at professional conferences. Our goal was to learn how others construed our data, and so on a number of occasions, we conducted workshops around the country and in Australia. We distributed copies of log excerpts, asking people to think about and discuss the patterns they saw in the teachers' thinking and writing. The confirmation we received was overwhelming, but even more important, it contributed to helping us make selections from among the participants.

Several criteria directed our choices as well. We wanted representatives from different grade levels. We wanted teachers who represented different subject area concerns. We also wanted to look at teachers whose involvement in the project varied according to when they had entered the program. Perhaps most importantly, we wanted teachers who illustrated the possibility of change. While we are aware that this decision is arguable, we believe very strongly that we can learn more by exploring what is possible than by condemning what is not. After rereading our chapter on democratic schooling, we also decided that we needed to understand the interrelationship of teachers' personal construct systems and the classroom climates that they created. If a democratic classroom is the goal, what kinds of attitudes, values, and beliefs make it possible for a teacher to create such an environment? What contribution were we able to make to the change process through our workshops and classroom visitations?

Much gnashing of teeth and chewing of nails followed. We started out with nine teachers and ended up with five, with a number of other permutations in between. We were helped in this selection process by returning to the data again. By now the conversations we had tape-recorded had been transcribed. These provided new sources of data to analyze, which contributed to enriching our interpretations of some of the teachers.

Not every teacher or administrator with whom we worked changed. Not everyone was "with the program." We have discovered no panacea, no magic, no cure for change, whether instant or gradual. To make the contrast clear between those who transformed their teaching and learning in dramatic ways from those who made, at best, cosmetic changes, we have chosen one teacher who, for us, illustrates a kind of stasis. We don't wish to condemn this teacher or any of the others for what didn't happen, but we do want to be clear about the role that a teacher's personal construct system and the present conditions of schooling play in thwarting change. We also want to present the power of the core construct as we understand it. In addition, we want to explore the role of the in-service project in the change process. So what follows is a chapter in which we contrast two secondary subject-area teachers, who are members of the original group; a chapter on a one-year participant, who is an elementary school teacher; a chapter on a high school English teacher who spent three years with us, and a chapter on another high school English teacher who spent two years with us. We hope through the selections we made, to emphasize the across-the-curriculum nature of this work as well as its impact across grade levels.

Chapter Three

The Nature of Knowledge: Two Views

Mr. Pfeiffer and Mr. Winberry are both high school teachers; Pfeiffer teaches social studies and Winberry science. Both of them are veteran teachers, having between them more than forty years of classroom teaching experience, most of it in Charmont. They share a commitment to familiarizing their students with a body of knowledge in their subject areas. They also share the pressure of having to "cover" their respective curricula in order to prepare their students for state qualifying and college entrance examinations. Neither of them volunteered to participate in the first year of the project. Their principal decided to persuade them to join based on his perception that they were both respected by colleagues and students, active in school affairs and activities, and interested in being exposed to new ideas.

We'll look at Pfeiffer and Winberry over the three years that they participated in the in-service program. We'll pay particular attention to the roles that their core constructs about knowledge played in formulating their beliefs about teaching and learning and how all of these connect to their understanding and implementation of language across the curriculum. We'll see them as teachers in *their* classrooms, as well as learners in *our* classroom, and the connections they made between the two. They'll show us clearly what they think school knowledge is, how it's generated, and the role they see themselves playing in building knowledge in, with, or for their students.

Teaching as Learning

Like all the teachers in this program, Winberry and Pfeiffer came to the workshops with an already formulated view of the world, in other words, a system of guiding beliefs about their classrooms and learning in general. Our goal, in part, was to encourage them to share their views and test them against new ideas about using language as a way of learning across the curriculum. In the second workshop we held with the teachers, we asked them to read and write in response to a passage from Noam Chomsky's *Aspects of the Theory of Syntax* (1965), chosen because it is difficult to read. We asked the participants to read the passage twice. The instructions for the first reading were to read through the passage without taking any notes, asking any questions, marking the text in any way, or talking to their peers. Once the entire group had finished reading, we gave them a multiple-choice, true-false test, with the objective of finding out "whether or not you had read the material." Our intention was to block personal meaning making and engagement as completely as we could. We also hoped to contrast this reading experience with a very different teaching and learning encounter with the "same" text and, thereby, to reveal more fully the elements of each learning process.

On the second reading, we asked the teachers to keep a learning log entry in which they would (1) summarize the excerpt, (2) make connections, and (3) raise questions. After reading and responding individually, they were divided into groups of four or five and asked to share and discuss their learning logs with one another. Once both activities were completed, we asked the group to reflect in their logs on "what" and "how" they had learned in each situation.

As it happened, Pfeiffer and Winberry were in the same group that day. While we didn't realize it at the time, the transcript that we have of their small-group discussion reveals who they are as learners and their spontaneous, uncoached ability to connect themselves as learners to their students. This contributes to a picture of who they are as teachers. The transcript opens with group members, in turn, summarizing the article.

> MR. WINBERRY: OK. About the only thing I said here is that this article is a confusing treatise on syntax and grammar [*Pause*], I think. End of quote.
>
> MR. PFEIFFER: I originally started by answering the wrong thing. I really answered number three. So, I decided to go back. My statement and summarization is that this deals with English grammar and the need to know the various aspects or nomenclature of the language which it has. And that knowledge is, in some cases, maybe a complicated technical knowledge involving syntax, or writing involving syntax or linguistics, etc. Or it can be the ability to write creatively

or generatively and realize that your writing contains the structure of our language? Now if that makes any sense [*Pause*] that's what sense it made to me. . . . My question: Is there a need for all of us to understand syntactic theory and English syntax and linguistics or is it enough to know, from my point of view not being an English teacher, ah, what and how to write no matter what the content is and the fact that this is contained in it?

MR. WINBERRY: I think your verbosity is too copious for my diminutive comprehension.

It's natural that using talking to learn in an initial encounter with a new field, a new vocabulary, and new ideas will produce language that appears incoherent and can be incomprehensible to others. However, one of the cornerstones of the belief in the connection between language and learning is that even language of that sort will make connections and meanings for the language user that can be built upon, refined, and contemplated. So, even though Pfeiffer's first statement seems incoherent, it contains the seed of an insight into Chomsky's theory, which is, in fact, quite sophisticated ("the need to know the various aspects or nomenclature of the language"; "realize that your writing contains the structural aspects of our language"). This seed appears in his second question as a more complete, more coherent thought about the connection between knowledge about language and ability to use the language ("is there a need for all of us to understand . . . or is it enough to know . . . what and how to write . . . and the fact that this is contained in it?"). In other words, in trying out some of Chomsky's terms, Pfeiffer finds his way to making them mean something for him. And, perhaps most important, he has used his "shaping at the point of utterance" to work his way to an important question.

Winberry, however, responds differently: he criticizes the article for being "a confusing treatise" and parodies Chomsky's high style in his response to Pfeiffer's question. Winberry was not mocking Pfeiffer. Instead, his responses masked his own uncertainty about gaps in his knowledge. Pfeiffer revealed the limits of his understanding; Winberry distanced himself from the process. Although Chomsky's style *is* difficult to read, it's clear from the different responses given by Pfeiffer and Winberry that Chomsky can be penetrated if a learner takes the risk of sounding unsure and inadequate.

Soon after these responses, Pfeiffer moves to sharing the connection that he made from the Chomsky excerpt to something in his experience. He says:

I'm sure the fact that we give our students — I do — material to read which to me is very simple to read because it's content area I'm so familiar with and *yet to them it's probably like reading this article*. I don't know. I was trying to draw a comparison to the fact that things that they're getting I'm sure create the same type of frustration I had reading this or that several of us had. (Emphasis added)

There are several other times in the transcript where Pfeiffer compares himself as learner to his student learners. We designed immersion activities hoping to evoke this kind of connection. If teachers could become learners again, we speculated, this experience might bring them closer to empathizing with their students' experiences of learning in their classes. Making the connection between self as learner to one's students as learners creates the affective bridge essential to moving beyond identification to enactment of alternative processes of learning.

But Pfeiffer goes beyond this to actually criticizing his own teaching for ignoring signals from his students that they're having trouble learning. We will see that this criticism will in turn cause him to raise questions about his teaching and his students' learning. Before we turn to those questions, we want to point out that we believe that the empathetic stance Pfeiffer takes may be an important aspect of his construct of teaching as coaching. Without inside knowledge of what it feels like to be a learner, a novice, a teacher can't be a master craftsman, an effective facilitator.

Winberry also makes some connections to teaching. During a discussion of the pros and cons of oral reading, he tells a story:

OK, Frederica could read beautifully. Better than anybody, practically anybody in this room. . . . Anyway she could read and read and read and read beautifully but she wouldn't know one thing she just read. [She] had the ability to read beautifully with nice inflection. She could go up and down.

This story seemed to serve as a way of illustrating a point that was raised by other group members, enabling Winberry to be a part of the conversation and to create a spirit of group consensus. He makes a connection to his classroom and his teaching, although he doesn't make a connection to how he learns himself.

By focusing in on learners, himself and his students, Pfeiffer naturally creates an opening for "talk back," which pushes him to raise questions about his classroom. About twenty minutes into the discussion, he appears to be questioning one of his practices:

MR. PFEIFFER: I've tried different ways of giving vocabulary words to the kids before they do a reading.
Ms. SCOTT: Does that help them do you think?
MR. PFEIFFER: I don't [*Pause*] Sometimes. I don't know. I don't know if it helps.

A little later, at the end of the discussion on why the choice of materials by teachers accounts for the difficulties students often have with reading, he moves the discussion to contemplating the effectiveness of reading aloud in class:

> MR. PFEIFFER: Is it good for 'em? Does it destroy 'em? Does it help 'em?
> MR. WINBERRY: Some people like it. Some people really. . . .
> MR. PFEIFFER: It's not a question of liking it or disliking it. . . . But is it something that should be promoted?

Winberry tries to answer questions; in contrast, Pfeiffer keeps asking them. Pfeiffer evidences his inquiring attitude in resolving some of his teaching dilemmas by sharing what he has tried out. In the conversation quoted earlier, he told his group that he tried a variety of ways of introducing vocabulary that was new to students, but contained in their reading assignments. Somewhat later, he shares his experience with having students talk to him individually about whether or not they understood their reading assignments, rather than asking them to read aloud in class.

By adopting an interactive stance with a "foreign" text, one through which he raised questions, revealed gaps in knowledge, tried out new language, and connected to his own experience, Pfeiffer was subtly revealing his approach to learning. While it's true that everyone in Pfeiffer's group was the "good" student, dutifully following the teacher's instructions, Pfeiffer went beyond answering the teacher's questions and set his own purposes for learning. He engaged in learning about and learning from the Chomsky piece with commitment and open-mindedness. He read as though what he was reading ought to make sense, so that rather than being cowed by the text, he used it as a springboard for discovering something new. The risks he took in exposing himself as a learner reveal that he sees learning as an activity that encompasses trial and error. Learning is something that learners work at, rather than something that simply happens to you if you're lucky. Learning is making meanings for Pfeiffer, not receiving truths.

Just the Facts, Ma'am, Just the Facts

Another way of talking about the difference between Winberry and Pfeiffer is to call Winberry an objectivist and Pfeiffer a constructivist. Winberry accords facts a completely independent status in the world. For him, "the truth of beliefs can be tested by their conformity to reality independent of anyone's way of seeing it; disagreements about empirical truth can be resolved, at least in principle, by reference to facts . . . " (Schön, 1987, p. 222).

By contrast, Pfeiffer can't even define knowledge in social studies without making reference to himself as a learner or to what the experience of learning social studies must feel like for his students. This is a theme that began to emerge as we analyzed the conversation about the Chomsky excerpt, where Pfeiffer exhibited himself to be in transaction with the known, to be quite literally a maker of the things he knows (Bentley & Dewey, 1949). In short, facts are equivalent to knowledge for the objectivist, whereas in the constructivist worldview, facts may be a part of knowledge, but without a knower, facts have no life. For a constructivist like Pfeiffer, facts are not disembodied entities, because "perceptions and beliefs are rooted in worlds of our own making that we accept as reality" (Schön, 1987, p. 222).

From the start, Winberry keeps his students and his subject separate. In responding to the notion that connection making in the form of expressive language (after Britton) has no place in the study of science, he writes that asking students to use their own voice and language to learn about science before memorizing the vocabulary is "a problem in science." "Gadzooks," he writes. While this may be an appropriate strategy in some curricula areas, it "leaves out the heavy academic (*new vocab*) courses." He suggests that the personal connection making embedded in expressive writing can be achieved in other ways: "filling-in-blanks and short-answer questions *do likewise*" (Emphasis Winberry's).

Both teachers are examining the possibilities of using expressive language to learn academic content with their students. Winberry argues against using writing to learn in his learning log; Pfeiffer uses it in his classroom, suggesting that his students "write their reactions to what we've been doing with the Constitution." The contrast between these two teachers' attitudes is reflected not only in their beliefs, but in their actions. Pfeiffer is already struggling to make applications in his classroom, whereas Winberry is still struggling on paper to find a use for expressive writing.

Pfeiffer cannot conceive of social studies as an entity independent of a learner and he experiments with new ways of connecting learners to the material to be learned. Our early observations of him with his students revealed his willingness to try a whole variety of new strategies all at once. Although he and the two of us found much to criticize in the ways he was implementing these strategies, we also found much to compliment because he was so willing to try approaches that were new to him, such as using small-group work, written responses at the end of class to evaluate what had gone on, and student-generated inquiry about textbook material.

Beliefs are not simply descriptions of an interpretive system, but are the structures of and for understanding, predicting, and acting. We observed Winberry in his classroom on several occasions early in the year and found a perfect match between what he was saying about what he believed learning in science entailed and what he was doing to help his students learn science.

He says, "Spontaneity in learning is important but so are the facts." What he does in his classroom is to engage students in a variety of copying activities, which leaves little room for spontaneity. All notes taken by the students during our classroom visits in October and November were copied directly from his carefully prepared set of notes, which he either wrote on the blackboard or presented on an overhead projector. Each day, the students were required to complete a preset amount of work toward accumulating knowledge of biology by the end of the term. Each of these predetermined steps had its accompanying carefully planned worksheets to be completed by the students: either a scientific diagram to be labeled, or a set of problems to be solved, or an observation sheet to be filled in. Unless a student was absent that day, these were not completed independently. Winberry either drew, labeled, or solved them on his transparency, which was flashed on the screen by the overhead projector he had with him at the front of the classroom. He occasionally asked students to help him complete the tasks. The students' primary activities were answering his questions or copying his work.

By January, 1986, Winberry was revealing more and more about his core construct of knowledge. In referring once again to his students' role in making knowledge, he notes in his log that "much writing in class is not personal experience but someone else's work—or an observation." He goes on to suggest that:

> I have written down the guidelines for responding to student writing since I wish to consider them. Some of these, "focus on writing's meaning, emphasize the positive," and "consider the developmental nature of writing," will have to be modified to include the fact that many of our writings include facts rather than just thoughts. Facts are important here. Some ideas and thoughts might be appreciated, but there are differences and they must be noted.

Both these entries suggest to us that he believes that facts have an independent and impersonal status. Human beings neither create nor perceive facts; they recognize, apprehend, and "learn" them. Although he acknowledges that someone does some kind of work, the students' task is to reproduce that work. He says that there are some things that are "facts" not "thoughts" and that facts have a higher status than thoughts. Thoughts are "*just* thoughts" (emphasis added). Observation, too, in his science classes does not entail an observer and so is not very different from "someone else's work," even though on the face of it, students are being asked to record what they see.

Winberry and Pfeiffer placed learners, whether themselves or their students, very differently in the learning context. If facts are the primary concern, if to transmit the information is the driving force behind teaching, then the learner will inevitably take a back seat. On the other hand, if, as a constructivist, knowledge is created and meanings negotiated, then learners must play a central role, since they are the agents of the construction. Pfeiffer not only puts himself in the role of learner on a number of levels, but uses his insider knowledge of learning to make applications of the new ideas he is confronting. His idea for having his students "write their reactions to what we've been doing with the Constitution" is connected to the fact that "I myself have even written a log entry on the subject." He is, therefore, a learner with and for his students. He recollects in December, 1985, after reading Fulwiler's (1982) "The Personal Connection: Journal Writing Across the Curriculum," the role that journal keeping played for him on a trip he took to China and wishes that he would make more use of journals in his own life:

> It was the only time in my travels I kept [a journal]. I'm amazed at the writing I did. I usually don't write much. Some of the stories bring back vivid memories. I wish now I had one for all trips.

The transition from using his own journals to learn to having his students using learning logs in his social studies classes was a smooth one.

Pfeiffer articulates the essentialness of bringing the learner's life and new ideas together in the classroom as a way of building knowledge and he does so in part through reflecting on his own experiences in school:

> To this day I have no idea why I took geometry and algebra. Although I studied like mad for them, they never had any practical applications. Probability did but never relating tangent, co-tangent, etc. is confusing [sic]. Maybe math teachers would find more success if they equated the problems to life experiences instead of handing out ten problems and theorems to do and memorize.

This kind of critical reflection raises some interesting questions for us. It's certainly clear that Pfeiffer had the experience of being set apart from and expected to passively take in the facts he was required to "learn" and that the experience was a negative one for him. What we can never know is how much his recollections were affected by the thinking and doing in the workshops. That is, did his learning during immersion activities result in a reconceptualization of his experiences as a high school math student? Or did his experience as a math student enable him to understand and connect to those issues being explored in the workshops in the first place? Or, even, did the workshops allow him to reconfirm an implicit belief? Perhaps all of these things occurred. Our raising them is a way of sharing the complexity of these issues. What we believe is that "history is possibility" (Freire, 1988, p. xxviii), that the experiences of one's life transact with one another to continually evolve our beliefs and knowledge. And, finally, as for Pfeiffer, so as for us, a knower cannot be separated from knowledge.

Facts and Disciplines

The current emphasis on accumulating information, the sort of emphasis that has placed Hirsch (1987) and Bloom (1987) on the best-seller list, is directly connected to the place of factual and conceptual information within the curriculum. Winberry's emphasis on teaching facts in order for students to be able to pass standardized tests places him in good company.

It's clear to us (and this locates us outside the popular view) that there wouldn't be any facts if there wasn't a theory, an interpretation, and that facts don't carry any meaning unless there is a theory to explain them. This suggests not only that facts are as reliable as the theory that explains them, but that as the theory changes, so do the facts. Since this is so, then science is a continually evolving field, where new questions raise new problems leading to new theories that will attempt to explain and interpret those problems through the identification and accumulation of new facts or the reinterpretation of already existing facts. Science is always open to change. Yet, if science is taught only as facts, then it's bound to be viewed as a static field, one where all the answers have been found, where no problems or questions remain. And, of course, this is just not true.

Consider the theory of biological evolution. Most evolutionary biologists have come to believe that biological evolution has occurred through a very gradual and extraordinarily slow process of change over millions of years. The facts that substantiate this theory and are taught as biological evolution include fossil evidence and carbon dating of fauna and flora showing the gradual changes that took place. Yet, there exists, even now, a debate within the field of biological evolution that suggests another theory, one that seeks to explain biological evolution as a process of very rapid spurts in which changes came about discretely and dramatically followed by long periods of no change at all. No doubt, such a theory, if it is to usurp the favored one of gradual change, would need to find its own set of facts or reinterpret the current set of facts to substantiate its claims for discreteness and rapidity.

If we teach only the facts of evolutionary biology to students without contextualizing the facts within a theory, then we are not only misrepresenting the field of science by defining it as a *fait accompli,* but we are also putting students at a disadvantage. They will have no organizing principle around which to understand the facts as they are now. Questions of *why* such facts have been chosen will not be part of the science curriculum if the theories of science aren't part of that curriculum as well. Knowledge of alternative explanations, that is, competing theories, is not made available to students either. Such knowledge is rarely, if ever, given a consideration in a curriculum that pretends that all the problems have solutions, since the facts themselves seem to be evidence that all the controversy, all the questioning, and all the intrigue have gone on, been dealt with, and settled long ago. McNeil's research (1986) showed us evidence of this sort of "defensive oversimplification" across the curriculum. If we have all the facts, then there's nothing much more to do but to memorize them and move on to the next set of facts. Students' natural stance of "incipient scientist," as Kelly (1955) calls it, a stance that sees human beings as continually exploring, questioning, testing out, and hypothesizing about their world from the moment of birth, is effectively shut off in a science curriculum that is conceptualized only as facts.

If thinking and acting like scientists were at the core of the science curriculum, then students could not only exercise their natural inclination to curiosity by exploring the "whys" of science, but they could also begin to attempt to ask and to discover the kinds of questions and the kinds of evidence that scientists use. If students were given the opportunity to explore a variety of theories and to build theories that account for the facts that they see, they might be in a better position to argue for the merits of one over another; they certainly would be able to read "critically" the facts used to substantiate the competing theories. They would learn in the process what theories are.

All the evidence we have points to fact-based curricula as the most common type of content organization and delivery. It's widespread throughout the United States and across the curriculum and grade levels. It's what happened to literature study, as we have asked students more and more to identify such things as, "Where did Silas bury the money?" It's Hirsch's (1987) cultural literacy test and dictionary. The problem won't be solved here, but it's crucial to begin to uncover the kinds of commonsense attitudes and beliefs and pedagogical theories that give credence to the primacy of facts in the curriculum.

Teaching vs. Learning: A Profound Confusion

A major implication that can be drawn from the contrast between a constructivist and objectivist view of the world is the classroom focus that inevitably results from seeing the world in these two very different ways. Judith Lindfors (1984), from whom the title of this section is derived, has argued that teaching and learning are not mirror images of one another and that if we focus too much on what teachers do and not enough on the learner's processes of coming to know, then we may confuse and distort the two acts. Lindfors suggests that what and how we teach ought to derive from what and how learners learn. Her essentially constructivist view leads us to focus on learning, whereas an objectivist view would focus on teaching.

The confusion between teaching and learning expresses itself in two crucial ways in these two teachers' classrooms. Where and in whom they believe purposes and intentions for learning are generated is one way they express their beliefs. How they come to see the role of language in learning is another expression of their focus on either teaching or learning. How they define the role of "teacher" is embedded in the attitudes that they have toward motivation and language. In the following sections, "Motivation vs. Negotiation" and "Integrating Language as a Way of Learning," we will look closely at Winberry and Pfeiffer's words and actions, as they demonstrate their constructs of teaching and learning.

Motivation vs. Negotiation

Up to this point, we have attempted to illustrate both Pfeiffer's and Winberry's beliefs about what knowledge is and how knowledge is generated. Given the differences in the ways each of these teachers thinks about knowledge in his discipline, it should not be surprising to discover marked differences in the roles they believe teachers ought to play with learners. We have come to see Pfeiffer as a "coach" and Winberry as an "examiner." By coaching, we mean exactly the role Dewey has defined:

> The student cannot be *taught* what he needs to know, but he can be *coached*. He has to *see* on his own behalf and in his own way the relationships between means and methods employed and results achieved. Nobody can see for him, and he can't see just by being "told," although the right kind of telling may guide his seeing and thus help him see what he needs to see. (Archambault, 1974, p. 151)

From such a perspective, teachers become not only listeners and observers, but facilitators and collaborators in learning with their students. And, of course, from such a perspective, it is the learner who is at the center of this enactment.

Winberry writes in his log that "I don't see anything meaningful in the 'metaphor of teacher as coach.' " Shedding further light on how he views his role, he states: "I'm still trying to teach science not analyze students. Teachers should resist the temptation to analyze rather than teach." He sees his job as teaching a subject and so questions or insights about what students are thinking are irrelevant. The role he chooses is diametrically opposed to the one articulated by Dewey because he believes that teaching is telling and seeing for students, not analyzing how or why students are learning. The most efficient way to determine whether or not students are learning is to test them for recall of the facts. For us, therefore, Winberry is an examiner. Examination also functions as motivation.

> "Evaluating as little as possible" is hard to do. Kids want motivation to learn, they don't work without it. They need to get paid or they won't work.

Payment for work done—the motivation for student learning—takes the form of good grades on classroom tests and passing scores on mandated examinations.

We find him at the end of the first year of the project viewing himself as the best person to provide the payment students need to be motivated to learn. He writes:

> Elbow [1983] makes a practical suggestion that "students will get more out of a lecture, a reading assignment, film, etc. if they free write after the event" [p. 234]. Good idea, but if you don't collect it many students may not bother to do it!!

He writes a bit further on in his log that "my experience has been that students accept very little direct instruction other than the basic ground rules of "what do *you* want" (emphasis added). Students, through their schooling experiences, have come to accept teachers who are examiners and consistently ask this most relevant question. Students support their teachers in maintaining an objectivist view by reinforcing teachers in their role as givers and examiners of knowledge. They have come to expect that the teacher will tell them what and how they have to learn.

Pfeiffer's willingness to take risks coupled with his view of knowledge, even within the confines of a highly structured curriculum, leads him to see the need for personal engagement in learning. In reflecting on his own learning, he writes in his logs:

> We learn most quickly when we are personally involved. This is also true for students. They are better learners when involved and we must involve them through language for more effective learning.

In a classroom where students are encouraged to share their own quests for knowledge, it becomes possible to negotiate students' and teachers' intentions. Instead of hoping that there might be some overlap between the purposes of learners and teacher, a negotiated approach ensures that a portion of everyone's intentions will be satisfied. As we explored negotiating the curriculum in Chapter 2, we looked at how the constraints of curriculum, time, and testing play a role in determining what and how learning will proceed. Pfeiffer's discipline of social studies, like Winberry's of biology, has a mandated curriculum and competency tests. We'll see that Pfeiffer, though operating under constraints and dedicated to helping his students achieve on standardized tests, is able to find ways of negotiating even the most formulaic curricular demands.

The principles of negotiating the curriculum had immediate appeal for Pfeiffer. They fit both his need to involve students' personal meaning-making stances and his view that knowledge is constructed by learners. Shortly after articulating his own need for personal involvement in learning and connecting that to his students, he planned a possible role for using negotiation to begin a new relationship with his students in his classroom. The in-service participants were reading an article by Peter Elbow (1983) entitled, "Teaching Writing by Not Paying Attention to Writing," in which he suggests that:

At the beginning of a course it's helpful for the teacher and students all to write rough, informal pieces telling what they want from the course, what their positive and negative expectations are, what it will take to maintain their commitment and investment, what they need from the teacher and from each other, and what special strengths they can offer. (p. 236)

Pfeiffer responded to this by writing,

This is a great way to start a new year. Could you also ask them what grade they would like and what they feel is needed to get that grade? A "pre-negotiating" session to lay ground-work and rules?

Elbow is suggesting that using writing to learn is a way of helping students and teachers to reveal their assumptions, to reflect on their own purposes for learning, and to suggest what they would like the classroom context to provide them. Going beyond that, Pfeiffer sees negotiation as a way to do what Garth Boomer (Green, 1988) calls "reading the whole curriculum," by recognizing that student involvement should include the whole range of decisions that constitute the curriculum, from what content will be learned to how learning will take place and be evaluated, and the means by which to work together. For him, negotiating evaluation becomes a major issue, and so he writes about it again:

Self-evaluation would be on the work they completed. How much they put into it. Again negotiating is possible. Then tests don't become the only vehicle for growing.

There's nothing mechanistic or recipelike in his understanding of negotiation. He's clearly not advocating any single approach to evaluation, but he seems to be recognizing that to negotiate all but the final grade would be deceitful. By maintaining total authority over grades, teachers undermine the collaboration that precedes it. This authority continues to perpetuate the existing teacher/student power relationship by giving teachers complete control over the ends of learning, no matter what the means, even if those means give the appearance of student ownership and participation.

On the other hand, turning over all decisions about grading to the students would also be destructive. All actors in a negotiated setting get to contribute and satisfy their intentions and must accept compromise by receiving input from the rest of the negotiators. This is what we mean by democratic schooling. And, further, there are negotiable but real criteria for achievement that distinguish levels of accomplishment.

Once Pfeiffer was able to imagine what negotiating might look like and entail for his students in his subject area, he was then able to try it out. As a result of his experimentation, in fact, his action research, he expanded and refined his use of negotiation year by year. At a workshop during the third year of the program, he tells a story of something that had just occurred in his classroom, which we believe typifies the integration of the principles of negotiation into his moment-by-moment practice in the classroom.

> A class of ninth graders had been studying a combination of the geography and culture of China. In a test I'd given them, there was a question dealing with "green" China, the eastern part which is fruitful, [and] "brown" China, which is the mountains and everything else, which is "dry" China. The kids looked at the [question] and they said, "Did we learn this?" And I said, "Well, in your mind think of the map of China." A girl looks totally confused. The kids were writing for awhile and one of the kids raises his hand and says, "Mr. Pfeiffer, I'm having trouble with this question. Do you think you could pull the map down?" And I looked at him and the first thing I said was, "No way." And then I thought about it and said, "Why not? Why not? Wait a minute. Why not?" . . . A couple of them just could not visualize it in their mind[s]. So, I thought, pull the map down and let them look at it. And the kids said, "Oh, yeah, right," now. What we expected of them was . . . tremendous. For some people it takes years upon years of knowledge to get, but looking at the map they could plug [in]. I sat there, and at first said, "No way. It's a test." And as I sat back, and I laughed, and they thought [that the student who asked to have the map pulled down] was the greatest kid going here because he helped them all. I said, "Why not? What is the big deal?" Some of the kids said, "This isn't fair. We already did the essay." "It doesn't matter. If you want to add fine, but just go back through your essay. . . . " And some of them said, "I sort of don't have this." It's true, when you get so set [in your ways of teaching] and you say, "This is a pop quiz," so you can't do anything to help.

We can see Pfeiffer "thinking on his feet" and negotiating an alternative route to learning about China. His understanding of exactly what he intended the test to evaluate was so deep that he could be flexible. He realized that what he had originally planned had become, in execution, contrary to his intentions. When he realized he was testing for memory—could students recall the regions of China—rather than testing their ability to apply concepts about the connections between geography and history, it was logical for him to abandon the restriction (seeing the map at the same time they were attempting to write the essay) and allow the students to display what they really did know and understand. Of all the many kinds of teaching and learning situations that are a regular part of classrooms, the test situation is usually the most difficult one to find leeway into. And, as a result, we are particularly impressed that he was able to "reflect-in-action" in a context that's usually so tightly controlled by an unspoken pact between teachers and students—that students won't ask for help, and teachers won't give it under test conditions.

To become a "reflective practitioner," a consummate professional as Donald Schön (1983) defines it, took Pfeiffer the better part of three years in this project. His view of knowledge, which gave rise to his willingness to take risks, to see himself as a learner and a coach, one who wants to facilitate the best student performances, combined with his continued action research and inquirer stance, were all properties contributing to his ability to become a reflective practitioner. The workshop immersion activities, the workshop activities that encouraged risk taking, and the distancing activities interspersed throughout the workshop sequence supported and promoted him in his learning and change.

Integrating Language as a Way of Learning in Science and Social Studies

We've already suggested that a teacher's construct of knowledge has predictive power. This construct shapes and determines a number of other constructs that link teachers' beliefs to their practices. The focus of the in-service program in Charmont was to influence and engender the practice of using language as a way of learning across the curriculum. In this section, we'll see how Winberry's and Pfeiffer's views of knowledge affect their implementation of language across the curriculum.

Whenever we visited Winberry's classroom, we were struck by the fact that he was attempting to use some strategies for increasing students' talking and writing. His students were writing more, but the writing was serving the end of memorizing data, rather than interpreting and understanding it. His students were sharing their writing more, but without learning from or with each other because the writing was either copied from the text or Winberry's notes, so there was nothing for students to comment on or question. He continued to view biology as mastery over a set of facts. He shared

his skepticism about what he saw going on in his classroom when he attempted
to try out these strategies and he tended to conclude that the strategies were not
particularly successful:

> My reaction to students talking and "making their own unsystematic
> explorations" through talking with one another is positive and trepida-
> tious. My problem is that students' ideas wander and attention levels
> vary. It's been very difficult for me to do this without wasting more time
> than we can validly use. If I discovered the *Rosetta* stone for this type
> of teaching I would jump right in. My problem has been the mire of
> quicksand of the few doing it all and the others not listening. . . . It's
> good at first glance but let's go beyond the surface.

The level of student engagement and participation was very limited according
to his own and our observations. Thus, his testing out of new strategies recon-
firmed what he believed about the limited usefulness of language to learn
when the subject to be learned is conceptualized as a transmittable set of facts.
Moreover, he believed (and from his perspective we think he's right) that time
spent on these activities was time off task.

What's ironic about all of this is the very different view that Winberry's
students have about using writing to learn. At one classroom visit where students were role playing different parts of a tree, but reading their roles from
material that had been copied from Winberry's lecture notes and the textbook,
it was clear that the students were not involved in the activity. They were using
neither their own voices nor their own words. They were plainly bored. One of
us asked if the students might not be able to speak in their own words. They
volunteered one by one to act their parts and, just as we suspected, they had
such a command of the information that they could do this with ease. Winberry
was pleased at the level of their understanding as well as their involvement
in the revised lesson. The students, when asked what happened as a result of
putting the information into their own language, said, "It shows that you know
the material."

Winberry encapsulates a number of his beliefs in the following log entry:

> I don't really think "objective tests harm instruction." As far as I'm con-
> cerned language is language. Objective tests take the personal prejudice
> from the test. It's either right or wrong. We all know that at the end of
> the topic and course there will be a short answer, multiple-choice test for
> which there is much recognition of merit and anticipation.

This entry affirms his use of tests to motivate students' learning. "Objective"
tests are particularly suitable because language does not have different func-

tions. No matter whose language or what purpose it's serving, all language is the same. Learners are, moreover, not harmed by using textbook or teacher language rather than their own. And, finally, knowledge of biology is quantifiable; it can be simply counted and measured and students can be readily rewarded. Winberry's beliefs about testing, about knowledge acquisition and knowledge demonstration, and, most especially, about the role of language in learning make it understandable why the basic premises of language across the curriculum had limited expression in his classroom.

Pfeiffer continually explored how he might integrate language to learn in his social studies classes. In a discussion early during the first year of the program, Team A was talking about how textbooks are organized with questions at the end of each chapter. Pfeiffer was criticizing the kind of learning that is supported by having the students answer preset questions raised by others and exploring how to improve students' understanding of the material that must be read in social studies. He wrote:

> Question of reading text and understanding it—How can we evaluate this assignment? Have students ask questions of the text as an assignment—then respond in groups.

Here he was both developing a writing-to-learn assignment—students write their own questions on the text they've read—as well as conjecturing about an alternative to evaluate their learning. With textbook questions, evaluation is simple and neat (the answers, after all, are provided in the teacher's manual). But when students ask their own questions, learning becomes more open ended, even messy, so evaluation is more difficult. The alternative evaluation strategy is using language to learn as well, since students will be talking as well as sharing their questions and answers with one another. This also suggests Pfeiffer's ease with collaboration as a mode of learning, a climate that is conducive to, supportive of, and indeed, dependent on rich language use.

He interprets writing to learn as having an additional value for his students. He begins to see that writing may give an edge to students who are often excluded from so-called "class discussions." But he also recognizes the risks in challenging the accepted ways of doing school.

> Participation is key [in learning]. Some students aren't vocal and feel they'll be punished. [Writing] gives them a way to participate.
>
> A student who does write with ownership could be punished in grading compared to one who is better at copying the answers from a text or magazine.

He is able to predict the consequences of adopting and enacting new ways of teaching and learning in his classroom. And so his understanding of both the gains and the losses is very thorough. To be able to recognize that students who "write with ownership" may be punished because their answers may only approximate the right ones, and what they don't know will be as clear as what they do know, allows him to adjust continually—to be a reflective practitioner as we saw earlier—before, during, and after teaching. Moreover, he is not only able to predict and adjust for his own classroom, he is also able to consider and take into account the consequences of what he does in his classroom in relation to the commonsense school culture at large. Like the successful football coach who always weighs the strengths of his own team against the opposing team, he can anticipate how new ways of teaching and learning will affect his students.

It was Pfeiffer's core construct of knowledge that allowed him to consider alternative possibilities. For him, the in-service project served to support his inquiry into alternatives by helping him understand the implications of his constructivist view of knowledge and find ways to act on his beliefs in his classroom. What changed, then, for him, were his satellite constructs, as he used his research and writing to explore how writing can be used as a mode of learning, how students can learn through collaboration, and how negotiation can replace extrinsic motivation.

If we abstract from the performances of these two in teaching and learning, we can draw some conclusions about how they each view knowledge. All of the characteristics Pfeiffer exhibits as a learner and a teacher rest on a view of knowledge as the constructional meaning by human beings through reflection on their experience. And because he views knowledge in this way, he is naturally attracted to and generally enthusiastic about attempting to use language activities to help his students learn. Since he believes that knowledge is constructed by human beings, he can see almost immediately that talking and writing are two essential means through which such constructions are built. He did it himself in response to the Chomsky excerpt, as he struggled "to shape at the point of utterance" meanings that he could understand and identify with and eventually employ in his own teaching.

Winberry exhibits characteristics that rest on a different view of knowledge as a commodity. He may not use learning-through-language strategies because, in his view of knowledge, they may not be necessary. It appears that he believes that knowledge is transmitted to the learner from the outside, rather than something the learner has to make himself.

Winberry finds it very difficult, therefore, to imagine a constructive role for talking and writing to learn. For him, language is used primarily to encode and decode.

Constructs in Context

We have presented two teachers' individual and personal views of knowledge and how those views shape the roles they take on in their classroom (coach/examiner), their attitudes toward learning (motivation/negotiation), and, finally, in what ways Winberry and Pfeiffer are able to use their new knowledge about language as a way of learning in each of their disciplines.

Another crucial issue is to take seriously the commonsense view of knowledge that is held by the educational community in Charmont. This view is consistent with what has been clearly demonstrated by educational research in the last five years for the vast majority of schools in the United States. The continued use and support, for the most part, of fact-based textbooks, internal and external short-answer examinations, teacher accountability based on achievement scores, and the like represent merely the tangible testimony to objectivism, a belief system that supports the transmission of facts, the banking metaphor of learning, the commodity metaphor of knowledge, and the mechanistic and utilitarian role for language.

When the overwhelming majority, including those with the greatest amount of decision-making power, supports, sustains, and rewards a particular view of knowledge—and thus of teaching and learning—we can account for the positions that individuals who either hold to such a view or don't will have within the school community. In short, we find Winberry fitting into the mainstream, institutional structure of beliefs. Pfeiffer is an exception, challenging, by dint of his beliefs and actions, the accepted and mandated order.

Both of these teachers have displayed their commitments to the language across the curriculum project by making presentations at local- and state-level professional conferences, something new for both of them. Both have been spokesmen in their school for the project, reporting on their ongoing learning at department and faculty meetings over the three years of the project. Their self-reports on the change process and the influence of the project on their teaching have been positive and complimentary. Their colleagues have noted changes in them, as have the principal of the high school and the district superintendent. But these similarities mask one of the essential differences in the ways that they have incorporated language into their curricula. Here's a portion of Winberry's summary of his learning over the three-year project:

> We were at the New York State English Council meeting in Syracuse last October as presenters. Our presentation was well received, especially since it was next to the last session, and people had already left the conference. Even so, our session was packed (SRO) by an enthusiastic group of attendance.

Personally, I have grown professionally in the program in many ways. I always believed in writing as a vehicle for communication, but I was unsure as to how I could integrate writing with the content material that I felt I had to offer the students. . . . it just didn't fit with science or math.

Now in Applied Math we do math problems and summaries as to why we did these problems or activities. At first students resisted the writing as not math but they soon found meaning in both the numbers and the words. They enjoyed the project more because of it.

In Biology, we use learning logs to take notes; we use focused writing to help draw out thoughts after writing in the logs. We use summary writing to help explain to ourselves how we understand what we are trying to learn. Each student is to have a summary of what the lab meant to them, and what did they learn from the lab positive or negative.

We have written word poems successfully to help students with vocabulary studies. We have written stories using the vocabulary words to help students integrate word meanings with terms that are new to the students.

It has also been helpful to meet with others in our group to get suggestions and support from other members. . . . We're in the idea business. Sharing these ideas with other faculty members similarly inclined have *helped me to keep thinking and working for new techniques to use.* The program has rejuvenated my teaching by allowing me to get *another view on conveying information to the recipients.* The program has helped me in many ways. I am grateful to all involved for allowing me to be exposed to the benefits that I never expected at the outset. (Emphasis added)

The fact that a thirty-year veteran of teaching could be "reinvigorated" by any in-service process is inspiring. Both we and his colleagues noticed his enthusiasm and we were all pleased by his public declarations about how important the in-service process had been for him. His relationship to his colleagues began to focus on sharing ideas and seeking support for new classroom practices. Evidence of such practices can be seen in every paragraph.

We believe, though, that his efforts to use language to learn were always hampered by his core construct of knowledge, which did not change. In his own words, "the program has rejuvenated [his] teaching by allowing [him] to get another view on conveying information to the recipients." This suggests to us that knowledge continues to be information that can be transmitted from teacher to learner. As a result, the thrust of his involvement in this project was to "help [him] to keep thinking and working for new techniques to use." Language across the curriculum does rely on certain techniques, but those techniques when used without a reconceptualization of learning and teaching result in limited changes.

In an excerpt from Pfeiffer's summary of his learning over the course of the project, he shares his concerns for the future.

> I think I'm sort of under the gun again, back where Mr. Winberry was when we first started, you know, concerned about time, concerned about getting done with the book. . . . I'm in a rush.
>
> Problems. In trying to integrate I've been pleased with some things that I've done in terms of integrating. I've also dropped a couple of things. And I think that the major issue is I'm just tied up with time because of coaching. And I haven't had the time to get to meetings with colleagues. It goes back to well I have 120 students and I'm constantly looking at papers and I'm happy with what I've done, although I know *I want to reevaluate while I'm changing*. I'm already in my mind thinking about things from this year. And in the same general area of change—to allow that. So it's trial and error. I figure, whether you're a first year, second, third, or fourth year person, to me it's going to take a few years until I'm happy with what I'm doing. I got that fear from reading one of the articles [Applebee, 1984] on the social studies teacher who thought he had the writing workshop down. (Emphasis added)

Pfeiffer finds himself struggling to accommodate the antagonisms between his own beliefs and the institutional practices of the school. He exemplifies the role that institutional practices play in thwarting the ability of any individual to fully enact his personal beliefs, especially those that are at odds with the institution's. We see him struggling to find time to meet with his colleagues now that the official project is completed. After all, the institution does not define collaboration among faculty as a professional necessity, and so teachers are left to find their own time to fit in such professional work. The number of students Pfeiffer has to work with each day also inhibits his ability to teach in ways that are compatible with his beliefs. Even though he is happy with the writing his students are doing, the institution doesn't reward that by reducing his load. He is clearly feeling the tension between a natural pace for learning and the pace prescribed by texts and tests. Even though every aspect of the institution that we've listed here is designed to inhibit a teacher from acting out his constructivist views, teachers like Pfeiffer strive to help their students construct knowledge actively anyway.

We're suggesting that the institution doesn't assert omnipotent control over the choices and beliefs that individual teachers can and do make. Although it may depress Pfeiffer from time to time, it won't prevent him from continuing to grow and change. As is evident from the final part of his look to the future, he is still a reflective practitioner. That stance, built on a constructivist view to grow and change. As is evident from the final part of his look to the future, he is still a reflective practitioner. That stance, built on a constructivist view of knowledge and a professional attitude of inquiry, will, for us, ensure that he will not retreat, but will instead continue to question, explore, and grow.

In the following chapters, we will look at three teachers who share some of Pfeiffer's views of teaching and learning. All have a view of knowledge as a human construction and, like him, all grow into being reflective practitioners, learners, inquirers, coaches, and negotiators. All of these roles and the constructs that underlie them have the potential for creating a teacher/leader, the teacher we look at closely in Chapter 6.

Chapter Four

The Teacher As
Reflective Practitioner

Winberry and Pfeiffer were members of the original team of teachers (Team A) who participated in the in-service program, so we were able to look at their learning over a period of three years. Ms. Sealy, a fifth-grade teacher and the focus of this chapter, was a member of the third team of teachers (Team C), and so we could only follow her learning over one year. While this limits our ability to predict as confidently what might happen to her in the future, it does allow us to explore how the change process might be set in motion and the kinds of initial paths that may lay the groundwork for continued learning.

We don't claim that the project by itself caused changes in teachers' views of teaching and learning. We know that change is too complex a process for us to say more than that the immersion and distancing activities that comprised the workshops along with other elements of the program, like the action research projects and the teacher/advisors, were designed to promote thinking, reflection, and action, and that our objective was to support teachers in building a philosophy of instruction through these processes. But engaging in this kind of learning and reflecting during her year in the project enabled Sealy to uncover and recapture her core construct that knowledge is constructed by human beings. Like many teachers we've worked with, the power of the culture of schooling exerted itself in such a way as to repress her alternative system of beliefs and to co-opt them. After teaching for five years, Sealy had adopted the school's culture and the beliefs that support it as if they were her own.

Through the various activities she engaged in in the workshops, through the collaborative sharing she did with her colleagues on the team, her action research, her willingness to look at herself in ways she had avoided up to this point, and, most especially, through her diligent reflection on her beliefs and practices, she was able to recognize and reevaluate her ideas about teaching and learning. We have chosen her to represent "the teacher as reflective practitioner" because the conscious recognition she achieved of the dissonance between her theory of knowledge and the theory that pervades her school and, therefore, her classroom, is central to the change process. Without the lens of the system of constructs that we've defined, what we will hear from Sealy might not sound particularly dramatic or profound. But once we identify the ways in which her reports represent an articulation of competing theories and the struggle to resolve the growing tension between them, her seemingly simple statements about ordinary day-to-day classroom situations take on real significance and, indeed, for us, are both profound and dramatic.

Learning from Our Stories

During the first two years of the project, the participants taught us how much they could learn about their own views of teaching and learning by telling stories about how they learn. Therefore, during the third year of the project, we used a storytelling activity early on in the sequence of workshops in order to begin uncovering teachers' implicit theories as soon as possible. We asked teachers to write about a time they learned something, either in school or out of school, either a positive or a negative experience. Such stories, Bruner (1988) argues,

> become recipes for structuring experience itself, for laying down routes into memory, for not only guiding the life narrative up to the present but directing it into the future. (p. 582)

Bruner helps us to see how what seem to be simple recollections of our experiences are instead and indeed much more profound than that. Stories are the representations of the systems of constructs that both predict and guide our actions. These systems begin almost from the moment of birth and our stories about ourselves constitute a way of knowing, a mode of thought, a view of the world. According to Bruner, although we normally identify thought and knowledge with what he calls the logicoscientific, he would like us to recognize that narrative is just as important a way of knowing. Sealy's story, which we will now listen to, takes us back to when she was seven years old so we can see how she "lays down routes to memory," and how her sojourn to the past "directs her into the future."

The first time I picked up a needle with a true purpose was when I was about seven.

My best friend Archer and I wanted to make clothing for our trolls. The trolls (wishnicks) were three inches high. Their bodies were one inch.

I remember cutting material to "fit." The only sewing involved was the sewing of a button. Somehow we both "knew" how to sew those buttons.

Our trolls were the best dressed trolls in town.

But it wasn't enough.

We needed to know how to use the [sewing] machine to make carry-bags for our creatures, so elegantly clad.

My grandmother was an excellent seamstress. She could look at a dress and copy it to the tee. I had spent many years watching her make clothes for both my mom and myself. (I always had the nicest party dresses.)

Both my friend and I knew how to cut the shapes we wanted. We had to figure out how to make a flap, how to close it, and where to put the buttons.

Gran showed us how to thread the big machine. It was too big—too dangerous. I was given a mini-machine [Kinner] with a real needle and bobbins.

We turned out doll bags by the dozen.

Eventually, we could use the "BIG" machine. My friend and I moved to halter tops—we were ten—triangular shaped scarfs that tied around the waist and around a ribbon that tied at the neck. There was MUCH trial and error. Boy did we do a lot of seam ripping. But we made our own patterns and eventually her little sister, my neighbor, she and I were clad in the grooviest halter tops you've ever seen.

A major step in my learning to sew was when Gran showed us how to use a store bought pattern. We made peasant tops. By now, we were in the seventh grade and had the support of a home economics teacher.

Still a lot of seam ripping. Still a lot of trial and error.

Eventually, we moved on to baby doll clothes complete with ribbon, lace, buttons, and bows. They really were good.

Then with still more coaching from Gran we began our own clothes that we would wear in public. I knew I had learned to sew and do so well, the first time I wore something and no one knew I had made it.

I remember many crooked products and ones that fell apart. I remember having to throw projects away. But I also remember the feeling of satisfaction the first time I bundled up my little troll with bright blue hair into her green satin dress and slipped her into a matching bag with a rhinestone button and carried her off to school.

We view this story as an emblem of Sealy's theories of teaching and learning.

Collaborative Story Making

While Sealy could have explored and analyzed what this personal story meant to her on her own, the force and generalizability of her insights might have been minimized had she also not had the opportunity to construct the reality socially with her colleagues. Such collaborative moments launch conversations, which become the basis for building a common vocabulary and ongoing conversations about learning. As a result of sharing and discussing their stories with each other, Sealy's group generated a list of common characteristics of learning:

- Our age was not a factor in the process of how we learned.
- Our purpose for learning came from within.
- We observed a model enacting the thing we wanted to learn and whom we respected or who inspired us.
- We were provided with the necessary materials and practiced hands on.
- We learned through trial and error.
- We were able to practice and take risks because learning was done collaboratively.
- We received outside positive encouragement.

This kind of collaborative activity is one way of breaking down the isolation of teachers and the erroneous separation of research from practice. In a sense, it is a way of creating a common text from divergent experience, building a consensus on the values that shape views of the world, and formulating a lens through which to view the world anew. At the end of this workshop session, Sealy reflects on the day's activities. She writes:

> I enjoyed looking at "How I Learn." I feel that in examining how I do things I will in turn look at how my kids do things. They are human. I think sometimes we forget that.

Partially, at least, this new lens that Sealy is adopting includes a shift from teaching to learning. Once her focus shifts, then she no longer separates herself from her students, but instead sees all of them as learners who have more in common than not.

By writing about learning, we hoped that teachers would abstract from what they know about learning to guide their teaching. The stories and the generalizations about learning that can be derived from them is one in a series of reflections that we asked teachers to make, which pushes a deeper and deeper examination and articulation of an individual's constructs. Here is what Bruner says about analyzing autobiography. It is in this spirit that we will analyze Sealy's story as well:

> Philosophically speaking, the approach I shall take to narrative is a constructivist one—a view that takes as its central premise that "worldmaking" is the principle function of mind, whether in the sciences or in the arts. . . . Just as the philosopher Nelson Goodman . . . argues that physics or painting or history are "ways of world-making," so autobiography (formal or informal) should be viewed as a set of procedures for "lifemaking." And just as it is worthwhile examining in minute detail how physics or history go about their worldmaking, might we not be well advised to explore in equal detail what we do when we construct ourselves autobiographically? (1988, p. 575)

The seeds of a theory of teaching and learning that are contained in Sealy's story and that give rise to creating her world of teaching and learning are as follows:

1. Learning proceeds from the inside out rather than from the outside in: "The first time I picked up a needle with a *true purpose* was when I was about seven. . . . We *needed to know how* to use the machine to make carry-bags."
2. Learning proceeds by transformation rather than transmission: "I *was given a mini-machine with a real needle and bobbin*. . . . Eventually, we could *use the 'BIG' machine*. . . . There was MUCH *trial and error.*'
3. Learning proceeds through coaching rather than testing: "My *grandmother was an excellent seamstress*. . . . I had spent *many years watching her make clothes* for both my mom and myself. . . . Then with *still more coaching* from Gran we began our own clothes that we would wear in public."
4. Learning proceeds collaboratively rather than competitively: "My best friend *Archer and I* wanted to make clothing for our trolls. . . . Both *my friend and I* knew how to cut the shapes *we* wanted. *We* had to figure out how to make a flap. . . . *We* turned out doll bags. Eventually, *we* could use the 'BIG' machine. . . . Boy did *we* do a lot of seam ripping."
5. Learning proceeds through negotiated control rather than teacher control: "*Both my friend and I knew* to cut the shapes we wanted. *We had to figure out* how to make a flap, how to close it, and where to put the buttons. *Gran showed us how*. . . . "

This piece of writing was an opportunity for Sealy to reflect on a personal experience and to discover her own theory of learning from it. It allowed us to begin to understand that she had within her a theory of knowledge that we could build on with her. Unlike other teachers we worked with, who needed continual attempts at reconstruing their theories of knowledge and learning, she revealed to us through this story that if we reminded her of her implicit view of learning, we could push her to act on it in her classroom and to resist her impulse to act in ways that might be more compatible with the culture of the school. In fact, the view of learning and knowledge that she presents in this story is very different from the one she was practicing, the one the school supported. We've been suggesting that the core construct of knowledge is the most reliable predictor of the patterns of growth and action for a teacher. Having this dissonance spelled out so early allowed Sealy and us, collaboratively, to use it as a benchmark for explorations in her classroom as we'll see as we move through the year's learning with her.

Making Tacit Knowledge Explicit

At about the same time as she wrote her sewing story, Sealy was also reading and responding to *Learning to Write/Writing to Learn* (Mayher, Lester, and Pradl, 1983). Her written response in her log echoes her earlier reflection on the similarities between herself and her students.

> I felt this chapter had many interesting points. Writing should require an active process of discovery. Very often students' only purpose in writing is to fulfill the teacher's assignment. As I've expressed . . . writing this assignment puts you into your students' shoes . . . it's a *great* idea. (Emphasis and ellipses Sealy's)

So far what we have seen her do is "construct" a picture of herself as a learner by telling a story that made her tacit beliefs about learning explicit. She reflected on that construction, both individually and collaboratively, which resulted in her considering a new focus on learning. She then took this new focus and applied it to her reading, which gave rise to an interpretation of that reading that allowed her to speculate on new ways of doing in her classroom. In a similar way to telling a story about her learning, the story that she constructed about her classroom, which follows, makes explicit her tacit beliefs about teaching. Only through the process of building these constructions does it become possible to move from "knowing-in-action," a hidden set of beliefs, to "reflection-in-action," a revealed set of beliefs. This shift is made possible by capturing in language moments in our thinking and doing. Schön (1987) speculates on the role language plays in reflecting on action:

It is sometimes possible, by observing and reflecting on our actions, to make a description of the tacit knowing implicit in them. . . . Whatever language we may employ . . . our descriptions of knowing-in-action are always *constructions*. They are always attempts to put into explicit symbolic form a kind of intelligence that begins by being tacit and spontaneous. Our descriptions are conjectures that need to be tested against observations of their originals. . . . (p. 25, emphasis added)

Schön is describing a back-and-forth movement between doing and reflecting, between thought and action. Again, although this may be a common occurrence in everyday teaching practice, when engaged in collaboratively and socially, where thoughts are shaped in order to be publicly shared, formerly spontaneous and implicit activities become the basis for the kind of knowing that is the mark of a reflective practitioner. Sealy told a story in a workshop in October, 1987, that illustrates the point she was making in her response to *Learning to Write/Writing to Learn.*

I asked [my class] to write something and the only requirement was that it was fictional. That was the only requirement. I didn't care how long or what it was about.

And I sat down to write one too and all the things they went through, I went through. So I said, "OK, now who is my audience?" And I wrote the story to them. If I read it to you, it wouldn't have been as effective. I had them in stitches over things that are funny to that group of kids. At 10:30 on Sunday night when I had to copy this 10 pages over—it was front and back five pages—I'm saying to myself, "Man, I wish I had done this here" and "I can't believe it's so long." I was reading it to my husband, "How does this sound?" and I'm squinting because I can't read my own writing, which is what the kids do, and I would say to them, "It's your writing. Can't you read it?" And there I am and I'm going, "I don't know what this word is but," and I'd go on.

And then when I read it to them, "OK, I'll read mine" and I finished and they just sat there. So I said [to myself], "Well," because they didn't do anything, and I wanted them to clap. I'm still going to make them share and I'm still going to do what I did, but now I understand why little Johnny was so nervous, because I wanted them to like it. I knew my husband had to like it because he knows [me]. But the kids didn't have to like it.

Problem Posing as a Social Activity

The cycle of reflection and action in which Sealy has been engaged plays a pivotal role in her learning and marks her as a reflective practitioner. The workshop setting is itself an integral component of this process by helping learners reflect on what and how they know. Anticipating that teaching and learning experiences will be shared with the group of colearners, Sealy can't help but be aware that whatever she does in her classroom will become a serious subject for discussion and exploration. And we believe that this awareness gives experience a different character. It may be that what Bruner finds in spontaneous narrative—its power to shape and predict as well as recall—may be heightened by the knowledge that a story will be shared. This may alter the experience even as it unfolds.

In Sealy's case, we might point to what she has chosen to highlight in her story. She did not choose to emphasize writing, in particular, even though she had been reading about writing. What she did emphasize was the connections between herself and her students. For us, this is not accidental, but the result of attending to her new focus on learning and the anticipation of sharing *that* with her colleagues. We would even speculate that the sum total of her reading, writing, talking, and teaching to this point has led her to pose a question to herself, against which all of her experiences are now analyzed. This question is, we think: How is my learning similar to my students' learning?

Another question that Sealy seems to be posing illuminates the growing tension between her personal beliefs about how she learns best and the attitudes and messages that the school culture sends about how students learn. Through this question, Sealy sets herself within an historical, social, and cultural context. The question, we think is: Why do I teach the way I do? Here's her speculation on this issue:

> I have always been proud that I'm a believer of the "Golden Rules"— kind of a new bearer of old ways. Grammar and basic facts and all that "stuff" I was taught seemed so essential to me.
>
> I think of my own class struggling right now with the concept of verbs and subjects of verbs. They *speak* using "complete sentences." They write using subjects and predicates. Yet even after much description and discussion, they have trouble matching the "simple subject" to the verb.
>
> A fellow teacher once said to me, "We teach the way we've been taught." I agree. It's extremely difficult for me to abandon the idea of "nouns," "verbs," "adjectives," etc. The thought of not teaching it sort of blows my mind. Yet by 5th grade, these kids have no problem (have *few*) getting complete thoughts on paper—Isn't that what I want? (Emphasis Sealy's)

What is happening here is a "reflective conversation with the situation." In other words, the situation is talking back to Sealy and this talk back conflicts with her spontaneous "knowing-in-action." The students, through their actions, are suggesting that they already know what she is attempting explicitly to teach. And even though teaching in this way is at odds with the learning scheme that she has outlined in her stories, it is compatible with everything she knows about the way learning does go on in school. When she says, "We teach the way we've been taught," she's not expressing a mindless adherence to tradition, but a pride in carrying on what the culture of schools says is a tradition of excellence. She terms herself a "new bearer of old ways" and a "believer of the Golden Rules." By the end of the story, she questions these characterizations. Reflection has given her, therefore, not only a chance to recapture her beliefs about learning, but also a critical perspective on where her ideas about teaching have come from and consequently why she teaches the way she does. This dissonance, spawned by her reflection, is the catalyst for launching her into action research.

Action Research in Teaching and Learning

From the very beginning, Sealy's stories began to reveal, through collaborative reflection, certain directions in her thinking. Her personal story of learning how to sew pushed her in the direction of uncovering her hidden beliefs about learning. Her story about writing with her students moved her in the direction of beginning to see that her learning and her students' learning had much in common. The last story we shared, her critical reflection on teaching grammar, seemed to be moving her in the direction of considering the dissonance between her beliefs about knowledge and learning and those that are imposed by the school culture and internalized by her. All of these might be what Schön calls "frame analyses." That is, each of these reveals the construct that is operating, gives an opportunity to notice and be surprised by what the situation is saying, and offers the possibility of trying a new strategy and monitoring what happens. These experiments and the accompanying analyses by Sealy were all spontaneous and unplanned, whereas the action research that we will now describe was, to a certain extent, more formal and planned in advance.

The net result of all Sealy's activities that we summarized before was to reveal to her that she had at least two competing hypotheses about teaching and learning. We will enter her problem posing at a moment that makes transparent the ambivalence she has about her two simultaneously held and warring positions. The first moment took place during a collaborative discussion designed to help the group participants formulate the questions they would research. She opens the discussion with her first articulation of the problem she will investigate:

Basically, I want to find out if my kids can get more from a social studies textbook if they are in little groups and discussing it for themselves, than if I lead the lesson. My assumption is that I don't think that they will. I think they'll get more if I lead them. I guess I'd like to prove myself wrong. That would be nice. But I'm very structured and uncomfortable letting them break up into groups like that. [But] I'm going to break them up into groups.

We want to quote Donald Schön at length on his definition of teacher as researcher. Although we will be separating the "moments" in Sealy's research from one another for the purposes of analysis, we do that with full awareness that such separation is a convenience for the interpreter, rather than an expression of reality.

The non-routine situations of practice are at least partly indeterminate and must somehow be made coherent. Skillful practitioners learn to conduct frame experiments in which they impose a kind of coherence on messy situations and thereby discover consequences and implications of their chosen frames. From time to time, their efforts to give order to a situation provoke unexpected outcomes—"back talk" that gives the situation a new meaning. They listen and reframe the problem. It is this *ensemble* of problem framing, on-the-spot experiment, detection of consequences and implications, back talk and response to back talk, that constitutes a reflective conversation with the materials of a situation— the design like artistry of professional practice. (1987, pp. 157–158, emphasis added)

Schön's use of the word "ensemble" struck us as particularly poignant for describing teaching events. The word suggests to us that thoughts and actions, past history and present moments act like an orchestra in telling us many things at once and in showing us the importance of a conductor or reflective practitioner who can ensure harmony and coherence.

The fact that Sealy is posing this question—can her students get more from reading a social studies textbook if they are in "little groups" and discussing it than if she leads them?—suggests that her belief in collaboration for knowledge building, expressed so clearly in her story about her own learning, needs to be tested in the context of her classroom. Once she shifts her focus from her own learning to her students' learning, then the power of the school culture comes into play. That may account for her assumption that, in school, learners need to be led. In the expert teacher role that the school demands of her, she can't imagine herself teaching as her grandmother taught her, through coaching and facilitating collaboration with her friend. Nonetheless, hope springs eternal. We have to believe her, based on her discovery of how she and her students are alike as learners, when she says that she would like her students to prove her wrong. We empathize with her when she expresses and shares her fears, because we know how powerful the school culture is in shaping the roles teachers feel comfortable playing. In her own words, Sealy confirms the inferences we've made when she writes:

> As far as my classroom research, I think it will be fun. I really didn't mean to seem so "self-glorifying" when I said I thought my kids would learn more if *I* directed them. I feel I am a very structured teacher—groups make me nervous. I know the kids will benefit from some small group activity. I just have to learn to be comfortable with it. (Emphasis Sealy's)

Such discomfort is a natural part of frame analysis. Whereas in the past Sealy's awareness of herself as a "very structured teacher" could exist without conflict alongside her belief, expressed in a log entry, that learners "usually do better when they have a say," once her frame is revealed to her, and, further, as she becomes more accustomed to reflecting in and on action, tension between these two beliefs is heightened. Action is the only way out of the tension.

She reformulates her question in the course of discussing it with her colleagues. Her new question, "What happens when kids read and discuss their social studies textbook?" becomes the basis for her action research, which she describes in a report she shared with her colleagues in a workshop:

> I thought that I'd try to let my class work in small groups of 3–4 students. I chose a four page selection for them to read. There was a worksheet that accompanied the reading.
>
> Previously, our social studies lessons from the text included reading aloud together, paragraph by paragraph. Following the oral reading, the students would complete a set of questions based on the reading. This set of questions was usually completed by each individual student.
>
> When I explained the assignment to the class, there were mixed reactions. I grouped them based on where they sat, so they began quickly. Some groups chose to mimic our whole group lesson and read paragraph by paragraph aloud. Others chose to read silently, then do the questions together. One child came to me in tears because she hated social studies and "it was too hard." I found that the other members of her group were not doing *any* work.
>
> I found that most of the class did fairly well in completing the worksheet correctly. The major problem was answering the questions by group. It seemed that they all put the same answers. Frequently this occurred even if one disagreed with the rest of the group. (In one case, the one who disagreed had been correct, but put the incorrect answer to follow the group.)

Since the initial experience, I have tried different variations. The kids enjoy doing the small group work. However, they also ask for the large group lessons.

I've been alternating the type of lesson—choosing easier selections for the smaller groups. (Emphasis Sealy's)

The first observation to be made about the report Sealy made on her action research is that even before she set out to experiment, she changed her research again. The question that guided this research is interesting because, in spite of her original open-ended framing of the question—what happens when kids read and discuss their social studies textbook?—she changes it by the time she brings it to her classroom and now asks "What happens when kids read and answer questions from a social studies text?" What began as an exploration of what might happen through small-group discussion ends up being a small-group attempt at a traditional large-group lesson. There really wasn't going to be a discussion, because the aim of the lesson was for the students to get the one correct answer to the textbook's questions. They were filling in the blanks rather than using their own language to learn. The questions, themselves, reflect the textbook's knowledge structure and point of view, so that the task for the groups is to reproduce that line of reasoning.

In fact, given such a framework for teaching and learning, the lesson would have been much more successful if it had been overtly dominated by the teacher. In this case, what's missing is that there was no teacher to structure the activity as it's occurring, nor was there any preparation beforehand for helping the learners learn how to learn from each other. While it shouldn't have come as a shock to Sealy that all the students' answers were the same, since that would have happened even in a large group, the fact, though, that some students changed their "right" answers to agree with their group's "wrong" answers could have suggested to her that the students have no understanding or experience of the negotiation process that is central to building knowledge and that being "correct" is more important than understanding. In her state of frame conflict, it's not surprising that she would undermine herself and her students in their attempts to change how learning proceeds in their classroom. We don't mean to suggest that she intended to cause this experiment to fail, but only that her adoption of the school's definitions of teaching and learning overrode the attempt to recapture her belief in student-centered learning. Evidence that she is still operating primarily within the school's definition of learning and teaching is revealed in her final two sentences, where her criticism of her attempt leads her back to traditional modes of rectifying the situation. If small groups don't work, then students must still need whole-class instruction. If students struggle in small groups, then make the work easier.

Learning from Our Mistakes

Probably the most essential characteristic of action research is that it allows the teacher/learner to take risks, and so cannot really be deemed a failure regardless of its results. Since the purpose of action research is to deepen and extend insights, even when things seem to go wrong, new understandings are likely to take place. This is certainly what happened to Sealy. In reporting her research findings to a small group of her colleagues, she and they were able to analyze them in such a way as to generate a whole new set of possible strategies for teaching, in particular, for supporting the small-group inquiry process for students. She wrote notes on her conversation with her colleagues, which was the "back talk" she needed to "give the situation new meaning" (Schön, 1987, pp. 157–158):

- Should check [learning] by discussion, not just papers.
- Some students just copy each other.
- Students not good at delegation of work.
- Next time—write.
- Art instead of worksheet.

This kind of debriefing also helped Sealy to evaluate her action research unemotionally. She wrote at the end of this same day that: "I always enjoy hearing about people's research. It's great that we are all looking for ways to improve ourselves. I'm particularly proud of myself as I did not expect to be so comfortable with my research." Her comfort comes, we think, as a result of her collaboration with a community of fellow seekers, others who are more interested in "looking for ways to improve," than in waging a defensive battle over their beliefs and actions. It's the spirit of collaborative learning that makes all action research an opportunity for growth and transforms mistakes and failures into progress and success.

A Second Cycle of Action Research

This exploratory experiment, however, did not occur in isolation from a whole range of reflections-on-action both in and outside of the workshops. In spite of the fact that her previous attempt didn't yield the surprises that she hoped for, Sealy continues to push herself in new directions. So, for example, she decides to explore journal keeping in the content areas. The tension between her own and the school's view of knowledge still asserts itself. However, she is now ready to examine her own role in either promoting or inhibiting her students' ownership and authority over constructing knowledge. She states:

It must be difficult to let journals work for students in ways *they* discover; I have trouble "setting up" the situations.

I'm uncomfortable executing some of the activities that deal with this whole approach. . . . I believe kids should have structure, and based on *my* experience, I have trouble connecting structure with all of these conferencing activities which take away from whole group activities.

Of course, I realize that this may be misconceptions on my part. . . . I just think that *I* need to feel comfortable and organized (structured) myself before I let the kids loose with their own language/learning. . . . I'm just nervous about diving in. (Emphasis Sealy's)

This stance is quite different from her almost automatic retreat to the traditional solutions she offered earlier. Perhaps at this point she is posing questions like: What is my role in enabling my students' learning? How can I support my students' attempts at making meaning? These questions reflect an acknowledgement of her construct that knowledge must be built by learners and also that teachers must create contexts for knowledge construction. Rather than blaming the strategy or the students, Sealy now seems to be seeking a way of understanding her own contribution to the successes and struggles students display, a shift from the teacher as giver of knowledge to the teacher as coach.

If we couple this reflection with the collaborative contributions of her colleagues to her previous action research, we can see her new action research beginning to take shape. Her notes included a suggestion for having the students write the next time, rather than fill in the blanks. This last suggestion became the beginning of a new experiment, one based on the hypothesis she developed that "kids could learn from their reading without teacher-guided questions," a remarkable leap of understanding and insight in a short period of time.

Following Schön's (1983) scheme for the sequence in which reflective practitioners naturally engage, Sealy decided to conduct her action research as a "hypothesis-testing" experiment. Schön goes on to say that such an experiment "succeeds when it effects an intended discrimination among competing hypotheses" (p. 146). Without perhaps realizing it, "the practitioner has an interest in transforming the situation from what it is to something he likes better. He also has an interest in understanding the situation, but it is in the service of his interest in change" (p. 147). The interest in change is a direct consequence of a deeper and more explicit understanding of the knowledge and beliefs that guide the choices a practitioner makes. Sealy's previously voiced ambivalence about wishing to be proven wrong by her students' success in learning in small groups has been transformed into an attempt to simultaneously understand and change her classroom situation. She couldn't have done this before the exploratory experiment that deepened her insights.

We already know that Sealy holds two competing hypotheses simultaneously in her belief system—that students learn best when a teacher controls that learning and that students learn best when they set their own agendas for learning. We can see the tension very clearly in the language choices she makes when constructing her hypothesis that "kids could learn from their reading without teacher-guided question." Deconstructing her statement, we find that the positive assertion "kids could learn from their reading" is juxtaposed with the negative assertion "without teacher-guided questions," suggesting that she does not yet have language to define the converse of teacher-guided questions. What she is clear about is what she doesn't want. What she does not yet have language to express, because she still hasn't experienced it with her students, is whatever would be an alternative to teacher-guided questions. Read this way, her hypothesis is clear evidence that she is still living in limbo with two views vying for supremacy in her construct system.

In order to test her hypothesis and, perhaps, resolve the tension between her two competing hypotheses, she began a new unit on Indian cultures with the intention to allow students to read and learn on their own and to use their writing as a way both to learn and to share what they had learned. All the stories she brought with her to share in the workshop exemplified a personal connection between the material and the students' storytelling repertoire. Each was a unique construction and represented the individual student's interest and understanding. Here are two of the stories the children wrote:

The Incas

One day I was walking in the Andes mountains. I lived around in that area so I decided to take a walk. I was near the mountain top when I came upon a terrace. There were crops there such as potatoes, peppers, squash, and corn. I went on looking to see if I could find something else.

I came upon a village. It was the village of the Incas. Once they saw me they came out acting like I was going to attack their village. They took me into a building that was made out of stone. There, in the room we entered, was their ruler who they said was descended from the Sun God. I could only understand some of the things they said and that was about it. The ruler didn't know what to do so he said he would let me go if I promised not to attack their village. I said fine. Then I saw some tin that had been carved and had pretty pieces of jewelry on it. I asked them if they had made it. They said yes. I had heard they had lots of jewelry but I never knew it was true.

Then they showed me out of the room and I started on my way home. When I reached my house I ran in. My mother asked where I had been and I told her the whole story. She said I was lucky that they let me go.

Then she added as she walked out of the room, "The Indians of the 1100's are so modern."

White Cloud

One day a little Indian boy was working in the garden. He was a Navaho Indian. He was growing vegetables like watermelon, squash, and corn. He went back to his family's hogan. His mother was making a vest made out of animal skin. The Pueblo Indians had taught them how to weave wool into cloth. The boy's name was White Cloud. White Cloud was a very lonely boy because Navaho Indians don't live in villages. One day White Cloud went off into the woods with his horse. He rode for a long time until he saw some tepees. He saw a little boy his own age. He went over to him. They played and become best friends. The end.

In reflecting on the students' learning, Sealy realized that the writing demonstrated not only that the students have learned a great deal about Indian culture, but that the stories themselves were a good way for the students to summarize and synthesize their newly gained knowledge. When she shared these stories with her colleagues, the first words out of her mouth were: "I'm eating my words. I didn't trust that kids could learn from their reading without guided teacher questions."

In Schön's sequence, action is coupled with reflection. It is through this "back talk and response to back talk" that meanings are solidified and understandings clarified. As workshop leaders, we see our role as both providing room for and encouraging teachers in their reflections on their actions. So, we constantly orchestrate the back-and-forth movement between the teacher's classroom and the teacher as learner in our classroom through "immersion and distancing." Thus, in addition to exploring her beliefs by allowing her classroom to talk back to her, Sealy is also exploring her beliefs by being encouraged to continue reflecting on herself as a learner. We saw this at the beginning when she wrote of a time she learned how to sew. Now listen to her as she reflects in writing on her own problem solving and attempts to connect these mental acts with a theory of language and learning.

This activity [solving a math problem] helped show much about language and learning. First of all it didn't show lack of structure which I fear. Second of all, it showed how important my language was to my learning. I read, absorbed what I could and read again. Then I tried making connections. I verbalized my connections and wrote down some things. Talking about the problem, reading the problem, writing information concerning the problem used *language*. *Everything* we do in school uses language.

What's important is that I *knew* I had to read it over, I *knew* I had to take notes, I knew I had to do certain things to solve the problem.

Getting kids in touch with their own learning means helping them to use their own language to learn.

Son of a gun! (Emphasis Sealy's)

To genuinely examine their core constructs of knowledge, teachers must return once more to themselves as learners, to reconstruct, reevaluate, and synthesize all that they have learned. This demonstration activity served to yoke together the two experiments that Sealy conducted and brought to light not only a resolution of the competing hypotheses—"getting kids in touch with their own learning"—but also resulted in her recognition, now stated in the positive, because she has experienced it from the inside out, that a teacher's task is "helping [students] to use their own language to learn."

Ms. Sealy Contributes to the District's Language Policy

Perhaps the best possible way of determining whether learning has occurred is to observe the learner applying new knowledge to a different situation from the one in which the learning took place. Listen in to Sealy participating in a collaborative revision of the district's language policy, the first and second drafts of which had been generated and revised by the first two teams of teachers:

MS. HART: [*Reading from a draft of the language policy*] "Language is the primary and principal learning tool."

MS. LONNY: [*Reading on in the draft*] "Students need to talk and write about what matters to them as well as to . . . ."

MS. KOSLOWSKI: Maybe, "students need to talk and write as they learn in addition to reading and listening . . . ."

MS. LESTER: Then you're putting the emphasis on reading and listening again.

MS. ONORE: [*Reformulating the original draft sentence*] "Students need to talk and write as well as read and listen as they learn."

MS. SEALY: How about if you take that sentence, "students need to talk and write about what matters to them." Learning occurs through talking, writing as well as through reading and listening. Take that whole sentence that was first and put it third. The first two sentences, "Language is a primary and purposeful tool. Students need to talk and write about what matters to them as they learn." Then you take that big sentence from the front. "Learning occurs through talking and writing as well as through reading and listening."

> MR. KARISH: Now you're really emphasizing the first two, which is what
> we want.

It is clearly Sealy's contribution that serves to provide just exactly the
emphasis that the group was trying to achieve. The problem the group
was having was making it clear that the language policy needed especially to
promote learning through talking and writing, language modes traditionally
neglected in their schools. It seems to us that she could not have made this
contribution had she not understood thoroughly and deeply the implications of
using language to learn. These are implications that we saw her struggling to
understand in both the context of her classroom teaching as well as in her experiences as a learner in the workshops. The development of the language policy
gave voice to all that she had thus far learned. We would even suggest that
her constructs about knowledge have now become an "overarching theory,"
because they are no longer tacit, dissonant, nor contradictory. In other words,
she has integrated and synthesized beliefs, attitudes, and constructs into a set
of ideas that have both predictive and explanatory power. Her commitment to
making sure that theory was as clear as possible, as well as articulated in the
school policy, is further evidence of the change she has experienced.

Her commitment is so strong that she now perceives herself as a kind of
insider, one who truly knows that knowledge and learners are inseparable. It
is interesting, then, to see her speculate on the role the language policy might
play in lives of teachers who have not experienced, from the inside, learning
as a constructive activity.

> I have a little problem. Just that if I hadn't been to the workshops, I
> would read this and look at the terms and I would look at it and say, "This
> is gobbledygook" and I wouldn't concentrate on it, because now that
> I've been in it, I've experienced it, I've opened my, oh, fluency. I've
> been through it. I've experienced things. It can't be comparable for
> others. If I wasn't in the workshops I wouldn't even care about it. Most
> teachers that haven't gone through it, it wouldn't mean anything to them.
> It means something to us because we've experienced, we've learned,
> we've changed, whatever. That's where I think it's going to be difficult
> for people who haven't experienced the writing workshop 'cause it
> doesn't mean anything to them. They haven't spent three hours arguing
> about fluency. Whereas we have. That's where I think you're going to
> hit a problem, not here, but for the people who haven't. . . .

The irony, of course, is that Sealy is correct in her skepticism about her
colleagues' ability to embrace the spirit of the language policy because the
policy is being generated separately from them. This irony takes on additional
strength from the fact that she is committed to learning coming from the

learner's own efforts and intentions to learn, not from knowledge being bestowed upon those who are not in the know. So she both wants to present her worldview of knowing as clearly as she can, while she also distrusts the ability of any document or decree to successfully carry her message. That, perhaps, represents the most sophisticated form of interpretative synthesis that we can imagine.

At least in Sealy's case, the action research and the taking on of the reflective practitioner stance were the keys to unlocking her views of knowledge that would be most compatible with language-across-the-curriculum efforts. Change certainly cannot be said to depend upon any one activity, but we have chosen to look at her learning because we believe that the role of the reflective practitioner took on particular significance in her change process.

Describing a teacher's stance as that of a reflective practitioner is problematic on a number of levels. We acknowledge that reflection occurs all the time in teachers' daily experiences, as they attempt to make on-the-spot decisions about students' learning and their own teaching and evaluate or assess the effects of any choice they have made. What distinguishes the kind of reflection that is the mark of "reflective practitioners" is that what has already been a normal part of what they do, and therefore unrecognized and undervalued, now becomes open to consciousness and contemplation. Teachers' knowledge is embedded in their actions, just as the knowledge of any skilled professional inheres in their actions. This is what Schön (1983) calls a "theory-in-action." Such knowledge is so routine in performance that professionals do not necessarily know what they know until and unless they attempt to bring it to awareness. Such a process has the potential to make that knowledge, or some of it, explicit, where it was once tacit, to make both the knower and the knowledge more valid in the scheme of things, and to create the possibility that that knowledge may be transformed.

If Schön is correct, then any professional is continually engaged in reflection, and that is what constitutes professionalism. That is what makes the activity of a reflective practitioner also seem so ordinary. But Schön also wishes us to acknowledge the art of reflective practice in its profound ability to identify, enrich, and deepen the knowledge of a professional as it also supports the continued evolution of a professional's actions. Herein lies the key to the uniqueness of the reflective-practitioner stance.

When the process of identifying and reflecting on one's beliefs is also collaborative, as it was for Sealy in her engagements with her colleagues, then it has the additional potential to both free the individual teacher to hold an alternative view and to work with others to change the dominant view. In that way, we think it also has potential for changing others. What we have just said makes the whole idea of a reflective practitioner more social as well as individual, uniting reflection with action.

Reflective practice has the possibility for helping teachers make constructs explicit, such as the ones Sealy wrestled with and, thus, to change them if they wish. She has revealed that her constructs are as follows:

- knowledge is built constructively by learners
- learning is best supported by teachers who are coaches and facilitators
- the language of the learners is the connecting link between the knower and the known
- learners learn best through collaboration
- teaching is learning

Finally, what we are really suggesting is that if classrooms are to be forums for critical inquiry and a real exchange of ideas, then teachers who know what it means to be knowledge producers, problem posers, critical reflectors, and colearners will have the abilities and understandings to bring their students into these processes along with them and build a democratic classroom.

We will end this chapter with a final piece of reflective writing that Sealy did in a workshop we had with her group in the fall of 1988. We asked the teachers to write as if they were professional researchers and consultants to a school district whose teachers had been involved in an in-service program on language across the curriculum. They were to write the piece in the third person, as if they were interviewing themselves. Their purpose was to describe what they had determined to be the most important piece of learning they had accomplished during their participation in the project and how that learning was applied to their classrooms. They were to end their piece with any questions they still had about what they had learned and attempted in their classrooms.

When Leslie Sealy first began attending the in-service writing program in the fall of 1987, she was less than enthusiastic. According to Leslie, she was downright disgusted with the idea of leaving her twenty-five fifth-grade charges to attend a workshop that was bound to be a waste of her time. What she didn't know, as she reflects aloud to this author, was that this year long in-service program would change her teaching style in a very positive way.

When Ms. Sealy was asked to describe *the* most important piece of learning that she had accomplished during the year, she responded at first with a smile. Then she sighed and said, "I've learned not to be afraid of taking a chance, not to worry about change."

One's initial response to Ms. Sealy might be "What does that have to do with her work in her classroom?" Leslie explained, "In my taking a chance and changing my teaching style, I opened many doors for my students. I gave them different kinds of opportunities to learn."

Leslie had been afraid to venture from her successful teaching style of the past. She had learned successfully the same way she thought her students were learning successfully. The in-service program helped her to understand that people learn in many ways and that a teacher-led discussion may not always be the correct way.

Leslie took her newly acquired attitude and "bravely" applied it to her class. Content area lessons no longer consisted in textbook reading and discussion. Instead "Life in the Northeastern States" became an experiment. Students were asked guiding questions and set free. They learned about natural resources and geographical features as they tried to discover what they would do for a living if they lived in the Northeastern states. The students learned about the history of the states because they wanted to and needed to in order to complete their own research and answer their own questions.

Ms. Sealy states that her students became hungry for the information and retained the information because it meant something to them. In the past, the information had been memorized, but meant nothing.

Leslie is pleased that she is now able to offer her students different ways of learning and truly internalizing information discussed in class. She does admit to being still a bit hesitant at times if the material is what she considers "difficult." She would like to learn to be a better question asker so that she can help her students learn more complex concepts. Being willing to change and able to take a chance in her teaching style has truly helped Leslie Sealy to improve herself as well as the learning experiences of her students. She does have questions concerning this "changed style." How much freedom can one give to students when one is trying to achieve the goal of teaching specific concepts? And how can teachers today get around teaching to tests when they are trying to change the type of teaching/learning experiences required for success in today's schools? (Emphasis Sealy's)

Ms. Sealy's piece of writing not only confirms our own analysis of her learning, but, with her questions at the end, convinces us that she has already launched herself on another journey in reflective practice.

Chapter Five

The Teacher As Learner: "Contradictions of Control"

Ms. Renda was a member of the initial district steering committee whose members had visited other writing programs around New York State. After reviewing the credentials of a number of educational consultants, this committee of teachers and administrators invited us to interview for an in-service writing project. Renda made her presence immediately felt by posing questions to us that had a decidedly different character from the sorts of nuts-and-bolts questions being put to us by the other interviewers. One question stands out for us still. She asked, "What would you consider the most influential books which you have read in the field of language education and composition studies?" Looking back on it, we would interpret this questions as signaling her commitment to teaching as an intellectual enterprise. For her, we think, knowing what we did in other school districts, what we'd written and published, and how we would organize a writing project were secondary to uncovering our philosophical and theoretical perspectives on language education, our beliefs about teaching and learning. We also know now, through coming to know her, that she was able to evaluate our responses, because she herself was thoroughly familiar with the field. Obviously, our answers stacked up right for her, and she became, from that moment, a committed supporter and participant.

Renda is complex. Perceived by many as bossy—a strong, articulate, and very stubborn leader, one who takes charge of every situation and charges right in—she is also very sensitive, easily hurt, and insecure. The way she is perceived might be linked to her being a woman, rather than a man. Although we won't be exploring this possibility as we analyze her learning, we believe that many of her colleagues' attitudes toward her rest on the fact that she is a strong woman in a male-dominated power hierarchy.

She is also a child of the sixties: rebellious, anti-establishment, and anti-authority. Born, raised, and initiated into the teaching profession in southern California, she brought these characteristics with her into this very typical New York City suburb. Like other suburbs of New York, Charmont has a dual personality: it's small-townish in its gossip and familiarity. There are no secrets in Charmont. At the same time, it is also energetic, up and coming, politically and culturally aware. In many ways, therefore, Renda fit right in, but her assertiveness, even for New Yorkers, and especially within the school culture, marked her.

Renda is a prolific writer and reader. She needed little, if any, encouragement or prodding to use her learning log as a real vehicle for exploration. She read avidly and thought deeply about new ideas as well as ones she was already familiar with. Her thinking on a variety of issues was fresh and insightful, and she always found connections among the readings she did, the writings she learned through, and the classroom applications she attempted. The rebellious side of her nature expressed itself in her intellect as well. A prolific questioner, a challenger, a person never satisfied with the simplistic, she always probed beneath the surface of an issue. She attempted to overcome her insecurities through her bullheadedness, which resulted in her being able to take many risks, both in her classroom and as an advisor in the third year of the program.

Another way to describe Renda may be to look at her from a critical feminist perspective. Citing the work of Belenky, et al. (1986), Elizabeth Flynn (1988) outlines the stages of intellectual development that are particular to women. Flynn suggests that "the quest for self and voice plays a central role in transformations of women's ways of knowing" (p. 427). At their highest level of development, which Flynn terms "constructed knowledge," women, like Renda, "begin an effort to reclaim the self by attempting to integrate knowledge they feel intuitively with knowledge they have learned from others" (p. 427).

Renda is no armchair intellectual. Her colleagues were put off by her assertiveness, but they also appreciated it when she led the way for more teacher empowerment through her assertive actions on the system. After all, they received the benefits of the forced compliance by the superintendent of schools with teacher requests for meeting times, workshop days, video equipment, book purchases, and curricular innovation, all actions that she initiated.

We've chosen the subtitle of this chapter, borrowed from Linda Mc-Neil's work (1986), in order to reflect a range of tensions in Renda's thinking and acting. In McNeil's work, the contradictions of control center on the fact that the more resistance there is within individuals or the institution to taking charge of teaching and learning, the more tightly controls are asserted over teaching and learning. So, in just those situations where controls ought to be lessened, controls were strengthened out of a fear of loss of control. In Renda's work, the contradictions of control center on her own contradictory needs to be in charge and to share power and control with her students. As the title of this chapter suggests, she is also a learner who focused her learning on resolving the contradictions that were interfering with her ability to establish a democratic classroom.

Renda came to the in-service project with a constructivist view of knowledge and a desire to make schooling democratic. She writes, "Can knowledge exist independent of the knower? The answer is *no*. The mystery is what does the knower know?" Perhaps what has given rise to her perspective on the central role of the learner as knower is her own experience as a knower/ learner. The story that follows reveals her insider's view of the richness of learning and the poverty of the way that learning is evaluated in school. She understands that the meanings learners make cannot be pigeonholed and that learners know much more than can be expressed through simpleminded factual recall.

> I just want to tell you a wonderful story. When I was a senior in college, I had to write a dissertation, a mini-dissertation, and my dissertation was on George Eliot's *Middlemarch*. I knew that book and I had to take the graduate record exam. And I took the English exam, and one of the multiple choice questions was: "The theme of George Eliot's *Middlemarch* is ____" I had it. I just had it. I just finished writing 50 pages trying to determine what the theme of George Eliot's *Middlemarch* was, and here it was A, B, C, D, and one of them was right. And the other three were wrong. That was the first time I just hit it, how totally the questions do not fit the material. There was no way you could answer that question in a five word item. You couldn't do it. And yet there I was. But the point is, the more you know about a subject, the more you know it doesn't work.

One of the things we can learn, therefore, from Renda is that the core construct doesn't function by itself, even though it does serve as a springboard to propelling the learner ever deeper into reflective action. Holding this core construct of knowledge, she is enabled by this project, to generate all of the satellite constructs that have more direct application to the classroom. In other words, we don't want to suggest that because she believes that knowledge is a human construction, that she does not want or need to grow further in her understandings. From our perspective, having this core con-struct enables a teacher to explore and reconceptualize the inevitable implications on teaching and learning that result from holding a constructivist view of knowledge. But the job of creating the means for acting on this construct in the stream of daily classroom life is still a difficult one and requires that the satellite constructs about teaching and learning, the role of the teacher in the institution, the building of the curriculum, and establishing a democratic classroom also be examined, mulled over, and tested.

The Rebel Grows Up: Teacher as Transformative Intellectual

> I believe "if students are discovering their own ideas, asking their own questions, and fighting hard to answer them for themselves" describes *utterly* my own experience. As a student, I stank. I was always trying to rephrase, ignore or radically alter the dicta of "authority." I learned best in seminars where we set our own goals, asked our own questions, selected our own directions. Why did I think I was unique? (Emphasis Renda's)

Renda's historical role of rebel, learning against the grain, gives her the possibility, once consciously shared and reflected on, to become a "transformative intellectual" (Giroux, 1988), teaching against the grain. What Freire (1988) means when he says, "history is possibility" is that history does more than simply determine the future. Because human beings are constantly reconstruing experience, they make and remake their own histories. In this reconstrual process is the rich potential to make meaningful and constructive use of the past, rather than to be limited by it. In Renda's recollections of her past as a student and from her vantage point as a practicing teacher, what may have been painful and difficult years have now become the seeds for helping students to discover their own learning processes in all of their rich possibilities. She could have damned her past, seen rebellion as too hard a road to travel for her own students. Instead, she is able to reconstrue that role, see its strength rather than just its struggle, its commonality rather than its uniqueness, in the sense that it is more common to genuine learning than not and that within a community of learners who are each seeking their own directions, there is intention to construct collective meanings as well.

And in reconstruing her history, Renda is also able to formulate a new role in the present. As a transformative intellectual, she is able to find ways, with her students' help, to set goals, ask questions, select directions. She can begin to articulate, if not directly to her students, at least in her log, the institutional practices that prevent all of them from engaging in inquiry. These beginning articulations give her a way of promoting student inquiries, not inhibiting them. Further, as a transformative intellectual, she has begun to find those places within the institution where she and her colleagues can push the envelope for critique.

In tracing Renda's development toward becoming a transformative intellectual, it's helpful to envision a democratic classroom. A democratic classroom does not spring from a set of alternative methodologies, but is rather a frame of mind that a teacher brings to the classroom. A key element in this frame of mind is a sophisticated understanding and recognition of the hidden curriculum of schooling. The real curriculum is veiled by a skin-deep rhetoric of excellence, which holds that students and teachers must be held accountable, they must be tested, monitored, and corrected in order to achieve a standard set by an authoritarian removed from the direct context of the school. There is a clear message, for those like Renda, who are able to read it, that achievement should be standardized and that real learning is unquestioning conformity. Standards, then, are really only a way to sort students into the hierarchy that exists outside of the school.

We heard Renda struggle as a student with attempts that schooling made to control her and her learning. Now we'll see her apply these same insights as a teacher, insights that have led her to understanding and recognizing the hidden curriculum as it presents itself to her students and her colleagues.

> I tend to be an Emersonian-Herndon-type guerrilla fighter. I believe that *real learners* have to be guerrillas—aware that schools, corporations, churches, hospitals don't really *want* them to analyze, think, or seek change. Within each institution are good people—mentors, friends, helpers. Find them. Use them. And then blow off the rest! So from my point of view, a student sooner or later must: 1) *own* his words, his reading, his ideas and 2) accept that most of the time in school, he will have to "play the game" in order to *be* "successful." However, once he "owns" his life, *he* can exercise control.
>
> We don't, as an institution, *really* want this—we just want [students] to "do the work." Responding and thinking takes so much energy. "Just answer the questions."
>
> I really think at least in part that our function is to "adapt" kids to boredom, frustration, and meaningless repetition—that being what so many of them will fall into the *rest* of their lives. Why else are these stupid tests constantly, constantly, pressuring teachers like me into schizoid "teach to the test" vs. "this is what we'd really enjoy"? (Emphasis Renda's)

This very political statement shows that Renda both recognizes and understands what schools are about for students: denying them the tools to conduct or practice critical inquiry. But it also reveals that she has developed a way to negotiate the system. For her, students' exercise of control involves both ownership over learning and developing strategies for "playing the game." Even more important may be her theory that if you have knowledge of the system that is attempting to control you, then that knowledge can help you control it.

Renda's recognition of institutional control is not limited to the role it plays in the lives of students. She is also acutely aware of how institutional practices block collaboration among peers, perhaps in fear of mutiny.

> This workshop has been the only significant collaborative exploration I've done in teaching and though at many junctures my "collaborators" have infuriated me, I can still glimpse the *power* of shared exploration. . . . One reason why being an advisor has been so frustrating— the institutional constraints separate us very effectively, don't they?
>
> [The other advisors] and I are feeling very frustrated. We need to talk over and try to resolve this frustration. We want teachers to come to us, we want to create a support network, we want a feeling of mutually exciting professional support and community. But this is all brand new in our building. There is a long history of mistrust, of closing the door and doing what we want to do and concealing our fears, anxieties, and mistakes from one another. (Emphasis Renda's)

So not only does Renda understand the ways in which the system prevents collaboration—and here she is writing specifically about not being given real time in her and her colleagues' teaching schedules to work together—but she is also aware of the subtle ways in which the rules of the institution can be internalized by members of the institution. This results in teachers acting in ways that are perfectly compatible with what the institution demands: isolation, expertise, and pride in rugged individualism.

Renda embodies all of the beliefs and attitudes that Giroux suggests form the frame of reference for a transformative intellectual. For him, a transformative intellectual must be able to see the ways in which counter-democratic forces manifest themselves in the schools' definition of knowledge, school organization, teacher-student relationships, teacher-teacher relationships, and teacher ideologies (Giroux, 1988, p. xxiii). Giroux goes on to suggest that "inherent in the discourse of democracy is the understanding that schools are contradictory sites; they reproduce the larger society while containing spaces to resist its dominating logic"(p. xxxiii). We have just seen Renda develop her own ways to both see and resist the counterdemocratic forces. She also has some fairly clear ideas about how to create and maintain those spaces in which to exercise the power of democratic schooling.

We discussed earlier that Renda has a very powerful way of reinterpreting her own history and applying that reinterpretation to her students. And so from her own vision of herself struggling to be free as a student, she is able to explore how she might make it possible for her students to exercise their freedom.

> Slaves can't think or speculate unless they can hypothesize freedom. Is this what held all of us "learners" back until we reached adulthood and were "free"? Is it worse for women than men? Can a child make a "free space" within herself even within conditions of imperialist domination and injustice? (Say, most high school classrooms?)

These questions were to become the touchstone against which Renda constructed all of her inquiries over the three years we worked with her. As Giroux stipulates, transformative intellectuals have a role to play in "develop[ing] counterhegemonic pedagogies that not only empower students by giving them the knowledge and social skills they will need to be able to function in the larger society as critical agents, but also educate them for transformative action" (1988, p. xxxiii). Toward reaching this goal, she writes:

> I read Kozol, Kohl, and Herndon while working in a ghetto school and later a school in ferment, with protests, fights, and overt racist confrontations. Again forcing me to ask, "Is what I am teaching helping us to live together? Learn together?"
> What needs fostering is not forms, but curiosity, autonomy of judgment, a climate in which individual viewpoints are requested.
> I think cooperative learning strategies would do a lot to demystify how "bright" kids do what they do. Also lead to sharing of the mysteries: Who is asking the questions? What kind of questions? Good signs: Voluntary student questions; Voluntary student reading; Writing or talk about tasks; Student-to-student explorations of task setting; Problem solving; Tolerance for uncertainty.
> To what degree have we made the classroom "safe" for exploration? In the learning logs students ask the questions. Not so much in groups. I don't think they know how or maybe don't know that it's acceptable.

Teaching as Problem Posing

In addition to all of the questions contained in the passages from Renda's logs and conversations that we've already quoted, here are a sampling of questions she raised during her participation in the in-service program, culled from three years of learning logs:

- If our students' curiosity, questioning, exploring, sequencing, connecting are either dead or dormant, how are they to be stirred to life?

- Yet, without the hunger to know, to make sense of the world/people/ language—where do the "what I don't know," "what I want to know" come from?
- Isn't "proving" you read it a valid (even if "constraint") purpose?
- Why must we waste what will understandably be hours wrangling over words when they won't produce any significant effects?
- They *can* write, wonderfully—but not the 5-paragraph essay, with no errors in punctuation of adverbial clauses! How are we to resolve this?
- Isn't "learning roots, prefixes, etymologies, derivational groupings, borrowings" time taken from reading, writing, talking?
- If I wait ten seconds longer during discussion following a student response, will the student amplify the response? Will a student step in to respond? If the teacher talks less, will students talk/interact/take control of the learning process more? How [do I] demonstrate or measure this?
- Ask kids to ask the questions about the novels. What questions could/ would kids ask?
- What do I want my students to learn this year?
- What are the strategies for learning?
- How can we demystify the strategies for learning?
- Why is it so hard to do what we preach (and believe)?
- Will students do as well on the Regents Competency Test if they learn to write through a process rather than through memorizing a 5-paragraph formula?
- Why do more able students make use of coaching than less able students?
- Do learning discoveries provoke joy and thus strong emotion?
- Why does Mr. F. have kids copy out the items in multichoice homework? Can I show him a better way?
- What *do* I want to be? Where do I start? What shall I do?
- Can we alter the perception that observation is not a valid, useful mode for research?
- Is there any way we can streamline planning our advisors' sessions? Could we bring drafts to the meetings?
- Why should teachers who were successes in school and bought into the system question it now?
- Each class is a new puzzle and (maybe?) this is why curriculum has come to be so compartmentalized?
- Given that I read the article a month ago, am I fundamentally accurate in recalling its message or did the layers of previous "myths" and assumptions operate over time to "change" what I read and align it with preconceptions, etc.? (Emphasis Renda's)

We can see that Renda not only asked a large number of questions, but that the problems she posed cover a wide range of topics. What they have in common is a rejection of the characteristics of what we have called an auto-cratic classroom. While all of her questions situate her in the role of teacher/learner, two of her questions launched her on a formal road of action research:

> If I wait ten seconds longer during discussion following a student re-sponse, will the student amplify the response? Will a student step in to respond? If the teacher talks less, will students talk/interact/take control of the learning process more? How [do I] demonstrate or measure this?

> How will students do on the Regents Competency Test if they learn to write through a process rather than through memorizing a 5-paragraph formula?

The research she designed to answer the first group of questions in-volved her in having students time the amount she talked in the classroom over a one-week period. Through a student's use of a stopwatch, she discovered that she talked from twenty-two to twenty-five minutes during a given forty-five-minute class period. In addition to discovering how much she talked, she also discovered "how little thought I have put into the kinds of questions I ask," and perhaps more importantly, the depth of the control she asserted over students' learning by doing the lion's share of the talk: "I discovered that as soon as I approached a table, [the students] glanced down shamefacedly at what they were supposed to be working on, or stopped talking altogether and waited for me to tell them what to do. This persisted, in spite of my efforts to avoid telling them what to do." As a result of her research, Renda reduced the amount of teacher talk and she hypothesized that if she talked less, her students would talk to one another more and take more responsibility for their own learning. She discovered that "by shutting up when students wish to share their journal thoughts, I actually witnessed a student-run and student-gener-ated discussion. . . . and all I had to do is stay out of the way." (See Onore & Lester, 1986, for a detailed description of Renda's classroom study.)

She continued to grapple with this last hypothesis and discovery as can be seen from the research she conducted to explore the second question. This research, which she submitted to the National Council of Teachers of English for one of its teacher-research grants and for which she was awarded $1,000 to conduct, involved her in examining the effects of setting up a writing/learn-ing workshop in her classroom. Although she was disappointed that she never achieved her stated research goal—to prove to her colleagues that students who engage in writing as a process can do just as well on standardized tests as students who do not—she learned a great deal more. She learned about the enormous complexities of "staying out of the way" and she also learned how much complicity in the system her students had. She found out that even if she enacted the role of teacher as a coach and negotiator, students put up resistance because they didn't trust that kind of relationship with teachers. For many students, collaborative learning and shared power with teachers are not part of "real" school learning. Allowing her students to take ownership over the means and ends of learning was a completely unique experience for them. The possibility that at the end of the semester they would be punished for the choices and decisions they made was very palpable. When you make the decisions, you are then responsible for their success or failure. When teachers make all the decisions, students don't have to be responsible. If their choices were not wholly successful, how would that go down with Renda?

She analyzed her failure as the result of her own inability to help her students "read the whole curriculum" (Boomer, in Green, 1988). That is, she never came clean with them: about what and why they were doing what they were doing; about how what they were doing might be different from what other teachers did with them; and about the fact that they could be partners in exploration, rather than antagonists. She wrote of her discovery in this way: "They see only me. They do *not* see the curriculum or the system" (emphasis Renda's).

The Inquiring Teacher as Learner

We want to use Renda to expand the normal definition of the teacher as learner and draw from Carl Rogers to enrich our understanding of that role. In *Freedom to Learn: A View of What Education Might Be* (1969), Rogers recalls a talk he gave to a group of teachers in which he described his feelings about teaching and learning. He seemed to have come to a point in his life when teaching was no longer of interest to him, or so he proclaimed, because it seemed to be either impossible, irrelevant, or inconsequential (p. 277). Learning was all he seemed to care about.

Paradoxically, Rogers's statements have a tremendous amount to say about teaching. He writes first that "only learning which significantly influences behavior is self-discovered, self-appropriated learning." Then he goes on to say that "such self-discovered learning, truth that has been personally appropriated and assimilated in experience, cannot be directly communicated to another." And he ends with, "I find that another way of learning for me is to state my own uncertainties, to try to clarify my puzzlement, and thus get closer to the meaning that my experience actually seems to have"(p. 277).

What we believe Rogers is essentially promoting is demonstration, particularly teachers demonstrating their own learning. Demonstration is not only a powerful teaching tool, because it reveals the processes of learning that an experienced learner employs, but it also shows students that anything that is worth knowing can be learned best through discovery. By demonstrating the processes of meaning making, a teacher/learner is showing that no one can make meaning for you. What Rogers is really saying is that demonstration illustrates learning as constructing. While all of this is true, there is one essential area that we would like to add, and that is that teachers can, and must become engaged learners of their students' needs, because learners can, in Rogers's words, "only be interested in learning things that matter, that have some significant influence on [their] own behavior" (p. 277). The following quote from Renda illustrates all these aspects of teacher as learner reconceptualized:

> I've learned (remembered?) that my most exciting years as a person and a teacher occur when *I'm* learning, and immersed in reading, writing, thinking, drawing, dreaming about an idea. Immersion to synergy to change. I've worked really hard on all aspects of these workshops—research, application, note-taking, sharing—and experience how "time flies" and drudgery becomes purposeful when the heart and mind are fully engaged. If this can happen for a few of my students through the classroom environment I've structured—it just might be an "epiphany"—"Oh, so *this* is what learning is all about!"—that will so galvanize them that they will not settle for less.
>
> I have really learned from my students' learning logs. They *can* and *do* connect fantastically—I'm so impressed with the growth in their writing. . . . I feel so much closer to my students' learning processes—it's worth the time to react and respond to learning logs.
>
> I still have a long way to go on the issue of control. (Emphasis Renda's)

Counterhegemonic Pedagogy

The special role that a transformative intellectual, who is also a teacher, might play in the classroom is described by Giroux as the struggle to support students in critical inquiry that can be best achieved by "educating them to take risks" (p. xxxiii). Given Renda's awareness of the barriers that the institution of schools places in the way of real student and teacher empowerment, her efforts to develop "counterhegemonic" pedagogies—alternative forms of teaching and learning—represent her attempts to resolve the conflicts inherent in schooling.

We've already seen Renda view her own learning as embodying a "counterhegemonic" approach. Now we will see how she translates her understandings of learning into the kinds of decisions she makes in her classroom. In a sense, it was easier for her to learn how to learn in ways that did not fit into the school's culture, because she was, as a student, a risk taker and a rebel, than it was for her to transform her teaching in order to match what she had experienced and understood as a learner. Moving from behind the student's desk to the front of the class involved her taking on some of the cultural myths associated with teaching. We observed her clinging to vocabulary lessons divorced from the context of the reading and writing that students were doing.

We also saw her taking a somewhat elitist attitude about literature: that there are some students for whom it is intended and accessible and others who need to be led to literature by an expert interpreter. Here are two of her early log entries that illustrate these attitudes:

> If I assign *The Scarlet Letter*, I'm going to have to check comprehension or they're not going to read it, or read it accurately. This is, in no way, child-originated or child-centered—perhaps no 15-year-old would ever choose to read something this difficult—yet I believe there is value in expanding your capacity, strengthening your thinking muscle. I will ask this of them.

> Analysis of poetry takes a fine eye, good ear, rich experience and a tutor/mentor to open the windows and adjust the lens—please, leave poetry to those who will work at it, and let cinquains be labeled another form of prose, which they are—fun, worth playing with—but not, ever, Wallace Stevens or Blake or Adrienne Rich or the *real*, awesome stuff. I'm inclined to save poetry for the gifted.(emphasis Renda's)

The satellite construct of teacher as learner included learning about teaching in addition to being aware of oneself as a learner. The satellite constructs of teacher as coach and facilitator, teacher as colearner, learning as transformation, not transmission are all a part of what Renda must grow into. At this point in her learning, she does not see a conflict between her attempts to push and demand excellence in her classroom and her desire to tap students' potentials more fully than she believes the school system really wants. What she hasn't yet come to see is how limited and limiting this view of excellence is. Only when she explores and formulates the satellite constructs we just mentioned will she be able to redefine excellence so that it can come to mean a demand on students to take responsibility for their own learning and to learn how to learn. In other words, only through experimenting with alternative processes of teaching and learning will she be able to get more students involved in the learning and also achieve the kind of in-depth understanding of and access to literature that she wants.

At the beginning of the in-service project, Renda reveals her limited investment in student-centered learning, but at the same time a desire to invest more. She writes in her log:

> Group work is the case in my classroom, though it has been (except in writing work) more form than application. I am attempting this year to structure reading, writing, discussion around small group work. What I would do differently: an opening unit in which we learn to talk with, question, collaborate with one another.

Her initial toying with an idea and the successes she has with implementing "genuine" collaborative work lead her to a full-blown image of what is possible in a classroom that is a real writing workshop. In this entry, she sounds like an Olympic athlete envisioning the perfect performance, using imaging as a tool for living through and with all the motions and choices that need to be made in order to succeed.

> I'm really beginning to see this classroom, a writing workshop. I imagine myself in my classroom during my 3rd period class and try to look around and try to answer the questions that arise as I look around. I see groups of three conferencing and responding. I see two baskets—one for comments, one for evaluation (selected at intervals from file?). I still want to read and respond to the learning logs, but now there is a computer in the corner with PFS Write and a disk with reading quizzes on it, so I can print out quizzes when I need them? And students are typing away, getting manuscripts ready for publication. In the other end of the room, students are reading and talking about what they are reading, comparing notes, consulting with one another in pairs. The center of the classroom is writing—individual carrels or desks where students can work in peace and quiet. I have set up my desk for conferencing and the first and last slots in the schedule are for log writing/general announcements. Each small group has decided on the book to read/the project to undertake and the "graded paper" requirements are posted, as are publication deadlines. Some days or even weeks are for group activities—acting out *Julius Caesar* or the French Revolution, hearing reports, making a videotape—but three of four weeks are workshop time, with each student reading, responding, and writing alone or in small groups.

In fact, in visits we made to Renda's classroom after she had done this writing, we began to see more and more of exactly what she described. In each successive visit, we saw more and more complexity, more and more layers, more and more independent learning than we had seen the time before. We found that without going around the room and chatting with each student or group of students, we wouldn't really be able to understand what it was they were engaged in. It was also difficult to find Renda, because she was not in the classic position at the head of the classroom. Most often, she sat at her desk (which was placed discretely, at the side of the classroom), either reading and responding to logs or conferencing with students. The imaging became reality!

She found that "negotiating the curriculum" provided her with a vehicle and a support for her frame of mind for creating and sustaining a workshop. By the third year of the program, she had experimented with the processes of negotiating sufficiently not only to be able to make a videotape of her and her students negotiating the curriculum to share with her colleagues, but also to argue convincingly with her colleagues about how and why to negotiate the curriculum. Let's listen to her explore, in a conversation with her colleagues, the differences between classrooms where negotiating the curriculum is the norm—democratic classrooms—and ones in which the teacher dominates and controls knowledge:

> Ms. RENDA: I have a quarrel with your metaphor of "giving." To me, that is really, really sinful. I think our traditional instinct of education has been that of the teacher giving the learning, the knowledge, the exposure, the fill-in-the-blanks. And, in fact, I think beginning with Lindfors, the fundamental assumption that we have to at least consider before we reject it is: that you cannot give learning, that the child must acquire it on her own. And that can only happen from the learner. That you facilitate, make easy, expose, but not give. It's not measles. They can't catch it from sitting next to us, unfortunately.
>
> Ms. HART: But it is contagious.
>
> Ms. RENDA: But wouldn't it spread more rapidly between six enthusiastic students than between one teacher and one student?
>
> Ms. KOSLOWSKI: The two ideas of "giving" and "sharing," to me, I can't share something until I have received something. I mean I can't, for example, if you put me with your husband to discuss the nuclear power plant, I might start out by saying, "I know a little bit about an atom." When we got into nuclear engineering, I'd have to say, "It's out of my field." I haven't got in my head enough information to be of any contribution to a group of nuclear physicists unless I go and study something. Unless I get information that I can share with you.
>
> Ms. RENDA: But you won't get the information unless you've learned to ask questions. And you won't learn to ask questions listening to lectures. In negotiating the curriculum, the suggestion is that you begin by asking them "what they know."
>
> Ms. TRINITY: Right, that's true. But sometimes there are topics, like a thing that you know nothing about and you have to give some kind of background before you can start negotiating.
>
> Ms. RENDA: I haven't hit a single topic yet that somebody in the class didn't know something about. And I have been astonished by how much they knew already. They have stored a great deal of information. And so sometimes, our assumption that they have no background is just that, an assumption.

What's so interesting about this conversation is that the processes of negotiation that Renda is defending are built out of her core construct about knowledge: that knowledge is constructed by knowers. But she is also connecting this core construct with her satellite constructs. There is one more leap that she makes that is critical to her continued exploration of an alternative pedagogy. She develops a theory that both accounts for why negotiating the curriculum is so successful and what excellence really is. Her once "writing workshop" now becomes a "learning workshop":

> This sort of class meeting and interviewing of experts might be an ideal format for new "learning workshops" in English 9/10. How do *you* study? Take notes? A chance to reflect at some length on how we learn, how our learning strategies are flawed, alternative problem solving schemata. (Emphasis Renda's)

Her new theory is that learning how to learn is, in the long run, more important than the stuff of their learning for students' achievement of excellence.

"Contradictions of Control"

While Renda's achievements may seem, as we have laid them out, automatic, consistent, relatively conflict-free, and predictable, given her core construct of knowledge, this isn't the whole story. When we described her personality at the opening of this chapter, we made a point of her assertiveness. What we want to explore in this section is the role of her personality in modulating the ways in which she could enact her beliefs about teaching and learning. We want to see her explicit struggles with the "contradictions of control," as she admits to her need for control, as she questions that need, and finally how she begins to alter her role in spite of her need.

In the immersion activity with the Noam Chomsky passage, she was, of course, a vocal participant in her small-group discussion. She reflected in her log on the role she played in her group after reading a transcript of the group's discussion:

> Nothing like reading over, at a distance, the inanely bossy "know-it-all" that you were. Don't know why anyone puts up with it. Next time, I'll shut up and listen more. (Yes, in classes, too. If kids can't even finish a thought, they'll either stop trying or I won't know what they have to say, really.)

This discovery led her to her first action research on teacher talk, which we described earlier. Neither the recognition or the research were yet to have a profound effect on changing her role in the classroom. She reflects in her log on her own struggles with her bossiness in the classroom:

> Rereading my learning logs for workshops, I see the struggles over giving up control, the lack of faith that students can/will find connections,

share them, seek them. The comments show me backing off—"Hey, look this is just not *possible*"—and you asking "Why not?" (Emphasis Renda's)

Even her attempts at giving up control don't cure her skepticism about students' abilities to take ownership responsibly. While she is willing to respond to students' complaints that "I must choose what I read or I don't really want to read it" by allowing students choices in selecting their readings, we will see that she is not completely comfortable:

> When I told them they had the option of choosing a book as long as it was on the suggested theme, they went to work, and so far we have accumulated quite a long list of possible titles. I'm not wild about all of them, but I'll go along with it and see what happens.

Renda did go along with her students' choices as well as trying to negotiate other areas of her curricula. The negotiation, as we saw earlier, became one part of setting up her classroom as a writing workshop. All of these activities gave her a rich tapestry to reflect on. How was she doing? Lucky for us, she made a videotape of the range of student activities comprising the writing workshop in action. She asked us to view and evaluate the tape, since she was considering sharing it with her colleagues. At one point, the student director zoomed in on a conference she was having with a student on revising a piece of writing. She let the student read the draft, and then asked her, "Well, what do you think?" The student, not having an immediate response to the question, sits for a moment, but says nothing. Renda jumps in at this point on the tape with a whole range of suggestions for revision. When we spoke to her after viewing the tape, we suggested that she look again at the part where she is having a one-on-one conference with a student. It seemed to us that she was able to orchestrate the other student engagements without taking ownership away from them, but that in face-to-face interaction with an individual, it was more difficult for her not to take over. We wanted to know what she thought was going on, especially because it was clear to us that she felt her conference had been successful. Following our critique, she wrote that "Preemptive, along with manipulative, major 'no, no' word. Yet in my desire for efficient use of time, for product, *I* preempt. Why is it so hard to *do* what we preach (and believe)?" (emphasis Renda's). This log entry confirmed our view of what we had seen. In many ways, this tape and our collaborative reflections on it spurred her to struggle even more with issues of control.

Another contradiction of control had come up once before when her classroom research on student writing for examinations faltered because of student resistance to taking ownership. Being a "successful" student in school means learning to give up and give over responsibility for learning. It is, therefore, no easy task for students to unlearn what has functioned for them more or less successfully in the past. Renda must find a way of helping students both understand their role in learning, but also the implications of that new role in becoming critical and transformative along with their teacher. It makes perfect sense to us that, given her own internal struggles to release control, her students' resistance to taking control only reinforces her inability to "do what we preach and believe." It's far easier to slip back when all parties are encouraging it. Her route to solving this contradiction comes about as a result of her writing to learn:

> Students need to write to discover how to write, to read in order to discover how to read, to talk with each other in order to learn how talk can be used. Yet they are so unaware of the processes of making meaning, clarifying meaning, communicating meaning. And if we use a period to talk about how talking and writing help us learn, then that period I talked a lot and I'm sick of the sound of my own voice. I know there is a sort of simple "reseeing" that could show me a way out of the "stuckness": OK—talk less. Listen more. *Give* students space to sort, ask, think. . . . I asked my students to reflect, etc. about above concerns. And they gave me some useful suggestions. I'll follow up. (Emphasis Renda's)

In the struggle to release control, Renda realizes that her theory that helping students learn how to learn may be the key to shared control. In learning how to learn, the students' own sense-making activities are central and, once the students have experienced such activities, they may be less resistant to taking control.

When Renda volunteered to become an advisor to the language-across-the-curriculum project, she didn't realize how important this new role would be in her learning to teach. Watching her colleagues grapple with the same issues, trying to support them in their struggles, and examining the role that she could play in her colleagues' learning all contributed to additional insights and a deeper understanding of the connection between control and learning.

> We *must* release control for learning to occur. When we wrest the process unnaturally away from the normal errors and confusions we deprive others of the opportunity to discover for themselves. If we intervene too drastically or too early (answering before the questions are asked?) aren't we short-circuiting real learning? (Emphasis Renda's)

Did Renda resolve the contradictions of control that plagued her for her entire teaching career? Here is her evaluation of what she learned:

> Because of my own style and the kind of person I am, I will probably always exert more control over my learners than might be ideal—but if I can look back, say four years, I see major shifts and major openings up

of options, choices, and opportunities. Like successful parenting, successful "teaching" using this model is successful to the degree that the students do NOT describe you as a "great teacher who really got me to understand." Instead, they become independent, self-confident, young adult writers and readers—and they say, "That was a good class. I learned a lot. I really learned to write better". . . . After all, I feel "good about myself" as a teacher, not because others tell me that what I am doing is wonderful (though that is nice), but because I believe deep within that what I am doing is the most important job in the world and I'm secretly contemptuous of those who don't get to do what I do, but have to settle for being mere millionaires on Wall Street. (Emphasis Renda's)

The Transformative Intellectual out of the Armchair

For Giroux, in order to be a transformative intellectual, a teacher must unite reflection with action: "Teachers must be able to shape the ways in which time, space, activity, and knowledge organize everyday life in schools" (1988, p. xxxiv). We've already examined in detail how Renda, through reflection and action, transformed her teaching and her classroom in order to make way for a new kind of learning. But she went well beyond the confines of her own classroom in attempting to reshape relationships, catalyze curricular innovations, and redefine the roles of teachers in creating a new quality of life in the school. We have already mentioned that she was a voluntary member of the original writing project planning committee, that she was a first volunteer in the program itself, and that she attempted to extend her work and her colleagues' involvement in the workshops by setting up informal meetings at the high school and videotaping her own classroom for other teachers as well as for the Board of Education. We would now like to be more detailed about some of the actions she took during the course of her participation in the project.

When we decided to transfer, in a formal way, ownership and authority over the project to a group of teacher/advisors, we were, of course both hopeful and confident that she would volunteer. Never one to choose a backseat role, she did come forward as one of two high school advisors. The range and quantity of her actions were enormous. We will touch on just a few of them in order to be able to share a sense of her commitment to action.

One of her chief contributions to the advisor role was her political savvy. She understood how one goes about getting things done in a bureaucracy. So, for example, when she saw a need for the high school teachers involved in the project to get together to share their successes, questions, and concerns, she wrote a memo to the high school principal requesting that he set up a meeting time. Interestingly, she understood that when the principal was having difficulty finding the time in the school schedule to set such a meeting, there were real reasons why this was difficult at the point at which she was requesting it. But as she states, "It *is* on record and his written response is affirmative. It *will* be scheduled" (emphasis Renda's).

At about the same time, the superintendent was sending signals that the district ought to start committing itself to developing students' critical thinking skills. Renda was concerned that the superintendent's intention would take resources and energy away from the language-across-the-curriculum project, and she was further aware that the project was already focusing on critical thinking. After reading and responding to Petrosky's "Critical Thinking: Qu'est-ce que c'est?" (1986), she wrote,

> Liked this article the *most*. And this is our route into [the superintendent's] good graces. Has he *read* this? If not, please send him a copy with a letter saying, "This article articulates the rationale and research behind your own sense that WAC is deeply connected to growth in critical thinking skills. Thought you might like to know that others share your commitment to these linked areas." (Emphasis Renda's)

Renda's language is subtle, as no doubt you have recognized. Rather than antagonizing authority through confrontation, she knows that the way to get support for what she considers important is to credit the superintendent with having thought of it first and to act as if he is already on her side. The strategy worked, too. Up to this point, there has been no separate critical thinking skills program instituted in the district.

Renda was also aware that her role as curricular maverick would be limited in its success, both inside and outside of her classroom, unless she found a way to institutionalize some of the innovations she was attempting to implement. Working deductively from her own and her students' classroom applications, she began to conceptualize the changes that needed to be effected in the English program at the high school. There were two significant areas she targeted: literature and composition.

> I took advantage of the extra time I had to set up a series of released time half days to work with the English Department to derive a new syllabus, so that there would be a degree of uniformity in the readings, speech, and writing expectations for each grade level. We began with the inventory, then set up novels, poetry, and short stories for each grade level, and ordered copies in, for the first time in 15 years through a department budget (rather than individual teachers submitting individual requisitions). For the first time, 9th grade students are now reading a Shakespeare play and four novels. For the first time, there is an American literature syllabus, so the 11th grade social studies teachers can be sure that all their juniors will have read *The Crucible*, *The Great Gatsby*, or

"Death of a Salesman." However, we were able to maintain a high level of choice, and curriculum can be negotiated early within the constraints planned.

Implicit in her description of what was accomplished is that she both requested and was granted released time for her colleagues to meet and work on the new curriculum and also that teachers would be empowered by this process to make joint decisions about expenditures as well as about content. Her efforts in the area of composition derive from similar commitments:

> The composition guidelines took longer. We met and each teacher brought sample writings from each grade level that he or she taught. Mr. M. did suggest, and the Department agreed to this, that we all meet and evaluate the Regents papers this year. I think this is a good move and I've gotten the office to approve it. I intend to distribute copies of the writing guidelines to board members, parents, kids, and other teachers—in short, parents and students can now hold in their hands a description of what is expected of student writers. If they do nothing with that information, then they deserve the inadequate level of instruction and practice that they are receiving.

Again, she takes political action both within the group of department colleagues, as well as in the school and community as a whole.

There is one more area where the force of her insights and actions could be felt. Given that she repeatedly refers to the isolation she and her colleagues suffered throughout their careers in teaching, it's no wonder that she expended most of her efforts in trying to break that isolation down for both political and professional reasons. Her political agenda helps her to recognize that teachers have more power if they work together to effect change and her own sense of professionalism suggests to her that decision making by teachers is a means to professional status. She also sees the role of collaboration in providing emotional and psychological support for the difficult act of changing. In her annual report describing her activities as an advisor, she wrote:

> In the high school, Ms. Lonny [the second high school advisor] and I continued to build support structures—for one another, and for members of the workshop teams. Often they sought us out to ask us to read over an assignment, suggest some approaches, or just "let it all hang out." By being there everyday in our rooms, the corridors, we could ask questions, listen to problems, serve as go-betweens. And when we reached a frustration point we could share our exhaustion. . . . Without a network of encouraging supports, the paper load and the sheer energy required to rethink and replan curriculum day after day can overwhelm

the best intentions. I think Ms. Lonny and I provided the nexus of that support network in our building—because we were there and because they knew that we, too, were juggling papers, essay questions, research logs, and meetings. We have credibility because we are in the trenches too.

Working with Team C teachers in our building has been a more structured relationship. Each of us has been responsible for assisting with the reading, research, and classroom experimentation of members of that team. This is a new experience for me—in all the years I have taught in Charmont I have never functioned as a mentor/buddy for a colleague. . . . I enjoyed conferencing and dialoguing with my colleagues, even when we disagreed, which we did. Unlike students, peers are not afraid to talk back, to say, "I don't think that's what's happening in my class." All of us learned a lot. We were even able to "infect" by example teachers who were not members of the writing workshops. Learning logs, small group work, brainstorming before writing, and revising test questions for clarity, are some of the strategies which have "percolated" into classrooms around the building.

Recalling Rogers' thoughts on being a teacher, we can see that Renda recognizes that sometimes the best learning happens by indirection, that demonstrating and acting as a nondefensive example can be the most powerful way to encourage change.

In thinking about the changes that Renda brought about in her learning and her teaching, there seem to be two key contributions made by the inservice project. The first has to do with being a learner herself and it is why we chose "the teacher as learner" to describe her. The immersion activities that constitute a large part of the workshops are expressly designed to put teachers back into the learner role. In this way, they have the opportunity not only to experience new ways of learning themselves so that they will be better able to understand how their own students will respond, but we also hope that being learners again will help them to recall and reconceptualize and reformulate in their teaching the experiences they had in or out of school when they were learners before.

For Renda, both learning new things as well as remembering her earlier learning experiences were at the heart of her change process. We've seen in this chapter time and time again how learning in these ways sparked new understandings, or raised new questions, or solved new and old problems. She is substantiating evidence that being a learner and exploring our learning histories are pivotal and crucial to change.

The opportunities for collaboration and cooperation that were provided by the workshop structure were another contribution to her change process. Because schools make it difficult, if not impossible, for teachers to talk to one another and share their experiences, these workshop opportunities were significant. From the feminist perspective we used to describe Renda earlier, collaboration is central to building personal voice and knowledge. It is clear that her route to transformation must involve integrating intuition with learning from others.

A proponent of a conspiracy theory would say that this action by schools is purposeful, that schools are fearful that if teachers collaborate, they will inevitably challenge the system. A house divided cannot stand, but a collective voice can revolt. And we know this. We know that the only way for teachers to take responsibility for teaching and learning is for them to do it together. They must, however, first learn to trust each other, to fight the institution's desire to keep them apart, to create competition, fear, and mistrust. They must be willing to open their classroom doors and share, not only their successes, but the risks they take that might not turn out so successfully.

This opportunity to collaborate with her colleagues gave Renda a renewed sense of purpose and professionalism. It also gave her a new sense of hope that schools might become places where teachers and students could learn together in democratic ways. And, finally, being able to collaborate with her colleagues allowed her to explore and act out alternative routes to control and power.

Through it all, Renda continues to be a learner and, perhaps, to value her role as learner above all others. She exemplifies for us all of the traits and characteristics of an engaged and committed learner and even shows us how that commitment forms the core of the transformative intellectual. We have used her own words to express our notions much more than we've used the words of any other teacher. That's because we think that she's not just a teacher who teaches writing, but a writer who teaches and a teacher who learns through writing. And in her role as an advisor, she appropriated another avenue through which she could learn:

> Being able to work closely with Nancy and Cindy and the other advisors was rewarding and they provided new readings, responses, and questions which allowed me to continue to learn as an individual. I need this, as perhaps we all do—it keeps me in touch with how it feels to be a student, and obviates smug complacency at my own "expertise." We have all grown together, in different ways than we might have predicted, and I suspect the others feel as I do that in many ways the more we know, the less we are sure of. I feel we provided an essential element in consolidating change and growth by the professional staff, as well as representing a new response on the part of the board and the superintendent to the question of "Who shall lead?" The writing advisors carried out much of the instruction and implementation of change with the members of the third year team—thereby satisfying one recurring criterion for meaningful staff development—ownership of the learning by the learners.

Chapter Six

The Teacher as Leader

It's currently fashionable to talk about teacher empowerment as the key to school reform. A variety of proposals, from increasing teachers' salaries to creating mentor teachers, has been offered as routes to empowerment. But there are few models currently being tried that might give us the opportunity to see what happens when teachers take on leadership roles or even what it means to be a leader. The only models that exist are those in which teachers are "promoted" to positions of power and, in most cases, this implies leaving the classroom behind. It implies, as well, a change in the collegial relationships among teachers, since teachers who become "leaders" in their schools are oftentimes viewed by their peers as sellouts to the existing school administrative hierarchy.

If change is to occur within schools, we reasoned, then structures and mechanisms would have to be established to support the teachers in their continued growth. Our experiences in other school districts had led us to conclude that without such mechanisms, only those teachers who are truly self-sustaining in their growth and change could continue to fight against all of the institutional and personal constraints impeding the development of democratic schooling. The role of a teacher/advisor is so foreign in a traditional school setting that by merely creating it develops an opportunity to discover what such a role would mean. Moreover, until new roles for

teachers are actually tried out and in place, we will be blind to their implications.

One model that has been around for at least fifteen years is that of the
teacher/advisor, a combined role that grounds a teacher's work firmly in the
classroom while allowing her time to support and collaborate with her colleagues. This model was developed at the Workshop Center for Open Education at the City College of New York by Lillian Weber (Albert & Dropkin,
1975). We were attracted to Weber's model because it seemed to encourage
peer collaboration, while at the same time acknowledging that structural
changes within the school setting were needed to accommodate new roles for
teachers that would engender empowerment. When we recognized that teachers participating in the in-service program needed to take ownership over the
program itself, we looked to Weber's model as a possible guide.

In this chapter, we will look closely at a teacher/advisor in order to
understand what collegial leadership looks like, how teacher/leaders might
work with their peers and the administration, the role that becoming a teacher/
leader played in both creating and sustaining change within this teacher herself, and how this particular teacher/advisor became who she is.

What Does a Teacher/Leader Do?

During the academic year 1988–1989, Charmont's superintendent decided
to create academic subject matter coordinators in the district. Because the
middle and high school faculties are so small that they have never had department chairs, there were never any curricular leadership roles for faculty. For
a brief time, there was a K–12 curriculum coordinator who was responsible for
leadership across the three schools, but the position was discontinued after one
year because neither the teachers nor the administration could see any benefits.
As state mandates for curriculum and testing have proliferated in recent years,
the need for someone to coordinate subject-area responses to these demands
developed. The role of teacher/advisor, created initially to serve the needs of
the language-across-the-curriculum project, had already proved to be a successful model for curriculum coordination. The superintendent, therefore,
based his call for faculty volunteers to take curriculum coordinator positions
in English, science, social studies, math, and the arts on the language-across-
the-curriculum teacher/advisor model. These positions would carry a small
stipend and released time of one-half day every two weeks. As you can see from
the positions listed above no provision was made for a coordinator of writing
or language across the curriculum.

After petition by a number of teachers involved in the language-across-
the-curriculum in-service project, the superintendent agreed to create two
special positions, a K–5 and a 6–12 writing-across-the-curriculum advisor.

He went so far as to agree to substituting additional released time for overload pay for those two positions. The teachers who petitioned wrote: "For people who see time as more of an issue than money, could additional released time be substituted in place of the appropriated funds?" Ms. Lonny, the teacher/leader whose story we will tell here, volunteered to take the 6–12 writing-across-the-curriculum advisor position. Here is a brief catalog of her activities during the first six months of the 1988–1989 school year:

- conferencing with 45 individual teachers on strategies for using writing
- arranging interclass visitations to observe "writing workshops"
- selecting and distributing professional readings
- videotaping model lessons
- conducting "sharing sessions" every two weeks with writing-project participants
- organizing interdisciplinary writing projects
- surveying staff about needs and concerns in order to set up after-school meetings for writing project participants
- planning a K–12 language arts assessment with building principals
- attending monthly curriculum coordinator meetings
- organizing a Superintendent's Day Conference workshop on writing across the curriculum
- proposing a series of full-day workshops for writing-project participants
- assisting Ms. K. in helping students use peer feedback

If this had been all that Lonny had done during this six-month period, it would have been impressive, but at the same time, she was also setting up a genuine writing workshop in her own classroom, negotiating the curriculum, conducting her own action research, and, in general, taking her own learning further and further. As we can see, the activities she engaged in as the writing-across-the-curriculum coordinator ranged from collaborative support and coteaching to an advocacy role within the district administration for supporting the ongoing work of writing-program participants. All of her activities have kept the spirit and the action of language across the curriculum alive and thriving in Charmont.

Who is a Teacher/Leader and How Does She Think?

Lonny's experience as the writing-across-the-curriculum advisor in 1988–1989 grew directly out of her experience as a teacher/advisor to the in-service project during 1987–1988. We described the advisor role in detail in Chapter 2, and we will refer to it again in the next chapter when we focus on changes within the institution itself. For now, we would like to look at the role through the eyes of one teacher. Asked to write an annual report of her work as a teacher/advisor over the 1987–1988 school year for the superintendent and the Board of Education, Lonny used it to define herself as a teacher/ leader and to sketch out the issues she deemed crucial in her learning and acting in this role. The entire report follows:

> I began this year as a Writing Advisor for Charmont's Writing and Learning Workshop with certain expectations about how I might be of help to other teachers. In attempting to live up to those expectations, I have actually broadened them during the year, as I realized that my value to other teachers is tied inextricably to my developing knowledge about my own, my colleagues', and my students' learning . . . that what I'm really advising is a cooperative effort to learn about learning.
>
> Being a writing advisor has first given me the opportunity to reflect on my own learning. In the beginning of the year, the advisor team agreed that one of our roles would be to act as "model" learners, reading and keeping learning logs on the materials Team C would be studying; in many cases, this reading would actually be rereading and re-visioning materials from my own experience last year. Far from being repetitive, the reading has encouraged me to reevaluate concepts I thought I fully understood; it has given me a chance to see the complexities of those concepts in light of classroom and advisory team experience I had since I originally did the reading. In addition, as the advisor team has met regularly to make lesson plans for third year workshops, I see all of us working cooperatively toward helping others learn new theories; our attempts to reach a consensus on how our colleagues might best learn what we have learned has sharpened again my own thinking and learning. This has also been the case in the actual workshops themselves, hearing and responding to other teachers' questions, theories, and arguments.
>
> As the year has progressed, I continue to gain appreciation for the great commitment the district and many of its staff members have made toward learning. Working with fellow teachers, both in workshop sessions and on a day to day basis, there are of course healthy disagreements about theories and techniques—as there must be, I believe, if true learning is to take place. The one thing, however, that has not caused any disagreement is the concept of the workshop itself; over and over again, workshop participants have expressed the benefits of the quality time that the district provides. This gives us the chance to learn together—not in isolation, as seems to be the case in most schools. Given the enthusiasm and commitment of my fellow teachers, it has been enlightening to be a part of their learning. Accordingly, I have been able to conduct lessons in other teacher's classes on writing response techniques, videotape model lessons taught by a fellow advisor, have teachers visit

my classes, help design, observe, participate in Team C classroom research, and serve as a sounding board and consultant for their concerns. By reading and responding to teachers' learning logs, I have also been able to model one of the suggestions we make for students.

While it is of course important to have the chance to work together with other teachers, ultimately our main goal is to enhance the learning of students in our own classrooms and throughout the District. As I continue to focus on my own learning, I gain a greater awareness of how long-term learning occurs; as I see my and my colleagues' needs to make personal connections with material, to have the chance to have our own questions answered, to actually see our teachers engaging in the same activities suggested to us, and to get trusted feedback on our writing, I realize how important it is for my students to have similar needs met.

As a writing advisor advocating such approaches, I know I must be sure these things are going on in my own classroom. In my work with my students, I am focusing on their learning: stressing the personal connections they make with the literature they read, encouraging them to find for themselves and suggest to others key ideas in materials, enabling them to assist each others' writing processes, giving them a chance to negotiate what we learn and how we learn it; in short, modeling a total approach to learning. Of course, in trying ideas that often run contrary to students' expectations of what school is like, I must deal with the day to day frustrations of not having things work out as they were "sposed" to—an experience which I can now share openly through my role as advisor, hopefully to the benefit of my colleagues.

In late October of this year, I had an opportunity to attend the New York State English Council pre-conference workshop sessions at Pace University. As I listened to teachers discussing and presenting their districts' writing across the curriculum programs, I realized just how far our own district had come; while most teachers are still limited to their own isolated attempts to try what's being suggested in the literature, I and my colleagues have a chance to learn and experiment cooperatively—seeing and doing first hand what we are theorizing will help our students. Being an advisor to such a program places me in what I now see as a circle of learning—my learning expanding as I work with colleagues to enhance the learning of our students who, in turn, teach us more about the incredible complexity of learning itself.

There are three dimensions of a teacher/leader role that Lonny focuses on that seem to be most important to her learning, her growth and change, and to her successful work as an advisor. These are the attempt to replace the isolation of teachers from one another with collaboration; to redefine teacher/ leader from the perspective of colearner and nurturer, rather than from the more common perspective of expert; and to build a student-centered classroom that will serve as a forum for a "total approach to learning" and will be seen by students and demonstrated to colleagues as a genuine alternative to a teacher-centered classroom. All of these dimensions embody not only a rethinking of school leadership, but also the possibility for real classroom and institutional change.

Isolation vs. Collaboration

Embedded in Lonny's learning logs are the seeds from which these issues have grown. In her annual report, she points out that the opportunity the workshops provided for peer collaboration among teachers may have been its greatest benefit. When she compares Charmont to other districts, Charmont emerges as unique. In one log entry, she critiques the isolation of teachers from one another and points to the fact that this leads to teachers being "afraid they'll be viewed as weak if they ask for help." In another entry, she tells a story of collaboration where seeking help is not only not a weakness, but a source of strength to both her and her colleague:

> I just came from a really neat meeting with Ms. Koslowski—we planned together a lab session that she's found the kids are usually confused by; we planned it by Ms. Koslowski observing as I talked through the directions, where I was confused, had questions, etc.—seeing how much "talking it through" had helped—we decided to try using a fishbowl in class, with a student doing just what I did, and the class acting as ethnographers, using that as the basis to do the lab themselves. I'm going to observe in class when she does it tomorrow. Ms. Koslowski has a good feeling for where the kids have had trouble in the past, so this should be a good experiment.
>
> I think Ms. Koslowski and I both really are excited to see what happens tomorrow—this is the kind of thing that I think is the best/most important about what we're trying to do as advisors.

Collaboration for Lonny entails enactment. That is, she and Ms. Koslowski are using the best of what they learned, demonstrating to and for each other and the students how writing and talking can support learning in science, but also acknowledging that what students need most of all is to learn how to learn. This last echoes her remark in her annual report that "advising is a cooperative effort to learn about learning." It is also very clear from this story that both Lonny and Koslowski contribute equally to identifying, understanding, analyzing, and solving a common teaching and learning problem. In short, Lonny demonstrates her deep understanding that learning proceeds best when we learn together. In spite of the fact that she has been working on and through these ideas longer than Koslowski, she knows she can continue to learn by working through problems collaboratively, rather than feeling the burden of always having to have a solution to someone else's problems that she must deliver and transmit.

Leader vs. Expert

In defining collaboration partly by seeing it as continued learning, Lonny is also suggesting that being a leader does not imply that the leader's own growth is something that must have already taken place; that as a result of her prior learning, she is now an expert and has nothing more to learn. In her words, as she wrote in her annual report, "I realized that my value to other teachers is tied inextricably to my developing knowledge about my own, my colleagues', and my students' learning." This attitude contrasts sharply with that of "expert," someone we would define as being a know-it-all, dispensing knowledge to others, never questioning why or what or how, demanding respect in equal measure to expertise, and working in a hierarchical model.

Lonny takes seriously the idea that the advisors should be model learners. She may not have realized when first taking on this role how powerful this modeling would be in her own learning. Her commitment to doing all of the work that she was asking the workshop participants to do had an unanticipated benefit:

> As I am personally rereading the text materials from last year, I'm noticing a lot of things in my own classroom that I want to get away from much earlier in the year than I did last year—especially teacher-centered discussion, parroting of answers, etc.—yet I also feel a conflict with setting up/establishing certain concepts/patterns that will be a basis for class content all year.

In addition to seeing new ways of approaching old classroom problems and reflecting on the benefits of rereading, she also finds in her rereading an opportunity to deepen her theoretical understandings. In her log in March of her teacher/advisor year she writes:

> My notebook just fell apart, and in putting it back together, I ended up rereading my log since September—God, I've really been a quivering mass of insecurity most of the year, haven't I? One thing I did see—or thought I saw—was a sort of progression of really internalizing the concepts. I do feel I've learned an awful lot (maybe not applying it any better, but one thing at a time)—am also at the moment handling the anxiety/distancing myself better.

Lonny also views her leadership to include being a demonstration teacher, which has a dual definition: on the one hand, she is actually using the theoretical practice she's advocating; on the other hand, she is taking risks and suffering the disappointments as well as enjoying the triumphs that she would wish her colleagues to experience. Such a way of viewing what it means to be a demonstration teacher is radically different from the standard definition. She doesn't do what she does in order to be mindlessly copied, or even admired, revered as someone whose achievements are unattainable by mere mortals. Instead, as she writes in her annual report, "As a writing advisor advocating such approaches, I know I must be sure these things are going on in my own classroom." She feels a real commitment to being a teacher who practices what she believes.

By admitting to be a "quivering mass of insecurity," she not only shares her insecurity, she uses it as another benchmark in her learning. Not only does she share these feelings with us, but she finds room within her role and definition of leadership to share her experiences, both successful and unsuccessful ones, with her colleagues. As she wrote in her annual report, "I must deal with the day to day frustrations of not having things work out as they were 'sposed' to—an experience which I can now share openly through my role as advisor, hopefully to the benefit of my colleagues." It seems to us that she doesn't want her colleagues to foist expertise on her either, but would prefer them to see her as a fellow struggler. She's constantly thinking about the implications of her role as they force both her and her colleagues to redefine power and authority within school settings.

Student-Centered vs. Teacher-Centered Learning

In her annual report, Lonny has identified some critical aspects of a student-centered classroom, which she has enacted both with her students and with her colleagues in the workshops. These include negotiating the curriculum, encouraging personal connection making, and posing and answering learner-generated questions. The ideas she has about democratic classrooms are central to how she thinks about her role as a leader and how she believes she can best support the learning of her colleagues. She makes a number of statements in her logs over the course of her year as an advisor that help us understand how her thinking has developed about this issue and account for how she made the decision to be a leader who orchestrates student-centered learning:

October 7, 1987:
I don't feel I'm getting away from teacher-centeredness (is that a word or just a mouthful?) nearly close to the way I should be—this year's freshmen seem really tied to that, and I'm afraid that rather than easing

them away from it—as I intended—they're easing me back towards it! After rereading the stuff on negotiation—I know I'm not using nearly enough grouping—I keep saying I'll get to it and I'm taking too long.

Re: The workshop—
[A couple of the teachers] have expressed a concern to me that we're taking a long time to get to the point—or that when we do, the point isn't definitive enough—I know that that's simply part of the process and that they need to move away from teacher-centeredness too.

November 4, 1987:
What a mass of confusion/lack of meaningfulness [students] attribute to school—for the most part, they really do perceive it as a maze that they'll just keep plugging away at—content not to know why/how— obviously we have to make it clearer, more meaningful—more *theirs* — but I'm really feeling frustrated by the institution. Is massive change possible? Can I make a dent? I've been grappling with these questions a lot lately.

December 9, 1987:
Since students over years develop this picture of teacher as "controller" they "coach" teachers to stick to this role; re: my feelings this year of being "pushed" by the kids into "teacher-centeredness."

May 18, 1988:
I need to figure a way that will help me get around what I believe to be the biggest problem in doing what I've been trying in a very traditional setting—the teaching for the test and every man for himself philosophies that these kids are *so* well trained in—they have learned that. I find this the biggest part of the temptation to say "Chuck it!" (but I won't). (Emphasis Lonny's)

Perhaps what got Lonny to the point where she totally committed herself to being an advisor and a teacher who placed the needs and learning goals of students first are the two revelations we see as most important in these writings she did over the year. The first occurs when she realizes that both her students and the teachers she is advising resist taking ownership over their own learning. But she has the courage to be firm in her insistence on learners taking responsibility when they don't wish to, because she firmly believes that learning won't happen otherwise. The second revelation she has is about the role of the institution in creating and perpetuating the myth of teacher as controller of all she surveys. We can conclude, therefore, that she knows she must think carefully about how she acts, about the messages she gives about learning, and, perhaps most importantly, about the way she construes her role as leader to ensure that it mirrors how she wants to be seen as a teacher and leader, as well as providing another forum to promote reflection and continued learning.

Building Theories of Teaching and Learning

> In my work with my students, I am focusing on their learning: stressing the personal connections they make with the literature they read, encouraging them to find for themselves and suggest to others key ideas and materials, enabling them to assist each other's writing processes, giving them a chance to negotiate what we learn and how we learn it; in short, modeling a total approach to learning.

What we see so clearly expressed in Lonny's annual report from 1987–1988 as a personal theory of how knowledge is constructed by learners and how to create a context in her classroom for knowledge to be built emerged much earlier in our work with her. During her first year as a workshop participant, she explained to the group how she learned best. She suggested that learning experiences where she was given the opportunity to work with her peers and to discuss and make meaning independent of the teacher were the most powerful and meaningful and long lasting for her. She suggested further that this insight about her own learning was helping her to place her students at the center of their own learning and to embrace the theories of knowledge we were reading and discussing in the workshops. Her constructivist view of knowledge is implied in the importance she places on the distinction that Mellon (1981) makes between language "competence" and language "performance" and the practical connections she sees as a result of making this distinction. For her, teaching and learning are distinct acts and her developing theory of knowledge is embedded here in her written reflections from 1986–1987:

> The distinction between language competence and performance skills— the idea of language competence—"naturally" acquired in preschool years, clearly fits in with previous readings and discussions because language competence is a given in all students, they are thus ready to acquire performance skills—but not through drill and practice—but through "natural" interaction with various forms of language.

While Lonny is willing to admit that she has not always been able to put into practice this theory of knowledge with her students, she is also aware that it forms the basis of her belief system. It was her inability to put her theory into practice, however, that eventually led her to rediscovering what that theory was. We noticed during her first year of participation in the workshops that she focused her attention almost exclusively on practical applications of the ideas we were working on. In the act of applying new "techniques," she began to explore the implications these techniques had for theories of teaching and learning, including the role of the teacher, the centrality of student ownership and intention, and the need for collaboration. Her first action research in 1986 gave her the opportunity to put into practice the kind of learning that she had talked about as being significant to her. She designs her project to focus on the following question: "Will having students write about initial responses to class literature reading (and having me comment on those responses) foster a more positive attitude about/perception of future reading?" Here's her description of what happened:

> In order to answer this question, I had students keep a journal in response to class readings (some of which were assigned, some of which were "free choice"). We discussed the fact that "acceptable" responses included summarizing what they thought they understood about the story, theorizing about possible meanings and themes of the story, relating the story to personal experience, and posing questions which they had about the literature. I responded by reacting to what they had written, suggesting possible answers, etc.
>
> I think I have observed a different approach by students to literature when they realize that their reactions are valid—that their questions and the theories they are posing are worthy of consideration. They have shown more enthusiasm toward approaching a new piece of literature and greater willingness to share ideas with the whole class.
>
> I feel as though I'm only just beginning to observe the possibilities of such responses, and that more than providing anything definitive at this point, I'm really just beginning to see what additional questions should be formulated.

What was successful in this piece of action research for Lonny was observing how shared meaning making could help students be more willing and able to interpret literature. She also learns that this willingness is based in great part on a validation of students' knowledge. Once she becomes confident in herself and her students as constructors of meaning, she begins to turn her attention to sharing responsibility with students for evaluating their learning. This new focus, which is briefly touched on in this piece of action research when she notes that she and her students talked about "acceptable" responses, gave rise to her answering some of those additional questions that are implied, but not explicitly stated in her report on her research.

Once again, she begins with the actual classroom technique and derives an underlying principle of learning from its application. Following a workshop in which the participants were asked to evaluate their own writing, she speculates: "I thought the self-evaluation sheet very clearly led up to the [writing] conference, and was a crucial step in putting the writer in control of his own writing (reinforcing his ownership)." This conscious theorizing about how self-evaluation is tied to ownership leads her to explore other implications for collaborative assessment. Through a cooperative action research project that surveyed students in the high school on their perceptions of the need for correctness in writing, she and her colleagues discovered that while students do believe that they will be judged on the basis of how correct their writing is, that alone is not a motivation for them to edit and proofread carefully. As a result of this research, she wonders how students can be motivated to correct their work:

> One possible answer is what we discussed about having them know a lot about us as evaluators, and also including them in establishing criteria for evaluation. . . . As a group we need to decide where to go with what we found out so far and how that act itself might be motivating to the students (simply through the act of including them).

Her own role as learner in the workshops also contributes to Lonny's growing understanding of student ownership over learning. In her reflective piece of writing at the end of a workshop day, she focuses her attention on what happens when learners are in charge of their own learning: "I was interested— fascinated—by looking at the various samples of student writing. I thought, though, that things kind of fell apart this afternoon—I guess I'm wondering if that sort of a possibility—and/or part of the process—when learners 'take control.' " Her commitment to enacting negotiating the curriculum, collaboratively deciding with students the whats, hows, and whens of learning, is a direct outgrowth of these explorations of shared decision making in the classroom in small ways during her first year of participating in the writing project.

Lonny's theories of teaching and learning were not always as congruent with her practice, or as well formulated as they appear in her annual report, or even in many of the log entries we've quoted. We've written earlier that it's often a conflict between competing theories or a dissonance between theory and practice that precipitates problem posing and problem solving, the stuff of reflective practice. Such dissonance and conflict was also a part of Lonny's learning history. We have just seen her problem posing and solving; what we now would like to look at briefly are those moments of conflict during her first year of participation.

> "The essential ingredient in finding purpose is the writer's conviction that she has something to say" is a very important concept that I have felt (experienced) myself but probably have not extended enough to my students.

I often feel sort of an inner battle between knowing I want a student-centered classroom and that irresistible urge to fall into the traditional teacher-centered role.

The conflict between theoretical understanding and practical application is but one kind of conflict she experiences. She also, understandably, feels pressure from the institution to work with her students in ways that may not fully embody her beliefs.

Important—"a final draft takes far longer to evolve than we usually allow for in school"—Aren't we all caught up in the "I've got to get to such and such" syndrome?

Re: the grammar teaching issue. I am and have been for years well aware of what the research says, yet I have still, in some courses, continued to teach it because of either "required curriculum" or the "teacher they'll be having next year" problem.

The last conflict that she gets herself embroiled in has to do with competing theories of teaching and learning, although she is unaware of this at this point. She may be compared to Mr. Winberry, the high school science teacher, who was able to borrow techniques directly from the writing workshop experience and fit them into a context that is totally at odds, theoretically, with the thrust and meaning of the technique itself.

One maxim I quarrel with in this chapter is the one banning formula writings—given the reality of Regents exams and similar student requirements, they do provide a needed crutch for students, and combined with prewriting, they can result in good papers.

How Does Being a Leader Make You a Leader?

We have attempted throughout Part II of this book to examine the factors that seem to contribute to and promote change in individual teachers. In this chapter, we have taken a different tack by presenting Lonny's history in reverse order. Rather than look at who she was when she entered the program and follow her progress throughout the course of our work with her, we've begun at the end of the story instead. This was a deliberate choice designed to stress that the central and pivotal factor in Lonny's ability to change was assuming the leadership role of teacher/advisor. This backward look helps us to see that without taking on the leadership role, she may not have changed in the ways she did. We'd like now to fill you in on a little bit more of her history so that you can better understand the person whom we met in 1986 and the one who appears as the writing-across-the-curriculum advisor here in 1988. Juxtaposing the final entry we quoted from her log with her annual report that appeared at the beginning of this chapter certainly raises questions about how and why she came to be what she is now.

Lonny is a high school English teacher with fifteen years of teaching experience. She did most of her teaching in the Midwest. In fact, when we met her in September, 1986, she had just moved from there and become a faculty member at Charmont High School. Unlike most of the teachers in the project, she did not volunteer but was strongly urged by Mr. Fallon, her principal, to be a participant. So not only was she new to the school, but she was drafted, without her knowing, into the project on her first day. Another disadvantage for her was that the group she joined had begun meeting during the summer before she arrived. She had, therefore, missed the entire first cycle of the in-service on language and learning and so had not had the opportunity either to form a sense of community with her colleagues or to explore with them the theoretical constructs introduced during that first cycle.

We know from interviews with her that she was acutely aware of her role as a new teacher in a small school where most of the faculty had been working together for upwards of twenty years. We questioned her about her almost unyielding focus during her first year of participation in the workshops on the "how-to's" of writing across the curriculum, some of which we shared through her log entries earlier in the previous section of this chapter. She explained that having not been part of the summer group, a fact we had entirely forgotten because of her commitment to the project and to becoming a leader, she had not been involved in theoretical discussions and was unfamiliar with the principles that were underpinning the immersion activities in the workshops. Just as important for her was her desire to be accepted by her new community as an excellent teacher. As she defined it, that meant that she was to be in charge of her classes. She felt that just as long as her classes ran smoothly, that the curriculum was covered, she would be perceived as competent. Again, we can hear this in the log entries. So all of her questions and comments about teaching strategies and the conflicts that emerged during that first year were, we believe, a direct result of her desire not to appear radical or different in order to blend into this new educational setting.

In her own words, from a reflective piece of writing in which she described and summarized her learning as a participant in the in-service workshops, she was able to reconstrue that first year, pointing out how important to her assimilation into a new community was her participation in that community:

> The 86–87 workshop was a marvelous experience for me—coming new into the District, it was the perfect time to initiate change—changes that I have never really been able to make comprehensively before—because

of the constraints/dictates of previous teaching situations, not having a "whole" to tie it all to. The workshop gave me a chance to put it all together. It also gave me an important sense of groupness. It made me feel good being at Charmont. Looking back—it gave me a whole philosophy—that was what was really fragmented about me as a teacher before.

Perhaps it was this sense of "groupness" coupled with what Lonny calls a "whole philosophy" that enabled her to move into an advisory role. But we believe that the advisory role itself was what crystallized this philosophy into the core of her as a transformative intellectual leader. After all, this piece was written after two months of being a teacher/advisor. And it's her most straightforward statement that there were gaps in her philosophy of teaching and learning. Prior to writing this piece, she had asserted time and again that she already fully supported the idea of a democratic classroom. Only when she assumes the advisor's role does she feel free to admit that her prior teaching had been fragmented and perhaps even atheoretical. As she wrote in an earlier log entry we quoted, being a teacher/advisor/leader frees her to share her insecurities, her questions, to admit her failures, which, in turn allows her to grow and change.

Our point in this section is that by acting as a leader, she becomes a leader. From a linear perspective, a teacher would have to prove her leadership capacities before being granted the status of a leader. We are arguing, by contrast, that from a transactional perspective, the role itself is a catalyst for the actions and beliefs we associate with leadership. Lonny taught us how important role taking can be in learning:

It's interesting how role affects what you're focusing on as you learn. I'm now looking at Cindy and Nancy re: *how* they respond to what's going on as opposed to what they are saying; so even though I still want to—and intend to—focus on the substance and theory—that's *not* my prime focus. I wonder if this will change as I become more familiar with my role as advisor.(emphasis Lonny's)

If we had looked at Lonny only during her first year, we might not have been able to identify her as a leader or even to find evidence that would account for the enormous leap she made from workshop participant, to workshop advisor, to district leader. Without becoming an advisor, she might have been content to focus on classroom strategies and techniques. But the advisor role enabled her to "focus on the substance and theory" and to build a "whole philosophy." By presenting her as a leader right away, we hoped to be able to demonstrate the transactional nature of role taking, and thus of learning. By acting as if she were a leader and by playing the role of a leader, Lonny is a leader: able to tap into the strength of her convictions about teaching and learning and able to prevent her insecurities from impeding her taking risks. She's literally able to see things differently from her new vantage point. In a way, she could not help but learn from herself as a leader because the role itself presents a whole new set of challenges that must be examined in new ways. We're arguing both that we shouldn't wait for leaders to emerge in school settings and that schools should make it possible for teachers to be leaders in order to understand fully the profound impact of such a role.

Even as we say this, we want to underscore the role that Lonny's constructs of teaching and learning played in the *kind* of leader she became. In the section entitled "Leader vs. Expert" earlier in this chapter, we suggested that the stereotypical leader is someone who dispenses expert knowledge to others, rarely, if ever, questions that knowledge and expertise, and is comfortable within a hierarchical model of power and control. We've argued throughout this book that teachers' constructs of the world of teaching and learning account for how they think and act as teachers. The same holds true for a teacher who becomes a leader: her constructs will inevitably define the kind of leader she becomes.

It should be evident from our analyses of Lonny's learning that she does not take on the stereotypical leader role. Instead, her constructs that

- knowledge is a human construction that must be built by learners;
- teaching is reflective practice;
- collaboration and negotiation rather than competition and isolation underlie genuine control over learning; and
- language is a mode through which she, her colleagues, and her students can learn best

create a very different picture of teacher as leader. Lonny is a leader who is continually learning from and with others. She is a collaborator and negotiator who seeks knowledge from others in order to build cooperative interpretations and meanings. She is a colleague who is an advocate and a facilitator. She talks and writes to learn and demonstrates for her students and her colleagues how language can help us learn. So while taking on a leadership role enabled her to become a leader, her personal constructs of teaching and learning defined the kind of leader she eventually became.

It would seem that she would rather not even call herself a leader. In the piece of writing that follows, where she was asked to write about her learning in the third person, as if she were a researcher writing an article about herself, she defines herself as a teacher/researcher. Listen to what characteristics she ascribes to herself as a teacher/researcher. They appear, to us at least, to be a new way of describing a teacher/leader:

Ms. Lonny's involvement in the Charmont Writing Workshop in 1987–88 was as a writing advisor; in an attempt to encourage local ownership of the program, she and three other teachers who had previously been involved in the workshop in-service were to act as "teachers," along with consultants N. Lester and C. Onore. During the course of the year, she focused on internalizing what ownership really meant; in doing learning logs both on the course content and her struggles as writing advisor. She was constantly struggling to "make a fit" between what was being suggested in the literature and in the workshop to her own activities in the classroom and with other teachers.

Perhaps the most difficult thing for her was to achieve a reflective distance about what she was observing in her work with other teachers and especially in her own classroom. She has a tendency to personalize in the sense that she considers a failure in the classroom a very personal failure, rather than looking at it as simply information which can help her students to learn better next time. Over the course of the year, as she worked with other teachers on their own research, and with the writing advisors on observation of what had happened in writing workshops, she was able to come to see herself more as a teacher/researcher, keeping careful track of what she observed, then reflecting on that in terms of what it said about student learning and engagement.

During the current school year, she is now the only writing advisor at the high school, and she saw her responsibility as twofold: to continue to support high school teachers with their own classroom research and to attempt to set up a pilot program in her own freshman English class which would truly incorporate the concepts of student ownership that she now believed to be essential to real learning. In her work with other teachers and in her own classrooms she has struggled with the problems of the kids taking real ownership when most of their school life encourages them not to. (We need to have reflective conversations about this.) Her own writing program is successful in that many students have taken control of their writing, do generate their own topics, and are seeking out their peers to help improve their writing. But she realizes that not all students are doing so, and that, often, she feels inadequate in her new role as "writing coach"—that is, supporting kids rather than directing them. Of course, this brings her back full circle to her old feeling of "personal failure," so the question at hand at the minute about her current and future work is whether or not she will be able to take the observations she is currently making and interpret them in a way that will encourage an even higher level of student ownership, rather than revert to her old habits of "it must be my fault."

Part III

Teachers Face the Institution

Chapter Seven

Teachers Face the Institution

In the last four chapters, we saw some of the effects, as described by the teachers themselves, of institutional practices on their abilities to transform themselves as learners and teachers: how mandated curricula, standardized testing, textbooks, isolation, workload, supervision and evaluation, lack of collaboration, and lack of control over decision making figured in the ways individual teachers thought about teaching and learning. In this chapter, we want to look at both the concrete and explicit, as well as the implicit and ephemeral, constraints that teachers face.

As we've already pointed out, teachers oftentimes internalize the rules of the institution and make them their own. Teachers, especially those who have been teaching for many years, like most of the teachers we worked with, not only come to accept constraints, but many come to argue that this is the way schools are and should be. Their mental models of schooling are what we have come to recognize as the norm. At other times, teachers bump up against what they perceive to be external impositions on their practices and beliefs. We discussed in Chapter 1 the conspiracy of silence that reigns in schools and pointed to the misperception many high school English teachers have about the Regents Competency Test requirements that results from keeping certain truths unexposed and unquestioned. By continuing to hide behind or not recognize the realities through questioning and challenging received truth, teachers often perceive constraints where there are none (Diamond, 1982, 1985). Sometimes, constraints that seem insurmountable, because we're fearful of confronting them, are, in fact, far less so when we come clean and work together to attempt to get around them. In addition, tradition, whether it be in how schools are structured or in how subjects are taught, lays its heavy hand over those who struggle to get out of its grasp.

Yet when we talk about teachers facing the institution, we are, of course, talking about people facing people. Teachers, administrators, and students are victims of the institution, as well as participants in it. In this chapter, we will not, then, be talking on an abstract level about those various and sundry characteristics of schooling that both define the place Charmont teachers teach in and impede their ability to change it. Instead, we're going to show how the human beings themselves—the teachers, administrators, and students—learn, most often collaboratively, to expose and open up to scrutiny some of the institutional practices that have constrained them, and through this process, how they have found ways to transform those practices to support rather than subvert change.

Our view will be political and social in the sense that we recognize that the reality of the language-across-the-curriculum program in Charmont is the conjunction of a variety of forces and that these forces transact. Within a school district, in other words, teachers, students, school boards, administrators, parents, and the larger community respond to rules and patterns of behavior of the environment in which they work, which are all simultaneously "caused by and realized in" one another (Searle, 1984, p. 12). While we have encouraged teachers to become aware of how much latitude they actually do have in the day-to-day conduct of learning in their classrooms, and as a result, how much they can experiment, we have also learned that a teacher's view of the day-to-day conduct of learning is already conditioned by the policies and precepts of the wider school community and that teachers' experiments will inevitably leak out from behind the closed classroom door and, perhaps, affect the life of the school in the same way that the standards of the community seep into the classroom.

But institutions can sometimes be supportive. We've already described the process by which this project was created, emphasizing both the grass roots nature of its inception, as well as participation in workshops and decisions about the project by higher ups in the system. To begin this discussion, then, it's imperative that you understand the dramatic and enormous commitment that the Charmont School District made to the in-service project. First of all, the district committed a total in excess of $120,000 over the three years of the project. Most of the money went to hiring substitute teachers, who took over participants' classes while they attended full-day workshops. This commitment is further reflected in the fact that a pool of substitutes was identified at the beginning of the school year, given all of the workshop dates, and asked to make a commitment that would guarantee that students would not suffer because their teachers would be out of the classroom so frequently. Giving released time to thirteen teachers each year for approximately fifteen days was another major support for teachers and their involvement in the program. It was agreed, at the time the program was being developed, that one administrator from each school would participate in the in-service program for the entire year and that a board member/parent would also attend the full range of workshops. This commitment of people, particularly people who are in positions of power within the system, is significant, and although more subtle than money, of equal importance.

The participation of school board members was particularly significant because those who participated became vociferous advocates of the program, arguing effectively for continued financial support, in fact, arguing oftentimes to support this program over others that were being proposed. Since the board members who participated also happened to be parents of students in classes of the participants, this provided another distinct advantage that contributed to additional financial and institutional support for the changes that were occurring in the classrooms themselves. If you couple these commitments with the creation of released-time advisor positions, then this is an extraordinary level of support and commitment to pedagogical change from a small district.

Teachers Learning About Power

In reviewing the data we had collected for this chapter, we noticed substantial changes over the three years in the ways in which the teachers took charge, not only of their own learning, which we documented in the previous section, but also in the ways in which the groups of teachers took charge of the project itself. In addition to making changes in how they worked with one another within the workshop setting, they also made changes in how they worked within their schools, with their building administrations, and with the Board of Education and the superintendent. These changes did not come easily or quickly. We'll plot the evolutionary nature of teachers' growth in taking power.

We want to begin at the end of the first year during a series of summer workshops for Team A. Team B is also meeting, participating in the first cycle of the in-service project on language and learning. Team A is continuing its work on language across the curriculum and also trying to plan their roles during the coming year. Here's a transcript of a discussion Team A teachers were having about continuing their own learning by bringing in relevant speakers during district-sponsored staff-development days.

Ms. GUSHIN: One of the things I thought of was for the superintendent's day conference that for those people who were interested in the writing that perhaps the District Planning Council could suggest a specific speaker for that day. Because I think that one of the things this article spoke about was having really dynamic speakers who sort of keep you, you know, inspire you periodically. They had James Britton who worked in the district, three days in each school. And I thought to myself that maybe one of our responsibilities could be as a group to try to think of someone who you think would be a good speaker. Even if it wasn't for the entire faculty, but those people which now would be 26 of us who are involved in this to hear somebody who is notable in this particular field to speak at one of those superintendent's day conferences. You know, and push that.

Ms. ONORE: Why don't you work on that?

Ms. GUSHIN: Well, I don't, I mean . . .

Ms. MARKS: It's done already.

Ms. ONORE: Is it done?

Ms. RENDA: Yes. What's her name is coming.

MR. WINBERRY: Madeline Hunter.

[*Short discussion of what she does, comparing her to Harry Wong and others who have previously spoken in the District.*]

Ms. RENDA: She's an inspirational person who can give you 95 different recipes for making your teaching more exciting. I thought that the most interesting thing about what they'd said about Britton's visit to the school was that Britton's conclusion was that if a teacher can't do it in the classroom it can't be done. He felt that his own presence in the school was only of value to the degree that a teacher found some things that she could use in her classroom. Which reinforces my high opinion of Britton. I suspect probably that people like Madeline Hunter and Harry Wong are somewhat less humble in their view of their impact on a school system.

I also, I must say I'm very disturbed by the emphasis that our district is placing on bringing in these outsiders. Everything we've read has said that it has to begin with students, where the student is, what the student wants to know, with how the student learns. And what do we do? We keep bringing in outsiders who don't even know that.

Ms. GUSHIN: But I'm speaking about an outside speaker for an occasion that would leave you with a feeling that what you're doing is good and is worthwhile. It's very nice to get the approval of our peers. I mean, when people say, "hey that looks really great." It might be nice to just be able . . .

Ms. RENDA: Maybe instead of having a speaker maybe what we want to do is bring in a consultant and kind of have a . . .

Ms. GUSHIN: Roundtable.

Ms. RENDA: Roundtable. And have the consultant say, "Oh my god, what you're doing is beautiful." Sure it would be great to hear that.

MR. PFEIFFER: The point is that the interest from this came from the Board, for the most part. You still have our so-called leaders . . .

MS. RENDA: But we own it now.

MR. PFEIFFER: I know but again the leadership here is saying: "I am impressed by the work you people are doing" but they really don't have that much knowledge of what we're doing until we come out with stuff. And that's the scary part of it. The fact that they, themselves, don't know what's going on. The fact that they, themselves, have not shown leadership. The leadership has come pretty much from one or two board members which has been filtered down through Mr. Fallon [the high school principal], and fortunately, they have brought in the project. But, what happens beyond the third year, to have support groups, to have this continue on and on and on? And that has to come from us. It has to come from the continued dedication. What happens to the third group who comes in and then Cindy and Nancy leave? Are they going to come back that fourth year to help them, like they're helping us with our second year. Or now they can say, "Well, listen, you now have the support group." Well, we have the support group, but do we have the hierarchy support? And this is what you're bringing up: the fact that they're bringing in Madeline Hunter, they're bringing in Harry Wong.

MS. RENDA: The money's there for that.

MR. PFEIFFER: Well, again, you have to understand the fact that they think they're doing the right thing, because this is what the teaching staff had originally pushed for. OK. Now the push by a select group of people is certainly in another area and, I'm sure, that we could get who we wanted.

MS. KRAMERMAN: I think we have the support if we show that we will follow through.

MR. PFEIFFER: That's it.

MS. KRAMERMAN: I think the whole thing will die if after three years everybody sort of goes their own little way and there's no . . .

MR. PFEIFFER: Because there's no leadership up there on which to base . . .

MS. KRAMERMAN: We have to have our own leadership.

MR. PFEIFFER: That's it. It has to be developed because we're not going to get it. Where is our resource after these people leave because this is not a three year program. It's a much longer program. It's a five, ten, or . . .

MS. RENDA: It seems to me that I have never experienced a group, this school has never allowed me to experience a group, where I did feel that we owned it. And I think that if we hold on to that, if we continue to say, look, this is what we need, get it for us. This is what we want, do it for us. Then, we are going to create a momentum and when we say in the fourth year, look you've got to bring Cindy and Nancy back at least three times. They'll say, right, what days would you like them? I think we got 'em trained.

MS. KRAMERMAN: I think we'll get that. I really do. I think they've been very supportive. And I think we'll get it. But we'll have to do it.

MR. MATTHEWS: It would be the same as a group of students in your class who come as a group and say, "look, we don't like this," and we'd listen. That would be wonderful.

MR. PFEIFFER: This is the first time this district has ever put together across the grade levels a group of teachers other than a confrontation of what are you people doing in there, what are you people doing up there. Well, it's always been a head to head thing of: over here sits the middle school, over here sits the high school, etc.

This sounds like a group ready to spring into action, a group ready to take responsibility for demanding that their needs get met. They seemed to be suggesting that if the district wants to bring professionals in to talk with the faculty, that those people should be people who have something compatible to say about what the faculty is working on and interested in. Here they are, later that day, discussing a perennial problem: the quick abandonment of district support for any project when a new educational fad comes along. This launches them into a discussion about what to call the newsletter they're about to send out to the entire district faculty about what they have been doing. They come across as particularly savvy about how to interest their colleagues in their work and how to prevent the district from abandoning their program and substituting something else.

MS. GUSHIN: One of the things we have to sort of try to get going also is that the district does not change their priorities in the next several years by suddenly saying to us two years down the road, "this is the year we're going to redo *math*." OK, and that's what happens here. (Emphasis Gushin's)

MS. RENDA: We have to be an advocacy group. We gotta go and say absolutely not.

MS. GUSHIN: Someone else will do that.

MR. WINBERRY: The only trouble with somebody else doing that is . . .

MS. RENDA: We want the money.

MR. WINBERRY: Well, that too, but we want to spread this program into math.

MS. KRAMERMAN: The point is that we want to spread this to the teachers who are at this point not interested and refusing to be interested.

MS. ROSS: I don't think you can do that.

MS. KRAMERMAN: I know you can't. But . . .

MR. MATTHEWS: Or you can invite those teachers to the forum.

MS. ONORE: What I think you're suggesting is that one of the arguments you're going to have to continue to make, it's not once and it will be over, is that it's not necessary for the district to spend money to re-vamp the math program, to teach critical thinking skills, all the kinds of things . . .

MS. RENDA: Writing across the curriculum does all of it.

MS. SHAPIRO: After reading that article which really supports very strongly my feelings about this workshop, and language in general, I think that's where we have to focus our attention. That is, that this is not a writing program. It's a language program. And as such, we are working to get children more involved, to be able to communicate and reach children in every single subject matter. It is not writing. It is communication. It's speaking, it's writing, it's whatever the students can do in order to communicate. And I really felt that, after reading the article, that we have a big obligation to educate this community continually, the administration and our own faculty, that we are work-ing not just in writing and writing isn't limited to one area. We are working on developing language. Children need to communicate. It's learning in every single subject. It's not just writing.

MS. LEWIS: I have a question. Since we're setting the newsletter and it's going to be printed up 600 copies, I'm supposed to be pressing on letters for a masthead for a title for this newsletter. I felt all along reluctant to use the word, "write" or "writing" on it. Now what would you like me to call this thing?

MR. PFEIFFER: Language and Learning. Writing Project: A Language and Learning Experience or something along that line.

MS. RENDA: How about "Language for Learning?" "Equals" a balanced construction.

MS. LEWIS: I thought Language for was kind of nice.

MR. WINBERRY: That sounds good.

MR. PFEIFFER: I like that too.

MS. RENDA: We're trying to show that there's a link.

MR. PFEIFFER: That's the reason for the reluctance of people in the middle and high school to get in, because they don't . . . they see it as writing. But it's language and learning, and it's a question of WHY to get in. In terms of the writing process, this math teacher who won't volunteer for the program says, "I don't teach that much writing." (Emphasis Pfeiffer's)

We would have expected that a group as committed to and insightful about language across the curriculum as Team A appears would be excited by the prospect of acting as helpmates to their peers. Listen to them discuss the proposal for setting up a buddy system with Team B teachers who were just beginning the program.

> Ms. RENDA: The scaffolding that we can offer is we know how quickly time evaporates and flows by. We know how scary it is to try something new. If we know that, if we felt that and lived that, then we know that these new people in the group are going to need support for change. They're going to need structure. In some ways, it's like classes need deadlines for their papers or they'll wait until next June to turn them in.

> Ms. LEWIS: I have another point. And I think it's unfortunate. I feel a little as if my buddy shouldn't have to be stuck with me as a resource person. In other words, if there are people that are really getting into these things and really have expertise and all I'm doing is, like, my first round of learning logs, I think, maybe, that it would be nice if we're going into the new year with some curriculum plans already in our minds, things we're going to try, I think there should be a resource list which each of the new people could see. Then they may not want to do a visitation. My buddy may not want to visit my room, my buddy may visit somebody's else's room.

> MR. MATTHEWS: Is there a consensus?

> Ms. RENDA: I would be willing to make the commitment at this time that I will definitely schedule regular meetings with my buddy.

> Ms. ONORE: Let's call it regular contact.

> MR. PFEIFFER: Yeah, I like that term better.

> Ms. KRAMERMAN: I don't see a problem with that really. I'm working next door to my buddy.

> Ms. O'BRIAN: What I would do because I always, rather than lay it on, because we're peers, I would say, "Would you like to have a meeting time?" or because I see her at lunch, "Do you want to set aside a special time or shall we try it just talking?" But from the things that people have said I made a sort of list of questions that you can use or not use, but
>
> > How are the workshops going?
> > How do you like the readings?
> > What interests you?
> > What have you decided to do for research?
> > Would you like to observe someone who's done X?

> Ms. ONORE: So we can tell Team B we will be contacting them on a regular basis. Just to check in with them and see how things are going. Let them know that we're available to help.

> Ms. SHAPIRO: Why does it take us this long to get to that statement? I thought that that was an assumption.

Ms. RENDA: Anita said that she didn't feel that we should have to be setting up formal meetings and there was quite a bit of support for that.

Ms. SHAPIRO: We're still not having formal meetings. There are many people that are still saying go informal. So, there's really no difference.

Ms. RENDA: What's the difference in meaning? I'm totally confused. What is the difference in meaning between formal meetings and informal ones? That doesn't strike me as ripping anybody's heart out.

Ms. ROSS: I think one of the problems may be that it sounds like a bigger deal than it is. Maybe they feel that—I'm now going to talk from my own personal viewpoint—when I think of this I don't think of it as necessarily going in there with a lot of information and being the great white savior here. But just sort of a kind of informal chat: "How's it going?" That's it. And if there's anything I can do, terrific. If there isn't, then maybe I can help them figure out where they can go for it. That's all I see it as.

Ms. GUSHIN: I never felt any point last year, whatsoever, a need to discuss the readings at all with anybody. I didn't, I mean, I think Toby and I spent a lot of time talking about the writing because we were near each other and she was . . .

Ms. RENDA: Then so you did have it.

Ms. GUSHIN: But it was, it would have happened regardless of this program.

Ms. ROSS: No. Because I didn't do it.

Ms. GUSHIN: But I'm just reflecting on Sally's statement. I think because of the nature of our staff and ourselves and what we do, we do in fact, spend so much time with each other, that we would have done it anyway.

From this discussion, you can understand why, even though the group spent forty-five minutes arguing this through and deciding somewhat reluctantly to institute a buddy system, it never actually worked. In the first two excerpts we have quoted, the teachers seemed able to challenge the potential undermining by the administration of their intentions. This last discussion leads us to believe that it was easier for this group of teachers to rebel against the administration than it was for them to collaborate with their colleagues. Possibly the teachers in this group feared that their colleagues would view them as "bosses," as just another arm of the administration. It's also possible that these teachers hadn't yet seen themselves as collaborative members of the larger school community since collaboration had not been a common practice in the district.

In fact, one of the pervasive myths about teachers is that they are "rugged individualists" (see Britzman, 1986, for a discussion of the "myths" connected to the roles teachers take on) who must develop their expertise alone and keep to themselves. To do otherwise would show weakness or haughtiness. The high value placed on individualism explains why "teachers' definitions of autonomy and control are frequently of a narrow scope and do not encompass a role in determining educational content and purpose" (Densmore, 1987, p. 155). The value of separation of teachers from one another that the culture of school holds becomes so much a part of teachers' work life that it becomes very difficult to imagine or to value a system that grows and functions precisely because people work together. This is one of the implicit controls and barriers placed in the way of teachers attaining true professionalism, and, thus, of changing themselves or the institution.

Even though the teachers had not yet learned how to collaborate with one another, how to support one another in their struggles, they did learn how to take control in a number of situations with the administration in the district. One of these was a direct result of the discussion we quoted earlier about bringing in guest speakers. About six months after that discussion, the group met again and here is one of the teachers talking about her learning and seeing a contradiction between what she learned and what the district was seeming to support through its choice of outside speakers:

> I think I'm getting a little bit better at allowing students more freedom and not having to be in such a high efficiency mode. I think over the years that I considered high efficiency, productivity, and such. This year the class that Leslie and I shared, the lower English class, they come to an elective at the end of the day, and I find it's extremely refreshing. It's the exact class that I've given the most freedom to, I probably look forward to the most and I don't attempt, maybe I don't even have energy, to impose all these efficient structures. And I have found that the results, the products, are really fantastic. Very exciting. And I think it's given me more ammunition to kind of loosen up a bit.
>
> But the thing is that I have a question, I have two questions, one little question and one big one. I think the Harry Wong, Madeline Hunter thing, from what I have noticed going to the workshop on Saturday, but I think the things I have been doing with the efficiency and use of time— the way to handle and get more papers and get papers corrected, and conceiving having introductory discussions and then activities you do as you go out the door—there is a movement in the school district to involve people more in that method. I'm not so sure that that isn't exactly counter to what, partly counter, to what we're talking about here.

It was this teacher who drafted a letter that was signed by all twenty-six participants in the workshops requesting that the District Planning Council— a group of administrators and teachers charged with planning districtwide professional development activities—consider the messages it was sending by its choice of speakers. The letter contained a brief description of the philosophy of the language-across-the-curriculum project and compared this to the philosophy being presented by the outside speakers. The teachers wanted to go public with their complaints and offer their assistance to the District Planning Council with choosing speakers in the future. As a result of their letter, their commitment to the program, and their new sense of power, neither of the speakers mentioned has been asked to present in this district again.

Collaborating for Control

Recognizing that there might be ways for the workshop experience to contribute to a fuller sense of community and sense of power for teachers, we began to reconceptualize some of what we were doing in the workshops themselves. Our goal in rethinking what we were doing was to heighten the sense of community teachers would have within the workshop and develop contexts which would tap teachers' intentions to support and be supported by their colleagues. We wanted to create a safe place where teachers could take on new roles of leadership. Having the advisors act as workshop leaders was an important experiment for those who became advisors as well as for their colleagues. We hoped that the advisors could be models of leaders who are colearners, rather than leaders who are authoritarian experts. We wanted to encourage people to reconceptualize leadership, so it would no longer appear to them, as it did with the buddy system, that teachers who are leaders are not trustworthy because they are not peers. We also wanted to make it apparent how limiting and disempowering isolation and individualism truly are. We believed that teachers could come to see collaboration as a natural way of operating, rather than necessary because a teacher is deficient, unsuccessful, and in need of remedial help. Finally, for us, new views of leadership and collaboration are essential because collective resistance to the domination of the school culture is the most successful route to change.

The next excerpt is a transcript of a workshop session in the third year of the project led by Ms. Renda. She and her fellow advisors decided to run a negotiating session for the second cycle on fluency. We will enter this conversation at the point where she is attempting to summarize what the group has generated about what they already know about fluency. She says, "At this point, I think we've agreed on the following assumptions." One of the assumptions she offers by way of summary is that "Learning, like writing, begins with fluency." And the conversation continues:

> MS. KOSLOWSKI: I'm sorry but I don't accept the first statement. I need to keep backing up. I don't think we agreed that "Learning, like writing, begins with fluency." We didn't talk about that. What we

said was "What do we think fluency means?" not whether or not we accepted that statement that you have to have it to start with.

[*Ms. Renda decides to move to the questions the teachers have about fluency before continuing to discuss what they know about fluency.*]

Ms. LEVIN: How can we help kids be comfortable with it?

Ms. SCHERFF: Why do the writers of the book [Mayher, Lester, & Pradl, 1983] think it has to come first? Why do they think you have to write even if you have nothing to say? I mean this notion that you have to say, "I'm stuck, I'm stuck, I'm stuck," isn't it irritating to go back to a lot of garbage that is unorganized? Isn't that as irritating as it is helpful?

Ms. RENDA: Could you rephrase that? Make it a more open-ended research question?

Ms. SCHERFF: Is generating a great deal of material of greater value than generating less that is more accessible and more organized?

Ms. RENDA: That's a statement not a question. What do we really want to know about this?

Ms. SCHERFF: I want to know, does it really help to write and write and write?

MR. KARISH: Quantity vs. quality. Is there a value to it?

Ms. SCHERFF: Are you ever expected to go back and read it again?

Ms. LESTER: Are you expected? No. Might you find it valuable?

Ms. SCHERFF: Might you ever find it valuable to go back to it?

Ms. RENDA: Is its value in the process of doing it or is its value discovered at some later stage?

Ms. SCHERFF: That's very good.

Ms. RENDA: Are there any other questions anyone would like to address?

Ms. TRINITY: How would you handle a student who isn't fluent?

Ms. SCHERFF: Just tell 'em to write. "I'm stuck, I'm stuck, I'm stuck."

Ms. HART: Why does Berlitz advertise that, "You'll be fluent after six lessons"? What's that definition of fluency? How is that definition distinguished from what we're saying? Could we have that as a first thing?

Ms. SCHERFF: How does the ordinary variety of fluency compare with this one? I think that's important 'cause otherwise we'll talk in circles.

Ms. KOSLOWSKI: Yeah, is it really the thing that we start with 'cause I don't care about encouraging it if we don't really need it.

Ms. SEALY: And I find they [Mayher, Lester, & Pradl, 1983] don't tell you what it is. [*She reads a passage to the group from the book.*] I know what the goal is, but I still don't know what it is.

This conversation had great value to all the teachers in helping them learn about fluency and in demonstrating how language itself is a mode of negotiating meaning. In addition, of course, they are reevaluating the role of a teacher within a democratic classroom in which knowledge is built collaboratively. We want to focus, however, on how this small exchange acts as an immersion activity in which teachers can try out collaboration and test new forms of leadership. The first teacher to speak presented a challenge to the direction Renda believed she was setting for the conversation. Renda recognized that there was not a consensus about the definition or value of fluency, and rather than sticking to her agenda, she switched from her interpretation of the assumptions agreed upon to questions that still needed clarification. By encouraging questions, Renda is acknowledging that she cannot, as a leader, make assumptions about others' interpretations or understandings and that her job is to become "a student of your students' needs" (McLaren, 1988). In other words, she needs to discover what her colleagues' assumptions are, which she does through eliciting their questions, before she can know how to help them.

The other teachers in the conversation are learning, first of all, that they do not have to passively receive others' interpretations. Once Renda's assumptions are challenged, and once she responds to that challenge by participating in it, rather than resisting it, other members of the group feel supported in their own meaning-making processes. This leads to the other thing we believe this group learned. That is, that meaning making can be enhanced and enriched through collaborative learning. There's no sense of competition either between the teachers or between them and Renda. In fact, the conversation grows more animated and productive as the teachers use each other's questions and comments to build collective meanings.

In mapping the change in teachers' perceptions of what power is and how they might wield it, we want to look at one more transcript that builds on the understandings about leadership and collaboration that we saw developing in the preceding negotiation section. Here, the same group of teachers, about six months later, is discussing the district language policy that was part of the writing all the participants from the beginning of the in-service were involved in. (See the Appendix for the complete document.)

> Ms. KOSLOWSKI: I think the district should decide to support the language policy, in a very specific and formal way. That would be my personal preference.
>
> Ms. HART: I agree.
>
> Ms. KOSLOWSKI: That's what we decided at that after school meeting.
>
> Ms. HART: Maybe that's not what everybody here thinks.
>
> Ms. KOSLOWSKI: I don't know what the feeling is. That's why next week when the administrators come, I'd really like to know from Mr. Simmons [superintendent] and the other administrators what they think about this. You know, is it just going to be a nice little summary

of what we got out of the writing workshops or is it going to have some teeth in it?

Ms. TRINITY: I think the people who have never been in the writing workshop, some of them would say that, "Well, I don't want the Board to accept this because maybe I don't agree with this." I understand exactly what you're saying, but I know some people on staff who would say, "Well, I don't want that to be policy."

Ms. HART: I think it should start some place. And then it should be called "proposed language philosophy of the Charmont Schools K–12" and then submit it to the three buildings. The whole school staff take it and they accept it or they reject and then you know where you're at.

Ms. MARKS: It says in the policy in the first few sentences that it's a living document, so these teachers who are not participants in the workshops, they can respond to it. If there's something that they disagree with, and I guess when we get together in ABC meetings and listen to these responses, we can make whatever changes that we all agree to. They certainly should be invited to the ABC meetings.

Ms. TRINITY: But if they haven't experienced what we're really talking about in here, will they understand it?

Ms. HART: But if it's carefully written, they will not have a bone to pick. They can either accept it or reject it.

Ms. MARKS: The teachers who have not been part of our workshop, when they look at this they're going to reject it or they're not going to understand it or whatever. You know it's the same thing as when they get a teacher's guide or curriculum guide. Not everyone accepts and believes in everything that's in the guide. They adapt it. What about our own professional growth. If teachers who are not part of the workshops can't be expected to, then we can't expect to be hand fed, all of us as professionals. We have to take some initiative and some responsibility for ourselves. We want it from the kids.

Ms. KOSLOWSKI: But if you really want this to happen, if you don't want to just say this is what I think, if you want this to actually *happen* in the classroom, then there has to be a commitment to say, regardless of whether you were in the writing workshop or you weren't in the writing workshop, the district has committed itself and believes that this is what we want to have happen in your classrooms. And you are not conducting your own school system. You are part of the Charmont district and the Charmont district would like its teachers to do this. Therefore, we want you doing this. [Emphasis Koslowski's]

Ms. HART: I know, but, in other words, you'd start with the base of the position paper, you'd expand it to the faculty, they say Yes, No, Maybe, Change, Go Back, Out, In, Present.

Ms. KOSLOWSKI: At which point you police. I think the word *policy* comes from the idea that you can police it. You can evaluate it, you can, I hate the word *force* when it's used as violent force, but I do think enforcing something is very important if you want it to happen. If you don't care what happens, then you can adopt 97,000 policies and nothing will ever change. Nothing will ever change, unless you enforce it. The same exact thing in my classroom when I want everybody to turn in their homework today, but if you don't turn in your homework it's OK.

Ms. TRINITY: You're thinking about presenting this to everybody and getting their reactions to it?

Ms. HART: In other words, you present a position paper and it's adapted, changed, fooled around with and then it comes back.

Ms. TRINITY: And made acceptable to everyone. I think it could take a long time and there could be a lot of argument, but I think it would be very wise.

Ms. HART: Because if somebody says, "What's fluency?" there are people on every staff who can stand up and say what fluency is I would hope. If there isn't it should be cut. If they can't define it, it should be cut. Then you get the thing and you come to an agreement. And then you take ownership. I think that's the only way you take ownership. I don't think you have to come to the district and this will be your language policy and you will follow it. I don't think it works that way.

Ms. SCHERFF: Once we do it, who would you give it to?

Ms. KOSLOWSKI: I just wonder how long it's going to have to be struggled about before we can get some consequences from it. Maybe one of the superintendent's days or workshop days that we have we could get to revise it. The district-wide faculty broken up into groups, some elementary, some middle and some high school and in each group we would have representatives from the writing workshop, previous writing workshop people in there, and whatever it is we come up with as a final product from our group, and say let's look at this, what's wrong with it, what could you not possibly accept and why, and people that feel comfortable in supporting this could be with those who think that there's some terrible work or something.

Ms. JAEGER: If you call this a policy, and you say that you're going to be using this to evaluate them, I'm wondering, because all I hear is union, union, I'm wondering if those people who have not been to the workshops, who have not had the opportunity to do this, are going to have the right to say, you can't evaluate me on something that I've only read on a piece of paper, and then if he's going to get a negative one, because number one, either he's incapable or unwanting to do it, and he's going to get evaluated by it, and obviously if he's not doing it, he's not going to get a good evaluation, I'm wondering if this is besides this group that that person is going to say, "Yes, I vote for this to be accepted," if you're saying it has to be accepted by each school, he might just say, "I'm not going to accept this policy because I'm going to be evaluated on it."

Ms. HART: They'll hire us that way. When you hire, you hire and say, "Here's the policy, can you live with it?" Maybe you have a grandfather clause for everybody else, but when you hire new people [you say,] "That's the policy, can you live with it?" That's what we want. We got a lot of people here that are about ready to go to the great beyond and they're going to be gone soon. The high school is going to be really wiped out. But when you hire, you present documents and you ask them about them. I think that's part of the role of the administrator. And if you can't cut it, you're gone. I think that's the way you do business.

Ms. JAEGER: I also have to tell you that what you need is to coordinate between sixth grade and twelfth grade. What's happening in six, seven, eight is, what is happening in four, five is going to be followed in six, seven, and eight. If a child has reached a certain point in something in science or in social studies and then it is not taken up in the high school or the middle school, what I think I look at personally is that, first of all, they have to get it so that it flows through.

Ms. MARKS: What you're saying really concerns me. It worries me when you say that this is an evaluative tool. I never wrote or helped write this policy [in such a way that] in my mind if it was to be used as an evaluative tool. It never entered my head. It was just to show the connections between language and learning and the way, the steps of this process.

Ms. KOSLOWSKI: For some people the word evaluation gives you the impression that it's a negative thing. To me it's not. But if I were a principal or whoever would be responsible for looking at what teachers were doing and I was committed to this, I would go in with the idea that am I seeing this at all in that classroom? And if I'm not, is there any way that I might encourage that person to try to look at this and see if there's a way that they could use some of it. Not to say, you don't use it, you got an F. To me that's not evaluation. Evaluation is attempting to improve and change and make better what it is you're looking at, if it needs to be made better or fitting in with your framework of education. So I don't see evaluation as a negative thing. That's a problem maybe we have to look at.

Ms. HART: My whole idea of any kind of administrative observation, if I were the administrator, it would be to help improve what is happening or for me to understand what was happening in a learning context, for both of us. And maybe we could get some good ideas going and whatever, and then my end of the year evaluation would be summing up what I learned and what I saw and what I didn't see.

Ms. JAEGER: But everyone should be given the opportunity to look at this and to consider, at least, as mature adults, teachers, who have the responsibility of our children, look at it and possibly be able to do something. But I don't want to give it to a teacher who is going to look at it and say, I'm too busy.

Ms. SCHERFF: I think there's an interesting sentence at the end. "This document continues to grow and change as we learn." Somehow that's written into the recommendations. It's going to sit there unless someone gets together to continue to grow and change and learn and write it up differently.

For us, this discussion is a far cry from the one with which we began this chapter. While this group, Team C, is also in their first year in the project, the project itself was in its third year. They are a very different kind of first-year group from the teachers in Team A who discussed the buddy system. We think there are clear reasons for this difference. In the first place, these ideas had been around for three years. Not only had teachers been talking about them informally, but their classrooms had become living demonstrations of them, so that the faculties in the three schools were influenced by their colleagues' work, both directly and indirectly. Students moving from grade level to grade level were beginning to bring with them expectations for teaching and learning derived from the participants' classrooms. And, as we mentioned, we had been rethinking how to conduct the workshops themselves, and we believe this contributed to teachers' understandings of leadership, collaboration, and power.

Out of the crucible of their experiences in the workshop, of which the negotiating transcript (the third one) is representative, new understandings of collaboration, leadership, power, and the implications of all of these for life in this school district have become part of the teachers' working knowledge. No longer are they afraid to act as resources for their colleagues. No longer are they afraid to act as leaders with their colleagues. They are demonstrating their understanding of how to share what they know, the processes of sharing what they know, and the consequences of committing themselves and all of the members of the workshops to a clear position on the connections between language and learning.

Their discussion begins with how to share the language policy with their colleagues, but quickly shifts to exploring far-reaching implications. They worry about how their colleagues who have not participated thus far in the workshops will be affected by the language policy, should it, in fact, become policy. And they're also concerned over what response the union would or might have were the policy to become district-sanctioned. The obvious tension in the group between treating the document as a philosophy or a policy generates a lot of discussion about how change might be possible. They demonstrate their understanding of the importance of ownership over ideas in order for change to occur. They recognize that students need to be in a school district that has an integrated philosophy in order for learning to be supported. They also see the value that having a real philosophy or mission would have when making hiring decisions. In fact, a new high school principal was hired at the end of that year, and the faculty committee who interviewed her asked her to respond to the language policy. Her positive and supportive response to it was pivotal in the decision to put her at the top of their list.

The discussion of the consequences for supervision and evaluation is emblematic of a new way that these teachers think about teaching and the resulting role of supervision. Not only would they like building administrators to be able to comprehend language and learning well enough to view all classrooms with understanding, but they are also suggesting that evaluation need not be limited to a simplistic assessment. They're coming to see evaluation as having the potential to support continued growth by teachers. The idea that administrators and teachers can work together to "improve and change and make better what it is [they're] looking at," is a truly radical proposal. Although there's not complete agreement on these issues and some fear is expressed as well, at least they're considering the implications of adopting a language policy, and finding ways to set up a genuine collaborative environment, not just between peers, but amongst all parties in the educational community. Understanding that there's power in having a collective mission is the great lesson that we have learned from their explorations. We know that they have learned it too because they have submitted the language policy to the school board and continue to have exploratory discussions in building meetings, keeping the document alive.

Administrators Learning How to Change Their Roles and Share Power

As we said before, each building administrator participated as a workshop member in each year of the in-service program. In this section, we'll look at all three building principals, as well as the superintendent, as they worked and learned along with the teacher/participants. We'll be sharing a set of illustrative anecdotes. It's not our intention to describe all of the changes on the administration and on school structure that occurred during the project, nor do we think it would be possible for us to be comprehensive in our description anyway. After all, we've been outside visitors, and so our vision of what occurred is limited to stories like the ones we'll tell.

Mr. Simmons: The Superintendent as Managerial Facilitator

We'll begin with Mr. Simmons, the Superintendent of Charmont School District for the past eight years. The size of Charmont School District makes the contributions of the superintendent both more important and more obvious. Simmons' office is at one end of the Charmont Elementary School, and it is there that board meetings are held. This also makes access to the superintendent quite direct. For example, teachers do not have to march through a series of steps in the hierarchy in order to make contact with him.

In many ways, Simmons plays a typical superintendent's role. He is the employee of a Board of Education to whom he must answer on every issue. Neither of us has yet met a superintendent who was either interested in initiating or playing an integral or collaborative role in educational reform and innovation. Like his professional colleagues, Simmons views himself as an administrator, not an educator. Although like other superintendents, Simmons could redefine his role, he chooses the route of pleasing the Board of Education even if this means he must be at odds with his faculty. In many ways, then, this superintendent is caught between appearances of ultimate power by those below him in the system and the realities of somewhat limited power when viewed from the perspective of the Board of Education. In these ways, Simmons is not very different from other superintendents we have worked with or read about.

Simmons *is* different from the superintendents who preceded him in this district because he is representative of the predominant political climate of the Reagan years. Until recent times, Charmont was a hotbed of liberalism and this was reflected in educational policy. There was an open-classroom policy at the elementary school, the middle school continues to have a team-teaching structure, and the high school has existed without department chairpersons, thus giving say to all members of the department. But times have changed. As the community has grown and as exclusively single-family dwellings have been replaced by multiple dwellings as well as less expensive condominiums, the population has changed to reflect a much younger and more conservative attitude. Simmons was chosen as superintendent precisely because he presented himself as a hard-line fiscal conservative, one who could stand firm with union demands as well as centralize power and authority in administration, not in the faculty. It was at this time, as well, that the back-to-basics movement was gaining momentum, and the open classrooms at the elementary school disappeared.

As we describe Simmons' contributions to the success of the language-across-the-curriculum project and to some of the changes in institutional practices that resulted, it's important to keep in mind that he was not making risky decisions. As a consummate politician, Simmons is able to read the preferences and priorities of his Board of Education, the parents in the community, and his administrative colleagues in the surrounding communities. We're fortunate that a lot of the messages he was receiving happened to support what was going on, but we must say that of the many conversations we had with him over the three years we worked in Charmont, we can remember only one that focused on the theoretical practices of language across the curriculum. We raise the question, then, of whether or not Simmons understood or believed in any of the major premises of this project.

To get a flavor of the kind of support and assistance that Simmons did provide, we'll share a contribution he made at a workshop during which the teachers were discussing how they might meet outside of the workshop sessions. The teachers wanted to continue their collaborative learning and sharing. They wondered if these ABC meetings as the teachers came to call them, could be held during district-mandated after-school meeting times, but were unsure about getting approval. Would ABC meetings be considered a legitimate curricular area? Simmons suggested the following:

> The union has one Wednesday a month, I think it's the first Wednesday. But we can't schedule anything on these days. If the teachers at all three schools wanted to meet the third Wednesday of each month or the second Wednesday of each month as part of their obligation here, I'm not sure whether there would be time to do it the third Wednesday every single month, because if we end up doing that, then there's no time at all left for the principal to have his meeting with other curriculum groups. But there, I think, out of the twenty Wednesdays or the twenty curriculum days, I think there was an agreement that half of them could be on days other than Wednesdays. Half of them could be on union days. Five could be on union days; five could be on days other than Wednesdays, as long as you had a certain amount of notice. So, if you want to work out a situation where you get together as a group, come up with some dates, take advantage of some of the non-Wednesdays and some of the Wednesdays, a combination of the two, I'm sure that could be worked out in terms of the three schools. I wouldn't use every Wednesday, but maybe half of the Wednesdays and half of the other days.

Simmons came in with this contribution at a time in the conversation when the teachers were feeling pessimistic about the possibility of having regular meetings. He solved their problem by coming up with a solution that would satisfy him, them, the building principals, and the union contract. This is consistent with the attitude he played with most of the requests made by the teachers and us.

He never turned down our requests for money or meeting time. He even went along with the radical proposal for teacher/advisors, which he then adopted as a model for curriculum coordinators. He always ensured that the building principals would attend the workshops and that they would play an important part in recruiting teachers for the project. Another question we might raise about Simmons's involvement, then, is whether he was intentionally handing over educational leadership responsibility to his building principals, considering this the appropriate site for educational innovation and reform. He helped us choose Board member participants by suggesting who might be supportive of in-service professional development. Although he only stayed for about an hour each time he came, Simmons did attend workshops regularly and seemed to recognize that his presence at a workshop would send the message that this was a project he believed in. He never interfered with curriculum innovations or textbook adoptions, even if these selections were progressive. He always made sure that the project was featured at Board of Education meetings at the end of the year. Here teachers and their students were able to show what they had learned.

We would characterize Simmons's support as safe. None of his support required him to take a controversial stand with the Board, the union, parents, or the teachers. None of our requests explicitly asked him to rock the boat or suggested formal sharing of power with the teachers. None of them even required that he agree with or believe in the project's philosophy. But one of the things we learned and that the teachers learned, too, was that even the safest decisions can hide the potential for substantial changes in the power structure. Simmons's solution to what appeared as an innocuous problem has become the richest source of teacher empowerment to ever exist in Charmont. Despite continued conflicts in scheduling after-school meetings, the ABC meetings have become an institutional practice, one that is owned and run by the teachers. The possibilities for change that these meetings represent continue to be explored. We can only tell you about the kinds of changes the group has advocated and implemented thus far, but we have no idea what other possibilities for change might be generated.

For two years, the ABC meetings have been held once a month. Between twenty-five and thirty teachers attend regularly. Not only are these meetings a time for teachers to share what they're doing in their classrooms and to help each other continue to conduct research on teaching and learning, but they have become forums for planning for change. Where to go with the language policy has been a frequent topic of discussion. They also discuss districtwide professional development activities.

It was at a meeting during the third year of the in-service project that the teachers collaborated on writing the letter to Simmons and the Board of Education in which they outlined a series of requests for continuing the project. One of these recommended that "a teacher from the elementary school and the high school be released from all or part of their classroom responsibilities" to institutionalize the teacher/advisor role. This request was met after some initial resistance, and Lonny took the high school position. The ABC Teams asked to be able to "retain our expert consultants to visit on an occasional basis with the teacher/advisors in order to help them stay current with research and developments in the field of language and learning." As a result, we continued to work in the district with both the advisors and the participating teachers. Another request concerned educating new teachers to the district. Instead of asking for more district-sponsored workshops, the teachers suggested that Charmont take advantage of its relationship to the local teacher center and request them to offer a course "for credit that is based on the principles and readings that provided the backbone of the writing workshops." This, too, has been arranged.

Not all the requests were met, but the fact that these teachers have learned what institutional support will help them carry on their work and that they can ask or even know how to ask for what they need, speaks very persuasively of the enormous changes they have collectively experienced through exerting their power. The irony, of course, is that Simmons's safe decision turned out to be a bombshell. We don't know whether he knew that he was helping them to share power, to make decisions over their professional lives, to not so subtly challenge the school culture. We can raise some further questions, however. If Simmons had been an educational innovator, and if he had a philosophy that opposed the theoretical practices of language across the curriculum, would he have been a constraint we and the teachers could not have gotten around? In general, should a superintendent be an educational leader or is change better supported if, like Simmons, superintendents are managers who facilitate the use of time and money to support teacher transformation?

The teachers could not have predicted that even with the smallest innovation (and we think that on the surface, the ABC meetings are just this), it is possible to make profound changes. This is an important insight, one that they can continue to exploit because more often than not decisions on scheduling, like the one Mr. Simmons recommended, will be the most common routes through which teachers will take control.

Mr. Fallon: The Principal as Facilitator

Mr. Fallon, the high school principal, conceptualized the language-across-the-curriculum project through leading the review of the high school English program and generating the proposal for the in-service program. But Fallon's commitment to the project did not end there. He was the first building principal to participate in the workshops and his role there was one of an active and collaborative colearner as well as constant supporter of the work his high school faculty in the workshops were engaged in. Having a principal in the group presented some problems for teachers initially. They were simply not accustomed to interacting with an administrator as if he were a peer. They were skeptical. Was Fallon a spy for the administration? Could the teachers freely discuss whatever issues were on their minds?

Through his wholehearted participation in all of the workshop activities—including collaborating on action research with his high school faculty, writing and sharing his ideas, divulging his questions and concerns, responding facilitatively to all members of the group, and using his perspective as an administrator to support, rather than undermine, the teachers' goals—Fallon convincingly demonstrated that an administrator could be trusted and respected. The aspect of his participation in the project that we want to focus on is how the role that he established within the workshop setting spilled over into his work as the principal of the high school. He centered his research questions on how what he was learning in the workshops about language and learning could inform his role as principal of the high school. So it wasn't only that he was genuinely interested in learning about language across the curriculum, but that he expressly sought to integrate that learning into his job.

Since Fallon defined his role as primarily that of faculty supervisor, which is unusual in itself, it isn't surprising that the area he wanted to explore was how his observations and evaluations of faculty might be affected by his new view of what an effective learning environment might look like. Fallon's new lens brought into focus aspects of classroom life that, according to him, would not have even constituted "teaching" if he had not been learning about the role of language in the classroom. Peer-group work, peer response and evaluation, negotiating the curriculum, student-selected readings and writing assignments, more student talk than teacher talk—in short a democratic workshop setting—comprised Fallon's new set of criteria for assessing teaching.

What's interesting is that Fallon was not fully aware that these criteria were operating for him until he went to visit Renda. By his own admission, had he entered this sort of classroom a year before, he would have told Renda, "I'll come back when you're teaching." Instead, he was able to evaluate, support, and make suggestions for her that reflected his new understanding of the connections between language and learning and the visible implications of this new model. He discovered in the process of observing Renda that the formal scheme he had been using for many years for evaluating teachers was itself an impediment to noticing that learning was occurring when students' language and experience formed the center of the classroom structure.

That formal scheme depended on looking at the teacher as the center of the classroom structure. Without reformulating the specific criteria he was accustomed to invoking, he literally could not "see" what was going on. There was no category in the form he was using that would have allowed him to reflect accurately what he was seeing. So, in effect, this observation of Renda was a critical incident because not only did it give him a visible model of a democratic classroom, but it also forced him to create a new model for supervision and evaluation. In broader terms, he was able to see how the formal institutional practice of teacher evaluation was an instrument of maintaining the status quo. In his reformulation of evaluation, he was lending institutional support and validation to democratic schooling. He was, in fact, enacting the kind of collaborative supervision and evaluation that the teachers were discussing earlier in this chapter. He must have been the model they had in mind when they discussed how the language policy could be used to gain collaborative understanding of what was going on in their classrooms.

For Fallon, the goal of this project was never just to improve writing instruction. He was interested in improving schooling. In what follows, we quote him describing the work that he had recently done as part of a Middle States evaluation team.

> I recently had an opportunity to observe some teaching in another school district. And I saw, among others, two teachers that I wouldn't hesitate to describe as outstanding from the lessons I saw. I thought a lot about why, what made me see teachers, and this is a subjective judgment I think, there's no evidence to support this, but I just had an instinctive feeling that what I saw was very productive, excellent teaching. Good things happening.
>
> And you tend to come up with the answer it's personality and style. And if you stay with that, it's very discouraging in terms of thinking about changing a school, because everybody can't have this magical chemistry with the kids that some people do have. It was just good stuff. But to try to pick out something that . . . what made it good was hard to do.
>
> On the other hand, when I looked at classes that were, that I would describe as not good learning situations, the things that were absent were the things we've been talking about in this workshop. Kids were not writing, they were not communicating with each other, rarely with the teacher, and if they were, it was a one-to-one teacher–student kind of thing. They didn't go into groups, there was no peer evaluation, none of that. And that would be the . . . what it did to me was reinforce the good feelings I have about the kinds of things we're learning in this writing workshop because I think it's going to be ultimately more effective in the classroom.
>
> The question still, I guess, would be how limited we are to really help each other be better classroom teachers.

This transcript demonstrates that the model of teaching and learning he was developing and applying to his own teachers had become so much a part of his worldview that he carried it with him into whatever classroom he observed. For him, the way to change schools is to change classrooms, and he suggests that his own role in this change process is "to really help each other be better classroom teachers," an uncharacteristically collaborative statement by a principal. Significant, too, is that the ways he's thinking about good teaching fly in the face of magical thinking. One of the pervasive myths of good teaching is that it is an art that some are fortunate to have been born with and others are unfortunate to have missed receiving the gene. He refuses, through his own questioning, to accept the notion that teachers are born and not made.

In other small, but powerful ways, he was using his principalship to lend support to the high school teachers' work and to suggest new roles for principals. He encouraged teachers to attend professional conferences so that they could present their action research by facilitating the scheduling of professional days. When teachers decided that they would like to visit one another's classrooms during the school day, Fallon supported this idea, not just in principle, but by actually volunteering to cover classes so that teachers could feel free to learn from each other. In this, he became a role model. The notion of interclass visitations in the context of commonsense schooling is a radical one. And while the teachers came up with the idea, they were fearful of the reaction of other teachers, the union, and the administration to institutionalizing such a practice. By covering classes himself, Fallon was leading the way to peer collaboration, "to really help each other become better classroom teachers."

Ask any teacher to react to the words "faculty meeting" and you can be fairly certain to elicit a groan and a moan. Faculty meetings tend to be oral memos, forums for administrivia, wastes of time. Fallon attempted to alter the purpose for faculty meetings by inviting members of the writing workshops to present their research and to share classroom ideas with their colleagues. By the time volunteers for the second year of the program were solicited, there was no one in the high school who didn't have some idea about what the workshops entailed and there were more volunteers than there were slots for high school faculty. Those teachers who presented their work to their colleagues were not only pleased by being asked, but were reinforced in their experiments and revitalized as professionals. Faculty meetings became places where educational issues dominated the agenda.

If principals are the only authorities and the sole decision makers, then chances are that many of their decisions will be arbitrary simply because they will not have all the information they need to make informed decisions. On the other hand, when administrators decide to share power and authority with their faculty, they increase the likelihood that their decisions will be better for the life of the school because they reflect cooperative and collaborative input. One incident at the Charmont High School illustrates this point very well. Once the district had decided to adopt the teacher/advisor plan, we used the workshops to help define the job of the advisor and to get volunteers. Lonny was someone we hoped would volunteer for the position. When she didn't, we met with her to try to understand why she hadn't volunteered and to persuade her to do so. What emerged in our conversation was that she felt that her schedule was too demanding to allow her to add the responsibilities of the teacher/advisor. By probing further, we discovered that the key was a "privilege" Fallon wanted to reward her. In recognition of the excellent work she was doing, she was given an honors English class to teach. This plum was usually reserved for tenured faculty. But from Lonny's perspective, this class would give her an additional preparation and demand new thinking because it was a class that she had never taught before.

Trusting that Fallon would be happy to discuss Lonny's schedule with her, we encouraged her to set up a meeting with him. Once they began to discuss the issue, to explore the problems, she discovered that he was trying to demonstrate to her how much he valued her work, that he wasn't trying to make her work harder. Fallon discovered that what he had intended as a reward for strong performance was, ironically, serving as an impediment to her decision to take on a leadership role. As soon as these paradoxes were brought out into the open, resolution was achieved: he reduced her preparations to two classes and she volunteered to be an advisor. Here's an instance of an institutional practice—the scheduling of workloads by principals—that could either inhibit or support institutional change. Here, as well, is an instance of the institutional roles of principal and teacher—principal as sole decision maker and teacher as object of those decisions—that inhibits institutional change, but when redefined can become a vehicle for change.

In summarizing Fallon's contribution to change, it seems to us that when teachers face the institution of schools, they face what appears to be an impermeable and inviolable structure. The structure appears to have a status, even a life, of its own that is independent from the human beings who make it up. What's interesting to us is how confronting the human beings that make up the structure—and questioning their implicit beliefs, their time-honored roles, and the parts they play in maintaining the structure—uncovers the possibilities for change.

Dr. Sandmeier: The Principal as Educational Collaborator

There were more volunteers from the elementary school than from any other school in the district. Not only did Charmont Elementary School teachers comprise 49% of the total number of project participants, but they also represented 49% of the total faculty in their school (compare this to 17% by faculty from the middle school and 27% from the high school). This fact was largely due to Dr. Sandmeier's enthusiasm and encouragement for getting his teachers involved in professional development. None of us realized the kind of domino effect that this project would have on the entire range of practices within this school. By their very nature, elementary schools are more integrated environments than secondary schools. Teachers typically teach in self-contained classrooms and they take responsibility for the whole curriculum. This implies that a change in any aspect of the curriculum has the potential to affect other aspects. Changes in pedagogical practice, too, can spill over from one area of the curriculum to another. In this way, then, it shouldn't be surprising that even though many of the teachers we worked with intended to contain their work in language across the curriculum to some isolated part of their work, they discovered that this was neither logical nor desirable.

In spite of our efforts to expand the parameters of the project from writing across the curriculum to language across the curriculum, the legacy of the agreement and initiative under which we were hired continued to assert itself in the ways teachers and administrators defined the focus of the project. Moreover, even though the potential for elementary school teachers to work across the curriculum with the implementation of any new idea seems to be greater than it would be anywhere else in the school system, the reality is that when teachers chose a focus for their action research or for their efforts in reconceptualizing teaching and learning, the majority of elementary school teachers chose to focus on the language arts. We need to keep these realities in mind in order to understand the significance of the changes that took place in the elementary reading program.

It was the reading specialist at the elementary school, Mr. Pollack, who articulated the contradictions that were piling up between the thrust of the language-across-the-curriculum project and the skills-based basal reading series that drove the curriculum in the elementary school at the time. Both he and Sandmeier were members of the B Team. Each played a significant role in transforming reading instruction at Charmont Elementary School. Mr. Pollack knew about an innovative language series for elementary school study because it was being used in his wife's school. Once he began to understand and enact the connections between language and learning, the value of *The Impressions Series* (1984) through its whole language approach became apparent.

He took the initiative to bring up both criticisms of the series being used as well as to plan and spearhead an investigation with a small group of teachers (some of whom had not been in the project to date) of IMPRESSIONS. This small group began to meet regularly. They reviewed the series, invited representatives from the publisher to speak with them, and visited schools where IMPRESSIONS was being used. All the while Sandmeier supported the work this group was doing. Eventually, the group wished to recommend adoption of IMPRESSIONS at the elementary school. They discussed with Sandmeier what kinds of procedures they would need to follow in order to bring in the series. Sandmeier made two suggestions. One was to invite other members of the faculty to meetings that would focus on IMPRESSIONS; the other was that he offered to communicate his own support for the series directly to his faculty. While he did not wish to undermine the initiative and authority that the teachers had asserted, he was also aware that his endorsement would be pivotal to faculty support.

Because he had been participating as an equal member in the project, Sandmeier's support took the form of an informed recommendation. Here's a paragraph from the memo he sent out to his faculty:

> From our two years of involvement in writing across the curriculum, we've learned that students can write words which they can neither read nor spell. So why shouldn't a similar, non-controlled vocabulary approach to reading be used? If we follow the developmental scheme of fluency, clarity, and correctness with reading, then we should consider this new language arts series which focuses on a whole language approach.

What we find significant about this adoption was that it was collaborative and built on shared experiences, shared philosophy, and a shared vocabulary. Had the impetus for adopting this new series not come from both faculty and administration the likelihood that it would be successfully embraced by the entire faculty would be limited. In fact, adopting IMPRESSIONS was not without its problems. For those teachers who had been participants in the language-across-the-curriculum project, the match between IMPRESSIONS and many of the other things they were attempting to do was apparent. For teachers who hadn't been participants, IMPRESSIONS raised their anxiety level. Being sensitive to this allowed Sandmeier and Pollack to jointly plan ways to support teachers in using IMPRESSIONS in their classrooms. Pollack made himself available as a resource by visiting classes and by holding meetings on using the series. Sandmeier did not force immediate and wholesale adoption by those teachers who were still uncomfortable with the whole-language approach. Many teachers, for example, refused initially to give up their grammar workbooks, even though the series lent support to teaching grammar in context. In addition, Sandmeier encouraged those teachers to participate in the third year of the project and they all did. The possibility for change in this school was intricately tied to both empowerment of teachers to initiate changes through a commitment to new ways of seeing teaching and learning as well as the involvement of an administrator in an intellectual understanding and commitment to the implications of those changes.

Sandmeier's knowledge of the principles of using language to learn across the curriculum as well as his support of his faculty in carrying out these principles had their impact on another institutional practice. The elementary school report card in this district, as in most others, divided achievement in language arts into specific subskills, such as spelling, vocabulary, and penmanship. Even the most courageous teacher, one who perhaps had decided to use a whole-language approach in the "freedom" of her classroom, would have to, at the end of each marking period, evaluate her students' language development by separating it into discrete categories. No matter how deep such teachers' commitments might be to throwing out the workbooks and phonics skills tests, their construal of the possibilities must be conditioned by how internalized these outside constraints have become to a whole way of thinking and viewing the classroom. So even if teachers could occasionally ignore the requirements that the institution imposed on them, such teachers would have a much harder time ignoring the invisible constructs they themselves have built that have already embraced those institutional constraints. Those are an inherent part of their world views.

On the other hand, when experimentation begins to occur in many isolated classrooms and when experimentation begins to reveal the impossibility of reconciling institutional demands with individual goals and to exaggerate the inadequacies and contradictions of an eclectic approach to learning, then the individual teacher's decisions or choices simultaneously begin conditioning the larger school community. Collective action and change on the level of teachers' worldviews can come to influence the institution. Rather than having a teacher's choices controlled by the institutional practice, the institutional practice can come to reflect the collective beliefs and practices of teachers.

This was the case at Charmont Elementary School when the faculty reviewed the standard report card. By this time, fourteen teachers from the elementary school had participated in the in-service program. There had been a great deal of discussion about how evaluation could or should reflect what was actually going on in their classrooms, so when the teachers began to review and revise the standard report card, the participating teachers were prepared to reenvision it in light of what they had learned. Here is the voice of the teacher who headed up the review and revision effort talking about what happened:

> We did redo our report cards in the elementary school. What happened was in the offhand way that such things happen, we were asked, generically, if we had any suggestions for redoing the report card since it was time to look at the way it was laid out. There was no push to go to any particular style or no mention about the writing workshop. But it certainly was very much in the back of my mind. And we talked more times about if we were really going to do this, then somehow or other we have to indicate it in the way we evaluate because the evaluative device wags the dog. So I said all right, I'll do the 3, 4, 5 one or I'll do one version of it and see what it's like. So I did.
>
> And I handed it in. And we had some discussions together two or three times. And what happened was that without my pushing the thing at all, I simply asked questions or answered questions; it was accepted. And it was laid out and Dr. Sandmeier made a couple of changes based upon his own views, so it isn't exactly as I wrote it, but pretty much. And then when it was used for the first time, the 3rd grade teachers who are in our block had a really difficult time with it. It was a terrific pain for them as a matter of fact. And it sort of got all wound up with their

feelings also about possibly being involved in a workshop in the future, their feelings about having to do the new math program.

Anyway these are the feelings that I've had. And when, to get back to the report card itself, because what this was, even for those of us who had done the workshop, it was a fair exercise to redo, what I did was to put everything under language arts, speaking, reading, and writing, and I wanted to have speaking first, but Sandmeier moved reading up to the top. But it was supposed to be speaking, reading, and writing and all of them follow the same pattern: from fluency, clarity, correctness. But that was a fair exercise for me to do it originally and I talked to some of the others about it. But for the teachers who hadn't been through it at all, to just have it laid out, this is the way the report card is going to be, and then to have to try to adapt their thinking about what they've been doing with children to it, it really was an unfair task, I think. And it had, as a result, a negative backlash.

We can see from the teacher's description of what happened when the report card was revised that this was not going to be a smooth transition. If we couple the report-card changes with the changes in the language arts series, it is clear that the teachers who had not yet participated were going to be feeling both pressured and cut off. But together, Sandmeier and the teachers who had participated found ways to work with their colleagues so that antagonism and resistance could be kept to a minimum. He made it clear to the teachers who were feeling alienated by these changes that they would not have to operate alone. Support both inside and outside the classroom was offered. These teachers were encouraged to try as best they could to use the new report card and to ask questions and help of their colleagues. They were also assured that there would be slots for them set aside in the third team of participants in the in-service workshops. By now, all of them have, in fact, participated in the program.

Neither adopting IMPRESSIONS nor changing the report card were without their problems. One option would have been, of course, to wait to make changes in the curriculum and in evaluation until all members of the school community had been initiated into these ways of viewing the world. But like many of the other changes we've talked about in both individual teachers as well as their schools, they are an organic part of the life of the school. For real change to occur, options must be explored and tested simultaneously. In reality, once teachers become excited about new ideas and once they believe that they have the power to shape reception of those ideas, it's neither possible nor desirable to ask them to wait. Sandmeier was forced to face and deal with those teachers who had not yet participated in the workshops, and while he was willing to be patient and supportive, he was not willing to allow their lack of participation to become an impediment to change in the school.

As was the case with adopting IMPRESSIONS, the revised report card represents a collaborative effort among the teachers and between them and Sandmeier. Sharing knowledge, even knowledge of vocabulary like fluency, clarity, and correctness, was at the core of the changes that were actually made. Rather than focusing on skills exclusively, the report card was divided into reading, speaking, and writing with room to assess each student under each of these categories according to fluency, clarity, and correctness. It is no accident that we demanded that administrators be part of the workshops, because we believed, and the stories that we are telling bear this out, that by working together, teachers and administrators will, indeed, develop shared views of the world of teaching and learning and from their collaboration find ways to make the institution reflect these views.

One question raised by the workshops themselves that can only be answered outside of the context of the workshops is how the spirit of peer collaboration among teachers and between them and their administrator can be reflected in the governance of the school. Everyone was safe inside the workshops to explore new roles and relationships to one another. Would everyone be willing to risk these transformations once they were back in their regular work day? And further, what in the school itself would have to change for these new roles to be viable? Sandmeier and the teacher/participants discovered how to do this. The teachers led the work of revising the report card and adopting the new language-arts series. Sandmeier participated fully in their discussions and, when necessary, lent the kind of support to the directions they were going in that could only come from someone with his status in the hierarchy. So he was not abandoning his role as principal as much as he was redefining it.

Mr. Chandler: The Principal as Hinderer

In every story, the protagonist faces a moment of peril. Some challenge is offered that must be overcome if the story is going to end with everyone living happily ever after. While we have a perilous interlude that challenged our heroes, we're unable to end it happily. But let's begin at the end. Nothing really changed at Charmont Middle School. We can't point to a single teacher, an administrator, or any institutional practice that was in any significant way touched by this project. We don't want anything that we say to sound like rationalization. We don't even know enough or understand enough to be able to rationalize. We do accept responsibility, on the other hand, for the absence of any real connection between us and this school. We acknowledge that there might have been things we could have done that would have made a difference. We will say that we didn't fail for lack of trying. When we recognized the limits of our own personal efforts, we enlisted the aid of a number of people: administrators from the other schools, teachers from the other buildings, and the superintendent. Everyone was aware of the problem. No one knew what to do about it. And, in fact, the lack of participation of the middle school in a whole variety of district projects and activities was well established. No one was really surprised, therefore, by the resistance we confronted. In this case, the institutional practices combined with the teachers' constructs of teaching and learning were impermeable for all of us.

Part of the problem is that we could only define the problem indirectly because no one was willing to share the history of Charmont Middle School with us. Here's a little of what we have been able to uncover and piece together. Quite some time prior to our coming to work in Charmont, a small cadre of the total of nineteen full-time teachers had formed with the express purpose of controlling what happened in the school. They established an unwritten pact with Mr. Chandler, their principal, that they would support one another unconditionally just as long as power in the school rested in their hands. This had effects on the curriculum as well as on those teachers who were not part of the inner circle. Those teachers who formed the cadre got the best classes and the best schedules. Only those programs and projects of which they approved were officially sanctioned. The teachers who were not part of this group were isolated socially and academically and they were afraid, afraid to do anything that might make them more of a target than they already were for exclusion. Even Chandler seemed to be afraid.

Right from the start, we had difficulty getting volunteers from the middle school to participate. Those teachers who made up the cadre had already decided they would not benefit from participating in the program. They said that they knew all this already. Those who were not part of the in-group, as you might imagine, were afraid to participate. Only pressure from the superintendent's office worked to produce any participants at all. This situation worsened from year to year. During the first year, there were three teachers from the middle school who gained a modicum of insight. One of them left the district after her first year in the in-service program and the other two continue to work on writing in their classroom and to participate in ABC Team meetings. By the second year, the two participants from the middle school were clearly members under duress. By the third year, the situation was embarrassing. No one would volunteer. When Chandler selected two teachers, which he only did because the superintendent wrote him a letter demanding that he recruit at least two teachers and reaffirming the commitment of the Board of Education to the program, both of them declined to participate. Chandler's next strategy was to hold a "lottery" to select two names from a hat. You can imagine, as well, how happy these two were to be there. Our vision of the teacher/advisor plan for the third year of the program was that one teacher from each school would volunteer. Not one of the participating teachers from the middle school came forward. In addition, by the third year, Chandler had no choice but to be the administrator representative to the program. He attended a total of three out of a possible twelve workshops and never stayed for the full day.

So what did we do to rectify this situation? We attended faculty meetings to talk about the program, where hostility to what we talked about was palpable. We offered our help to individual teachers and teams of teachers whenever we were in the school. We even met with the cadre separately. Here are Cindy's notes from one of those conversations with the ingroup:

> Met with the seventh grade team (English, math, social studies and science). Asked lots of questions and listened as they told me about their students and their interdisciplinary projects. Their notion of writing across the curriculum is definitely grammar across the curriculum. But I knew I couldn't tell them that, so I listened, racing madly ahead in my mind to determine how I could keep the dialogue going—get them to trust me. So they complained about the research papers, the usual stuff, and I said, "Oh, I have a strategy that you might try." And I described dialectical notetaking. And one by one they say it's a good idea. Subject is dropped and we move on to another one. At the end the science teacher says, "I'm going to try that. Suppose the students go to the library and try it for their next paper?" And I say, "Suppose you bring some outside reading material to class and show them *how* to do it?" I said, "Sometimes just telling them to do something isn't enough" and she said, "Good idea." I ended the session by telling them that I hoped they would think of me as a resource, that if I could help them in any way, just to ask. And they all, once again, invited me to their classrooms.
>
> So a dialogue has begun. I don't know where it will go. (Emphasis Onore's)

This conversation occurred a year and a half after the program began and a year and a half after we had attended faculty meetings at Charmont Middle School, talked informally in the teachers' room, and been in the school at least once a month. Our optimism that this conversation was the beginning of something was misplaced. Even though we saw these teachers regularly after this conversation, we were never invited into their classrooms and never asked to speak formally with them again.

Still we were undeterred because we knew that Chandler himself would be a participant in the program during the third year. And so several months after Cindy's conversation just quoted, she went to speak with him about the implementation of the program for the third year, including the selection of an advisor from his school and his participation in the workshops.

> Mr. Chandler assured me that he would "support" his teachers who wished to be advisors. He asked me about the administrator's involvement in the third year team. He wanted to know what he had to do since his "boss" had volunteered him. I told him that the advisors could do much of the work. His main responsibility would be to attend the workshops. He said, "I'm not interested in writing. I'll find every excuse

not to go." I told him I didn't want him there if he didn't want to be there. [*The following exchange is recorded in field notes.*]

MR. CHANDLER: It's not an interest of mine. I have other interests.

MS. ONORE: We just want you to learn about the program.

MR. CHANDLER: I don't need to know what my teachers do. I support them. I find ways to help them do what they want. But I really am more interested in reading.

[*Mr. Chandler goes on at great length about his Sustained Silent Reading program, extolling its virtues.*]

MS. ONORE: Then there is a good reason for you to learn about writing across the curriculum because it's about reading, writing, speaking, and listening. It would help if you knew that.

MR. CHANDLER: I'm just being honest with you. If my "boss" says I have to go, I have to go.

Several things were made clear to us as a result of this conversation. We knew we were doomed. If Chandler believed he had to participate in the workshops only because Simmons demanded it, if he simultaneously believed that he didn't need to understand what his teachers were doing in order to support them, if the district commitment to language across the curriculum couldn't persuade him that there was a reason to participate, then we really had no hope of ever penetrating the impermeable facade of Charmont Middle School. How different Chandler's beliefs are from both Fallon's and Sandmeier's.

As we said earlier, we enlisted others to help us turn the tide at the middle school. Both Sandmeier and Fallon discussed with Chandler the unproductive relationships that existed between the middle school and the project and the middle school and their two schools. Before the teacher/advisor plan went into effect, several participating teachers attempted to make informal connections to the teachers at Charmont Middle School. We guess our final hope was that the teacher/advisors, especially Renda and Lonny at the high school, whose advisor responsibilities included the middle school, would be able to establish collaboration and support through working with individual teachers at the middle school. It seemed to us that, especially in Renda's case, knowing the history and the people for a longer time than we did would give her the edge we lacked. Here is Renda's description of her work with the middle school from her annual report:

> At times it [the advisor role] was frustrating, especially working with the middle school teachers whose schedules and constraints are, in a sense, a "separate world." Through the logs and the workshops, we became closer and better able to share and trust, but the importance of being in

the same building was underlined by the awkwardness and difficulty of exchanging so much as a phone call with a middle school teacher in the course of the school day. The voluntary abstention of the middle school from the ongoing implementation of the writing workshop philosophy creates important problems for those of us working on either side of the Great Divide. I hope in the future some means can be found to resolve this difficulty, as the three years of the workshops have produced a remarkable commonality of goals and methods between the elementary school and high school teachers.

The possibilities for change can manifest themselves through a number of avenues. In saying this, we are also acknowledging that resistance to change can take a number of forms. Our experience in Charmont has made us optimistic that even if only one avenue is open, the possibility of change will exist. But as we've seen in the case of the middle school, each and every avenue seemed to be blocked. Perhaps this is more common than we realize. What may be more common is the kind of control and power that this small in-group of teachers seemed to wield. It's certainly ironic to us that in a book that has talked about teachers taking control over teaching and learning, that we are critical of a group of teachers who have done just that. The kind of leadership that these teachers did exert, however, is exactly what we defined as expert, know-it-all leadership in Chapter 6. It's clear from the conversation we quoted earlier that the in-group is not interested in participating in the language-across-the-curriculum project because they believe they already have all the answers. They know what to do, they can't learn anything new, and they don't want to share what they know. Just as Lonny defined the kind of leader she was to become, so, too, have these teachers. We're critical of them because their definition of leadership and empowerment does not seem to include continued learning, collaboration, demonstration, facilitation, and advocacy.

But we've learned that taking one step can lead to unknown consequences. Suggesting this implies that we, indeed, do construct the world that we see. Real stagnation and impermeability in any context depends on all of its elements being impervious to change. Renda's final plea for shaping and sharing common goals throughout the school district is in danger if paths to dealing with the resistance and impermeability are not found. We hope in the next section to show how students can be significant players in changing teachers and the institution's expectations and attitudes about learning. Perhaps they are the only avenue left for penetrating the resistance at Charmont Middle School.

Students Learning About Power

In the course of our three years in Charmont, we learned from and about students regularly. They helped us see the consequences of all the kinds of changes we've discussed in the place where they ultimately matter most: the classroom. Finally, if the work of the project is to be evaluated on the basis of its power to improve teaching and learning, then no matter what teachers say about what they believe or what administrators do to enact and support change, it's meaningless unless there are tangible changes in the ways students see and engage in learning. We've already placed central importance on power relationships and roles that teachers play with one another, with their administration, and with their students. Our focus here on students will also center on how they reconceptualize their roles and their understanding of their power to learn and their power as members of the school community. We believe that once students begin to see themselves as full-fledged participants in schooling, that they, too, can be agents of change.

To look thoroughly at the changes in students and the changes they helped to bring about would require another whole book. Teachers were continually bringing in and sharing evidence of student transformation, student growth, and student achievement. And certainly, for the teachers who were participants in the workshops, there was little, if anything, as powerful a support for the work they were attempting than to see the results of this work for student learning. In fact, this is the initial manner in which students are agents of change. It's difficult to argue forcefully against an approach to teaching and learning when it so clearly engenders ownership, pleasure, and success for learners.

Teachers also perceived the power of student work to change minds. Many of them, as we've pointed out before, made presentations at professional conferences in which they shared the work their students were doing. Student work played other roles as well. Each year during the June Board of Education meeting, we were asked to prepare a presentation for the community. From the first of these meetings, student work was the central attraction. Teachers put up displays, showed videotapes, read from student work, and shared stories about learning in their classrooms.

By the end of the second year, the persuasive thrust of student work was so apparent to the teachers that they organized a presentation by students for the Board and parents. This presentation, which was based on a collaborative high school English/social studies project, involved students in a peer-response group. Unrehearsed, the students demonstrated a sharing and feedback session. Students read drafts of their writing; peers listened, took notes, and responded spontaneously to the writer; writers asked questions of their respondents, and discussions of the writer's intention, audience, and suggestions for revision followed. Awe and respect were palpable in the silence that followed this presentation. Silence was replaced by testimonials from Board members about the success of the language-across-the-curriculum project. Parents raised questions about how their children could be assured that their teachers would provide them with similar experiences. The message to the Board was clear that parents wished to see language across the curriculum institutionalized in Charmont.

We know from participating teachers' reports that students sometimes resisted new ways of learning and, like the principals who refuse to acknowledge student-centered classrooms as "real" teaching situations, they, too, often perceive their teachers' efforts to share ownership and authority over learning with them as not constituting "real" learning. After all, their views of the world of teaching and learning have been internalized through year after year of consistent messages about what learning is, what knowledge is, who the authorities are, and how to play the game of school as smoothly as possible. For them to be able to envision alternative views of the classroom and participate in an alternative model of teaching and learning requires, initially at least, a great leap of faith and afterward a commitment, supported by their teachers' unwavering commitment, honesty, and trustworthiness, to taking on responsibility for their own learning. In the same way that internalizing a view of the world of teaching and learning that is traditional can be the source of resistance, could internalizing a view of the world of teaching and learning that is democratic also give rise to resistance? If students come to believe that they own their work, that they construct knowledge, and that they can negotiate the means and ends of learning will they no longer accept classrooms where these principles and beliefs are not practiced?

Pfeiffer and Renda were working together during a workshop in the third year of the project. The topic of student expectations came up and a discussion ensued about what students had learned from previous experience in participating teachers' classrooms.

> MR. PFEIFFER: I will say this, the kids, because they've gone through a few years of writing workshops, they were sophomores last year, so that's it, when I talk about two, three, four drafts, there's no more of this ughs or oohs. They're ready for it. They're prepared. You can go back and see it.
>
> Ms. RENDA: Definitely, by the time they're juniors they've got that part clear. They seem to have a good understanding, even though they may not do it in class, they do it in the cafeteria, because I've seen them. They read their papers to each other. "Wait, wait, I've got this essay due for X, can I just read it to you?" And they do it very informally, but that's basically what they're doing.
>
> MR. PFEIFFER: I will say this, my seniors almost everyone to a tee, with an exception of a couple, on some of the papers when we negotiated topics and deadlines, they all have gotten away from copying the way they used to. You know, getting away from the truncated, right out of

>the book papers. I got some really good material from students in the past who were reluctant to write, who are doing it now, who've gone through two or three years in the program.

Pfeiffer and Renda seem pleased both that students are showing that they have learned a great deal about writing and learning and that they no longer have to spend time to teach them how to learn in new ways. We would infer, further, that these same students, should they find themselves in classrooms where teachers have a different view of how to build knowledge, would question having the teacher's knowledge imposed on them. They might question, as well, missing the opportunity for drafting, sharing, and revising their writing. Students have been observed, as Renda says, sharing their writing in the cafeteria even when they're not encouraged to do so in their classes. So not only do students have the power to support their teachers who are trying alternative methods, but they may also have the power to put pressure for change on their teachers who use more conventional and alienating methods.

Just as important as the power students might develop to change others is the power that they have already seemed to assert here as independent learners. The goal, after all, of a project like the one we've participated in in Charmont is to help students become lifelong learners. Once they glimpse the opportunities that they can create for themselves to learn, we are optimistic that they will carry these lessons with them throughout life.

At the last workshop during the third year of the program, we distributed an article by Grant Wiggins, Director of Research on Curriculum and Teaching for the Coalition of Essential Schools, entitled "10 Radical Suggestions for School Reform" (1988). Lonny, who had been working all year with her ninth-grade English students to establish a democratic classroom, felt that they might like to be aware of how professional educators were thinking about educational reform, particularly the structure of schools. Trusting that her students had already learned a tremendous amount about alternative education and that from their insider's perspective they could envision how an entire school might be reorganized, she distributed copies of the article to her class. Once they read the article, the students suggested that they write their own proposal for school reform.

What follows is a verbatim report the students collaboratively researched, wrote, revised, edited, and had published in the high school newspaper. Their understanding of what is wrong with the ways schools are presently organized is as insightful as much of the literature on reform that has been published in the last several years. Their suggestions for change are also perceptive. Their model is rigorous, demanding, and requires a high degree of discipline. According to Lonny, discipline was included in their statement because one of the students' major concerns was to build accountability into their model. It is also a democratic model, with power being shared equally throughout the school community. Equally important, this is not an elitist educational model, but one that embraces everyone. As we've suggested, teachers and administrators need to experience a collaborative environment for their own learning before they can create such environments in their classrooms and before they are willing to take new responsibilities and create new roles for themselves. This is the case for students, too. Having experienced collaboration and empowerment themselves, it is possible for them to imagine what a school could look like if its structures were transformed to support and engender collaboration and empowerment. And they seem right when they conclude that the school they have imagined would attract the best teachers.

"Reform in Education"
Written by All Students in 7th Period English

"The Crisis in Schools"—"A Nation at Risk"—"What's Wrong with American Education?"—these headlines indicate a growing public concern with the quality of education in this country. Such reports about the sorry state of the American classroom often are accompanied with many suggestions for solving the problems. But these suggestions are not always made by the people who would know the truth: the kids and teachers. Accordingly, after much time spent discussing, debating, and shaping our theories about what ought to happen in schools, we decided to propose the following reforms. We do believe that in schools that followed them, lasting learning would take place for a majority of students; however, we are not so naive as to believe that our suggestions could be enacted either easily or in a short period of time, but we hope that we can start a dialogue which could be the beginning of real change.

We propose three levels for the formation of school criteria. First, there will be a state-wide conference for the determination of core curriculum. These will be the basics that people need to know as a base for their own needs. This core will be small, being less emphasized in the higher grades. The committee will only be setting the bare bones as the more local level will adapt the "meat" of the courses to the area in which the students live, the individual classes themselves putting the flesh and skin to finish it off. By keeping the criteria and required courses to a minimum, students can have a larger say in what they learn.

The students' special interests are very important to develop, as they are the areas where we have the most potential. When somebody has a gift for a foreign language, communicating in our own language, or the liberal arts, they sould be allowed to develop that skill. Presently only a few of these can be adequately developed through schooling. But we want to see these come out whatever they are. Such skills cannot be allowed to go undiscovered.

Once the skills are found, the specialized groups screened and selected, there comes the process of learning and experience. Some places would offer practical experience for the class that goes there, be it a few days in an observatory for potential astronomers and astronauts, or a camping trip for the biologists and poets (though probably not together).

But then there is homework. Many argue that more homework makes better education. Barely. It makes for sore students up at midnight amid complaining parents. Often the work will have nothing to do with what students need to know. So homework should not be given for homework's sake.

Once the core curriculum and the special interests groups are in place, we propose a student/teacher council to control the day-to-day running of the school. The council would be half students, half teachers, elected by teachers and students. An administrator would be appointed to oversee the council.

The council's members would vote on a topic as to how it should be dealt with from the suggested possibilities. In the event of a tie, the overseer would vote. Some items that would be handled are disputes, changes in scheduling/courses, planning of special programs, and other occurrences of daily school life. For instance, a teacher and a student might have a dispute. If this matter is brought before the board, they can suggest appropriate measures and occasionally check up on whether these measures are being followed. Anyone who feels the need to bring up an issue could do so.

We propose to establish a system of scheduling for classes to avoid the typical, inflexible daily schedules which mire the students and teachers in a sea of routine. The core curriculum we have proposed would be scheduled more traditionally, meeting for a certain amount of time during the morning of each school day; these classes could rotate time slots on a weekly basis. However, for the special interest classes, the class itself would schedule the length of time for class and the number of class meetings per week. This might include running the school day up to five o'clock, but decrease in traditional homework would offset this. The entire special interest schedule would be coordinated by the student/faculty council.

In a school environment, we can solve learning problems by lowering the sizes of the classes. During the course of the school day the effects that large classes cause cannot be overlooked; special help cannot be given, and a potentially intelligent child fails. But the question is: What can we do about this problem? Students need to have individual attention from teachers, and teachers need to have a sense that they can have an impact on their students. Each day teachers have to face so many people. In an inner city school, think of how teachers may feel faced with 200 plus students a day? We propose an average class size of 10 to 15 students with no more than five classes a day.

We feel that testing and grading, common activities in any school system, do not always accurately reflect a student's performance because it is hard to represent in a single percentage or letter grade all the components that make up that performance. The idea that we present would be beneficial to both the parents and students involved, particularly in a school which adopted the core/special interest curriculum we described earlier. For both of these groups, we feel that giving one grade four times a year does not work. We suggest that conferences be set up between parents, teachers, and students discussing where the students' strengths and weaknesses are. For reasons such as providing colleges with records, numerical grades would be given out only for the classes in the core curriculum.

Another thing we think should be altered within our schools is the way we are tested. Whether it be after a unit, or a topic of study, we are usually given some sort of written exam. We don't think this is the best way to determine if a student has learned the material. Just because a student didn't do very well on a multiple choice test is not always evidence that he didn't absorb anything in class. Some people just get "blocked" out of fear for the test; a better way to show how much someone has learned could be by essays, in-class discussions, or projects. We think that there should be more applying of knowledge and less *re*-producing of knowledge.

We feel that there must be more discipline incorporated in the education of our society. With the introduction of discipline comes respect, organization, and productive scholastic activities. There should be in the ideal school harsher punishments for the frequent incompletion of assigned work on time as well as for tardiness. Such restrictions at early stages of scholastic development would encourage effective work habits while establishing the scholastic disciplinary relationship. Changes in the restrictions of general, inappropriate classroom behavior are also necessary with rules tailored to be more strict. Educational discipline should be regulated in fairness by a committee composed of both students and teachers. All affected by disciplinary codes shall have a say in the creation of these codes. With such educational innovations we shall be capable of competing with the systems of education of foreign countries. Today's students represent the future of the world. Ours must be taught discipline.

We believe that teachers should be well trained in the area or field they teach. An English teacher should be able to help students understand how to use the English language. A social studies teacher should know what a map of the world looks like. Gym teachers should be physically fit, and should have to pass a fitness test just like their students. A music teacher should know how to read music, and if they teach band, then they should be able to play a musical instrument fairly well. An art teacher should be able to draw.

Teachers are all role models, but the teachers of classes that require hands-on experience have modeling as their primary goal. If the teacher is unable to do something, then how is the student supposed to learn? It is discouraging to the students if their teachers are unqualified. We hope that when we make the changes we discussed elsewhere in the article, we will attract many competent teachers.

Epilogue

The Possibility of Change

What Makes Change Possible?

Substantial change is exceedingly complex. It is individual as well as social, personal as well as collective, historical as well as experimental. We believe that teachers' personal construct systems can be both a support for change and an inhibitor of change. Teachers' personal construct systems reveal who they are now and what they might become. We have found that teachers' core construct of knowledge lies at the heart of their thinking and acting, but because it is a core construct, it's difficult even to make contact with it, let alone alter it. In the cases where teachers' core constructs could be brought to light and could be examined by them, something happened.

It would be a total distortion of what we have learned and intend if our understanding of the role of personal constructs to effect change is applied mechanistically. The nightmare we envision is that after reading this book, some teacher educators or curriculum developers will either use a Kelly Repertory Grid, a test that has been designed to reveal a personal construct system, or devise a test of their own designed to reveal a teacher's construct system and use that test to accept or deny admission to any teacher education program. We don't want to imply that we ought to know what teachers' beliefs and attitudes are before beginning any professional development work. In fact, we believe that the process of uncovering and critically examining the constructs that teachers hold is the major work of any in-service project. Our goal in researching for this book was to account for what happened in Charmont, and by understanding what supported or inhibited change, to be better able to help teachers make the kinds of changes they wish to make in themselves and their school districts.

We began with a vision of a democratic classroom, one that we attempted to enact in our in-service program. By bringing teachers into this classroom, we hoped that they could create a similar climate in their own classrooms. We saw that some teachers could do this more easily and more successfully than others and so began our quest to understand how we could account for the fact that the same set of experiences would produce such divergent responses. Pfeiffer and Winberry presented the clearest example of contrast. From them, we learned that at the center of the meaning of the experience of the in-service project was a set of beliefs about knowledge and the roles of teachers and students in learning. They taught us that their views of knowledge, constructivist or objectivist, gave rise to a number of satellite constructs that guided their views of teaching and learning. These satellite constructs define the role of the teacher, the role of language, and the role of the student as well as the relationships among all of these.

Having defined the personal construct system most directly responsible for attitudes and beliefs about teaching and learning in a democratic classroom, we were able to apply this scheme to other teachers. In so doing, we were able to understand the role of reflective practice and the part played by action research in revealing and recreating the construct system of Sealy. From Renda, we learned about the power that resides in a teacher seeing herself as a learner and through her learning experiences how she could help her students learn with one another. Lonny is for us the teacher as a professional educator and leader. By taking on the role of leader, Lonny became a leader. From her, we discovered that action can precede and engender belief.

Recognizing that we could not separate these teachers from their context, we then examined how the institution either contributed to or constrained change. We looked at how teachers learned how to read and critique the school culture, and how by doing so they were able to transform some time-honored practices by redefining their roles, rights, and responsibilities. We saw how administrators could also redefine their roles and become full and collaborative participants in the change process. The teachers discovered that the superintendent, without having to change his beliefs or his authority, could support what they needed. They learned they could get what they asked for, but that they must take responsibility for asking. We also saw that there are some structures that could not be penetrated, that history, though oftentimes possibility, is sometimes inevitability. Students, however, might even be able to break down the most impenetrable barriers to change. We saw how their views of the world of teaching and learning could change their experience of school. We don't know enough about the long-term effects of changes in teachers' attitudes and beliefs on the students, but we do know that such research would be valuable extension of our work.

Reflection on beliefs is but one way into transformation. We have also seen where reflection on action has transformative power. Combining reflection on beliefs with reflection on action probably has more impact than either alone would have. While we didn't have this language to describe what we did when we began this project, we now understand that underlying our model of immersion and distancing was just such a notion. Believing and doing are the two inextricably linked parts of a whole process for change. Our model is not just a model for in-service education. Both of us practice immersion and distancing in all of the teaching we do and strive toward democratic classrooms, no matter what the setting. We have not finished exploring the potential of this model. We've learned so much from doing this research and writing this book, and we can't imagine that we will not keep on learning and experimenting as we move on.

That we would count our experience a successful one in Charmont does not imply that we believe we've discovered a universal panacea for school ills. Lest we give you the impression that all the teachers who participated in the in-service program were Lonnys or Rendas, a number of teachers were affected very little by their participation. And, certainly, one entire school was affected not at all. We chose Lonny, Sealy, Renda, and Pfeiffer because they illustrated the possibilities for change. We made a strategic decision. So much of the current literature on school and teacher change focuses on what is not possible that we felt and hoped that a focus on what is possible might in this historical period be likely to better support change. We see these teachers as demonstrators of what can happen, and perhaps the stories that we told about them and they told about themselves can "develop a language of possibility that can address the issue of creating alternative teaching practices" (Giroux and McLaren, 1987, pp. 278–279).

What Limits Change?

We want to add a few realities that we haven't touched on yet that can get in the way of change. As of this writing, four teachers who participated in the program along with Fallon and Sandmeier have all left the school district. It is probably impossible to make up for the loss of Renda. In replacing Fallon, the teachers were able to use the language policy to guide them in what we think was an excellent choice for principal. The new principal is not only helping to support teachers in continuing the work they already have begun, but she is attempting to effect even more changes, such as cross-disciplinary teaching and interschool, interdistrict visitations. Sandmeier's replacement has been more problematic, and at this point, the teachers and the new principal are at odds. Sandmeier, however, has exported his knowledge to a new district where he is currently the superintendent.

Such changes in personnel are inevitable, but they present new challenges. The teachers who remain in the district have already made good use of the language policy as an interviewing device. They also intend to use it with new faculty, not as a sorting procedure as much as an educational touchstone and a focus for discussion.

We are also aware that the political climate of the times can have a broad and dramatic impact on schools. Our crystal ball, then, is limited in what it can tell us. We have cause to be concerned right now as "cultural literacy," the "new" basics, and a "return to the traditional cannon" begin to assert a stranglehold on attitudes, resources, and energies. We do know that while a three-year in-service program may appear to be a luxury to some, it is a necessity to achieve even the limited results we describe here. We can't possibly stress enough that the possibility of change is intricately connected to time. But time is money and money has become scarcer and scarcer for education. And the future in this regard continues to look bleak. Nonetheless, three years in Charmont has been long enough for internal supports for continued growth to be established. We don't know if these will be enough to keep things growing. We do know that the systems that are in place—teacher curriculum coordinators, ABC meetings, and the like—are vastly superior to what we've seen in other places where teachers have to figure out on their own how to sustain themselves and their work. But these, too, need money and each has to be rationalized for budgetary approval.

Demythologizing for Change

If myth is "an integral, often unexamined part of our contemporary culture, including our professional discourse in teacher education and teaching," (Cornbleth, 1987, p. 187) and if we see myths as "commonsense empirically established fact or natural law" (p. 187), and if they, therefore, generate labels and elaborations that direct practice, define expertise, and contribute to professional identity (p. 204), then changing schooling requires demythologizing its culture. Teacher educators have a responsibility to uncover, to confront, and to excise those myths that stymie change. This means changing themselves before they can help change others. We see the establishment of democratic schooling as a frontal assault on such myths as the teacher as expert, the student as empty bank account, knowledge as a commodity, and teaching as testing. The job of working in and with schools to promote or to explore the possibility of change is risky because so much is at stake in the deconstruction of each myth. We recognize that every time teachers question their practices and beliefs, they need as much support as they can get. One characteristic of a community is a shared vocabulary. A shared vocabulary helps teachers to discuss their concerns with one another and to defend their practices and beliefs to others. The task that we have set for ourselves is to help teachers generate a shared vocabulary and to establish a philosophy of instruction that they can articulate and enact. In Charmont, the language policy became the vehicle for developing a shared vocabulary, building a sense of community, and generating a philosophy of instruction. No process of examination and reexamination leads inevitably to one unified philosophy of instruction for all members of the group. But learners will be more willing to examine their beliefs if they trust that they will be supported and helped to reaffirm or to change those beliefs.

Howard Margolis (1987) sketches a pattern for what he calls "the appearance and spread of a radically new idea" (p. 172), which we believe defines where Charmont has been, where it is now, and where it is going. The "uphill" stage is one in which conflicts between what has been taken for granted and something new emerge. During "consolidation," confidence that the new idea is viable begins to grow. In the final phase, "downhill," extending and modifying the new idea is coupled with figuring out ways to persuade others that the new idea is viable. Charmont's future may show that "a new view triumphs less by converting the old guard than by outliving it" (p. 184). Another possibility is that leaders will be insiders who "have at least somehow been spared from becoming active opponents of the new ideas." The possibility we have hope for in Charmont is that the initial resounding, "it's absurd," the skeptics' assertion "it's wrong," will be replaced by a collective cry of "it's obvious."

Appendix

Charmont Language Policy

Learning Through Language Across the Curriculum

During the academic years 1985–1988, teachers, administrators, and board members, representing the district's three schools, participated in a series of workshops on learning through language across the curriculum. This working paper reflects the thinking and learning in these workshops. It is a living document which all members of the Charmont educational community are invited to rethink and reformulate through ongoing discussion and classroom research.

This document on Learning through Language rests on four key philosophical assumptions.

1. Language is central to learning.
2. Language is the mirror of the mind: it is more than surface structure.
3. Through language, learners form concepts, solve problems, organize information, and make connections between previous learning and new ideas.
4. The entire educational community influences the learner's language development.

The Role of Language in Learning

Language is a primary and purposeful learning tool. Students need to talk and write about what matters to them as they learn. Learning occurs through talking and writing as well as through reading and listening. Students at all grade levels and in all subject areas need to talk in order to share new information, to organize ideas, and to ask their own questions. They need opportunities to use informal writing to summarize, question, and explore answers. Students must become active participants in their own learning.

Language use contributes to critical thinking. When learners have opportunities to use language, the quality of their thinking improves. To develop hypothesizing, problem-solving, analyzing, and other thinking processes, students need to practice these processes in their talk and writing. The learning process is short-circuited when students have the impression that there is always one right answer to a question.

Critical Components of Learning Through Language

Fluency

Fluency is ease in using language, either spoken or written. It is the free flow of ideas and thoughts. Learners develop fluency in all subject areas by linking what they already know to the new material being explored. Ideas flow best when the learner is unafraid to take risks. Fluency involves guessing, questioning, speculating, and exploring without concern for the correctness or final form of the exploration. Trusted peers and adults are the best audiences to engender fluent writing and talk.

Clarity

Clarity is the ability to communicate what is intended by the speaker or writer to a listener or reader as effectively as possible. Learners need to become aware of audience. Changes in language and expression must occur in response to the needs of readers and listeners. Talking to peers encourages rethinking or revision of a written piece. The goal of revision is clarity in thinking and language.

Correctness

Correctness in writing refers to accuracy of thinking as well as compliance with the rules of Standard Written English. Correctness matters most when a work is finished and is ready for sharing with a reader. Since errors and mistakes distract readers, correction becomes most important for those pieces which will be shared with an audience and have as their purpose a public communication of ideas.

Research shows that the separate study of English syntax and usage does not lead to better or more correct writing; research also shows that frequent, purposeful writing leads to better writing and the learning of English syntax and usage is best achieved in the context of the student's own writing.

Evaluation

The total process to be evaluated includes fluency, clarity, and correctness. Evaluation is a necessary part of the learning process and should not be confused with grading. Rather, evaluation is an assessment of the student's progress in using language to learn. Grading should be used discriminately and should not become a barrier to the development of fluency, clarity and correctness. Students should know and help to develop the criteria for evaluation whenever possible.

Revised by Team C April 20, 1988, and signed by all members of Teams A, B, and C.

References

Albert, B., & Dropkin, R. (1975). *The open education advisor*. New York: The Workshop Center for Open Education.

Apple, M. (1982). *Education and power*. London: Routledge & Kegan Paul.

Apple, M., & Weis, L. (Eds.). (1983). *Ideology and practice in schooling*. Philadelphia: Temple University Press.

Applebee, A. (1984). *Contexts for learning to write: Studies of secondary school instruction*. Norwood, NJ: Ablex.

Archambault, E. (1974). *John Dewey on education: Selected writings*. Chicago: University of Chicago Press.

Aronowitz, S., & Giroux, H. A. (1985). *Education under seige: The conservative, liberal and radical debate over schooling*. Granby, MA: Bergin & Garvey.

Bannister, D., & Fransella, F. (1971). *Inquiring man: The theory of personal constructs*. Harmondsworth: Penguin.

Barnes, D. (1969/1986). Language in the secondary classroom. In J. N. Britton, D. Barnes, H. Rosen (Eds.) (1st ed.), M. Torbe (replaced Rosen in 2nd ed.), *Language, the learner and the school* (pp. 11–87). Portsmouth, NH: Boynton/Cook.

Barnes, D. (1975). From communication to curriculum. Harmondsworth: Penguin.

Bastian, A., Fruchter, N., Gittell, M., Greer, C., & Haskins, K. (1986). *Choosing equality: The case for democratic schooling*. Philadelphia: Temple University Press.

Belenky, M. F., Clinchy, B. M., Goldberger, N. R., & Tarule, J. M. (1986). *Women's ways of knowing: The development of self, voice, and mind.* New York: Basic Books.

Bentley, A. F., & Dewey, J. (1949). *Knowing and the known.* Boston: Beacon Press.

Bloom, A. (1987). *The closing of the American mind: How higher education has failed democracy and impoverished the souls of today's students.* New York: Simon & Schuster.

Boomer, G. (Ed.). (1982). *Negotiating the curriculum: A teacher-student partnership.* Sydney: Ashton-Scholastic.

Bowles, S., & Gintis, H. (1976). *Schooling in capitalistic America.* New York: Basic Books.

Boyer, E. L. (1983). *High school: A report on secondary education in America.* New York: Harper & Row.

Brause, R. S., & Mayher, J. S. (1982). Teachers, students and classroom organizations. *Research in the Teaching of English, 16*(2), 131–148.

Brause, R. S., & Mayher, J. S. (1983). Learning through teaching: The classroom teacher as researcher. *Language Arts, 60*(6), 758–765.

Britton, J. N. (1969/1986). Talking to learn. In J. N. Britton, D. Barnes, & H. Rosen (Eds.) (1st ed.), M. Torbe (replaced Rosen in 2nd ed.), *Language, the learner and the school* (pp. 91–130). Portsmouth, NH: Boynton/Cook.

Britton, J. N. (1970). *Language and learning.* Coral Gables, FL: University of Miami Press.

Britzman, D. (1986). Cultural myths in the making of a teacher: Biography and social structure in teacher education. *Harvard Educational Review, 56*(4), 442–455.

Bruner, J. (1988). Research currents: Life as narrative. *Language Arts, 65*(6), 574–584.

Bullock, A. (1975). *A language for life.* London: Her Majesty's Stationery Office.

Chomsky, N. (1965). *Aspects of the theory of syntax.* Cambridge, MA: The MIT Press.

Cook, J. (1982). Negotiating the curriculum: Programming for learning. In G. Boomer (Ed.), *Negotiating the curriculum: A teacher-student partnership* (pp. 133–149). Sydney: Ashton-Scholastic.

Cornbleth, C. (1987). The persistence of myth in teacher education and teaching. In T. S. Popkewitz (Ed.), *Critical studies in teacher education: Its folklore, theory and practice* (pp. 186–210). New York: The Falmer Press.

Cuban, L. (1984). *How teachers taught: Constancy and change in American classrooms, 1890–1980.* New York: Longman.

Cuban, L. (1986). *Teachers and machines: The classroom use of technology since 1920*. New York: Teachers College Press.

Densmore, K. (1987). Professionalism, proletarianization, and teacher work. In T. S. Popkewitz (Ed.), *Critical studies in teacher education: Its folklore, theory and practice*, (pp. 130–160). New York: The Falmer Press.

Dewey, J. (1933). *How we think: A restatement of the relation of reflective thinking to the educative process*. Boston: D. C. Heath.

Dewey, J. (1938). (Paperback edition, 1963). *Experience and education*. New York: Collier Books.

Diamond, C. T. P. (1982). Teachers can change: A Kellyan interpretation. *Journal of Education for Teaching, 8*(2), 162–172.

Diamond, C. T. P. (1985). Fixed role treatment: Creating alternative scenarios. *Australian Journal of Education, 29*, 161–173.

Elbow, P. (1983). Teaching writing by not paying attention to writing. In P. L. Stock (Ed.), *Fforum: Essays on theory and practice in the teaching of writing* (pp. 234–242). Portsmouth, NH: Boynton/Cook.

Elbow, P. (1986). The pedagogy of the bamboozled. In Peter Elbow (Ed.), *Embracing Contraries* (pp. 85–98). New York: Oxford University Press.

Ely, M. (1984). Beating the odds: An ethnographic interview study of young adults from the culture of poverty. Paper presented at the Seventh Annual Conference in English Education, New York University, New York, NY.

Fine, M. (1987). Silencing in public school. *Language Arts, 64*(2), 157–174.

Flynn, E. (1988). Composing as a woman, *College Composition and Communication, 39*(4), 423–435.

Freire, P. (1970). *Pedagogy of the oppressed*. New York: Seabury Press.

Freire, P. (1988). Editor's introduction. In Henry A. Giroux, *Teachers as intellectuals: Toward a critical pedagogy of learning*. Granby, MA: Bergin & Garvey.

Fulwiler, T. (1982). The personal connection: Journal writing across the curriculum. In T. Fulwiler & A. Young (Eds.), *Language connections: Writing and reading across the curriculum*, (pp. 15–31). Urbana, IL: National Council of Teachers of English.

Geertz, C. (1988). *Words and lives: The anthropologist as author*. Stanford, CA: Stanford University Press.

Gere, A. R. (Ed.). (1985). *Roots in the sawdust: Writing to learn across the disciplines*. Urbana, IL: National Council of Teachers of English.

Giroux, H. A. (1988). *Teachers as intellectuals: Toward a critical pedagogy of learning*. Granby, MA: Bergin & Garvey.

Giroux, H. A., & McLaren, P. (1987). Teacher education as a counterpublic sphere: Notes toward a redefinition. In T. S. Popkewitz (Ed.), *Critical studies in teacher education: Its folklore, theory and practice* (pp. 266–297). New York: The Falmer Press.

Goodlad, J. L. (1984). *A place called school: Prospects for the future*. New York: McGraw-Hill.

Goswami, D. (1984). Teachers as researchers. In R. Graves (Ed.), *Rhetoric and composition: A sourcebook for teachers and writers* (pp. 347–358). Portsmouth, NH: Boynton/Cook.

Goswami, D., & Stillman, P. (Eds.). (1987). *Reclaiming the classroom: Teacher researcher as an agency for change*. Portsmouth, NH: Boynton/Cook.

Green, W. (Ed.). (1988). *Metaphors and meanings: Esssays on English teaching by Garth Boomer*. Australia: Australian Association for the Teaching of English.

Grice, H. P. (1975). Logic and conversation. In P. Cole & J. Morgan (Ed.), *Syntax and semantics, Vol. 3: Speech acts,* (pp. 41–58). New York: Academic Press.

Guber, E., & Lincoln, Y. (1985). *Naturalistic inquiry*. New York: Sage.

Harste, J., Woodward, V. A., & Burke, C. L. (1984). *Language stories and literacy lessons*. Portsmouth, NH: Heinemann.

Hirsch, E. D. (1987). *Cultural literacy: What every American needs to know*. Boston: Houghton Mifflin.

The Impressions Series. (1984). Toronto: Holt, Rinehart & Winston.

Johnson-Laird, P. (1983). *Mental models: Toward a cognitive science of language, inference, and consciousness*. Cambridge, MA: Harvard University Press.

Kelly, G. (1955). *The psychology of personal constructs*. New York: Norton.

Langer, J., & Applebee, A. (1987). *How writing shapes thinking*. Urbana, IL: National Council of Teachers of English.

Lester, N. B., & Onore, C. S. (1985). Immersion and distancing: The ins and outs of inservice education. *English Education, 17*(1), 7–13.

Lindfors, J. W. (1984), How children learn or how teachers teach: A profound confusion. *Language Arts, 61*(6), 600–606.

Maloney, H., & Dunning, S. (1984, February 22). *The Dunning report*. Unpublished report to the Board of Education, Charmont School District.

Margolis, H. (1987). *Patterns, thinking, and cognition: A theory of judgment*. Chicago: University of Chicago Press.

Mayher, J. (1989). *Uncommon sense: Theoretical practice in language education*. Portsmouth, NH: Boynton/Cook.

Mayher, J., Lester, N. B., & Pradl, G. (1983). *Learning to write/writing to learn*. Portsmouth, NH: Boynton/Cook.

McLaren, P. (1988). The liminal servant and the ritual roots of critical pedagogy. *Language Arts, 65,*(2) 164–179.

McNeil, L. (1986). *Contradictions of control: School structure and school knowledge.* New York: Routledge & Kegan Paul.

Mellon, J. (1981). Language competence. In C. R. Cooper (Ed.), *The nature and measurement of competency in English,* (pp. 21–64). Urbana, IL: National Council of Teachers of English.

Mohr, M. M., & MacLean, M. S. (1987). *Working together.* Urbana, IL: National Council of Teachers of English.

National Commission on Excellence in Education. (1983). *A nation at risk: The imperative for educational reform.* Washington, DC: U.S. Government Printing Office.

North, S. M. (1987). *The making of knowledge in composition. Portrait of an emerging field.* Portsmouth, NH: Boynton/Cook.

Oakes, J. (1985). *Keeping track: How schools structure inequality.* New Haven: Yale University Press.

Onore, C. S. (1984, November). Hurry up, please. It's time: Why we must find paths out of the wasteland. Paper presented at the annual meeting of the National Council of Teachers of English, Detroit, MI.

Onore, C. S., & Lester, N. B. (1986). Learning about teaching and practicing learning. *CSSEDC Newsletter,* Fall, 1–3.

Ortony, A. (Ed.). (1979). *Metaphor and thought.* Cambridge: Cambridge University Press.

Petrosky, A. (1986). Critical thinking: Qu'est-ce que c'est? *English Record,* Third Quarter, 2–5.

Polanyi, M. (1966). *The tacit dimension.* New York: Doubleday.

Rogers, C. (1969). *Freedom to learn: A view of what education might be.* Columbus, OH: Merrill.

Salmon, P. (1985). *Living in time: A new look at personal development.* London: J. M. Dent.

Salmon, P. (1988). *Psychology for teachers: An alternative approach.* London: Hutchinson.

Schön, D. A. (1983). *The reflective practitioner: How professionals think in action.* New York: Basic Books.

Schön, D. A. (1987). *Educating the reflective practitioner.* San Francisco: Jossey-Bass.

Searle, J. (1969). *Speech acts: An essay in the philosophy of language.* New York: Cambridge University Press.

Searle, J. (1984). *Minds, brains, and science.* Cambridge, MA: Harvard University Press.

Shor, I., & Freire, P. (1987). *A pedagogy for liberation.* South Hadley, MA: Bergin & Garvey.

Shuy, R. (1987). Research Currents. *Language Arts, 64* (8), 890–898.

Sizer, T. S. (1984). *Horace's compromise: The dilemma of the American high school*. Boston: Houghton Mifflin.

Smith, F. (1975). *Comprehension and learning: A conceptual framework for teachers*. New York: Holt, Rinehart & Winston.

Sperber, D., & Wilson, D. (1986). *Relevance: Communication and cognition*. Oxford: Basil Blackwell.

Thomas, L. (1979). *The medusa and the snail: More notes of a biology watcher*. New York: Viking.

Torbe, M. (1976). *Language across the curriculum: Guidelines for schools*. London: Ward Lock.

Torbe, M., & Medway, P. (1981). *The climate for learning*. Portsmouth, NH: Boynton/Cook.

Vygotsky, L. S. (1962). *Thought and language*. Cambridge, MA: The MIT Press.

Wiggins, G. (1988). 10 radical suggestions for school reform. *Education Week, 7*(24), 28, March 9.